The Shape of Fantasy

The Shape of Fantasy is an in-depth look at Heroic Epic Fantasy. It depicts structural and narrative patterns with models stemming from science and philosophy. Although Fantasy fiction is generally defined by its impossibility, it is not an illogical form. It is, in fact, governed by a sense of rules and structure, one that reflects our current understanding of space-time and cosmology. These models are an integral part of the structure of Heroic Epic Fantasy itself. Thus, this book introduces new ways of perceiving current productions of the Fantasy genre. In doing so, it also explores how Fantasy Fiction exhibits a conscious awareness of its own form.

C. Palmer-Patel is Head Editor of *Fantastika Journal.* Having completed her PhD at Lancaster University, UK, she currently resides in Alberta, Canada.

Routledge Research in American Literature and Culture

Wallace and I
Cognition, Consciousness, and Dualism in David Foster Wallace's Fiction
Jamie Redgate

Articulations of Resistance
Transformative Practices in Arab-American Poetry
Sirène H. Harb

Poetic Encounters in the Americas
Remarkable Bridge
Peter Ramos

The Shape of Fantasy
Investigating the Structure of American Heroic Epic Fantasy

C. Palmer-Patel

NEW YORK AND LONDON

First published 2020
by Routledge
52 Vanderbilt Avenue, New York, NY 10017

and by Routledge
2 Park Square, Milton Park, Abingdon, Oxon, OX14 4RN

Routledge is an imprint of the Taylor & Francis Group, an informa business

© 2020 Taylor & Francis

The right of C. Palmer-Patel to be identified as author of this work has been asserted by her in accordance with sections 77 and 78 of the Copyright, Designs and Patents Act 1988.

All rights reserved. No part of this book may be reprinted or reproduced or utilised in any form or by any electronic, mechanical, or other means, now known or hereafter invented, including photocopying and recording, or in any information storage or retrieval system, without permission in writing from the publishers.

Trademark notice: Product or corporate names may be trademarks or registered trademarks, and are used only for identification and explanation without intent to infringe.

Library of Congress Cataloging-in-Publication Data
A catalog record for this title has been requested

ISBN: 978-0-367-18914-3 (hbk)
ISBN: 978-0-429-19926-4 (ebk)

Typeset in Sabon
by codeMantra

This book is dedicated to my family for their incredible support and especially to Alex. One day I will look back at the madness of submitting a final manuscript less than two months after your birth and remind us all that "chaos is the womb of life" (N. Katherine Hayles, *Chaos Bound* 100).

Contents

List of Figures   ix
Acknowledgements   xi

Introduction – Defining Heroic Epic Fantasy   1

1   The Shape of a Hero's Soul: Interrogating the Destiny of the Hero in Lois McMaster Bujold's *The Curse of Chalion* (2001)   19

2   Forks in the Road: Assessing the Paradoxical Nature of Fixed and Fluid Time in Mercedes Lackey's *The Fairy Godmother* (2004)   35

3   Building Layers of Character: Analysing the Construction of the Hero in Robert Jordan's *The Great Hunt* (1990)   47

4   The Ou-Hero: Considering the Possibility for the Hero to Become Villain (and Vice Versa) in David Farland's *The Wyrmling Horde* (2008)   67

5   The Messianic Hero: Exploring the Hero's Willing Confrontation with Death in Gail Z. Martin's *The Summoner* (2007)   84

6   Breaking into Fantasyland: Investigating How Fracturing and Entropy Motivates the Plot in Terry Goodkind's *Stone of Tears* (1995)   100

7 The Hero as Portal: Examining the Hero's Role as Reversal of Entropy in James Clemens' *Shadowfall* (2006)   118

8 Perfect Epic Empires: Appraising Cycles of Utopia and Anti-Utopia in Brandon Sanderson's *Hero of Ages* (2008)   136

9 Chaotic Cycles: Evaluating Patterns Within and Between Sequel Series in David and Leigh Eddings' *The Seeress of Kell* (1991)   158

Afterword – Probing the Potentials of the Heroic Epic Pattern with a Brief Look at Anne McCaffrey's All the Weyrs of Pern *(1991)*   175

Index   181

Figures

0.1	The Heroic/Epic Graph of Fantasy	9
0.2	Textual Examples on the Heroic/Epic Graph of Fantasy	10
2.1	The Hero's Path, Before Choice	40
2.2	The Hero's Path, After Choice	40
4.1	The Path of the Hero and Ou-Hero with Bifurcation Points	74
5.1	The Fulcrum Tipping Back into Balance	92
6.1	The State of Entropy in Parallel Worlds	103
6.2	The Movement of Entropy When Two Parallel Words Are Bridged	103
7.1	The Hero as Maxwell's Demon between Parallel Systems	122
8.1	The Cycles of Sanderson's *Mistborn* Trilogy	143
8.2	Increase in Turbulence Creating a New Equilibrium	147
9.1	Differences in Cycles	160
9.2	Chaotic Patterns	160

Acknowledgements

Thank you to all the helpers on my journey: to my parents, Bharti and Dinesh Patel, for being my safety net; to my husband and best friend, Toby Palmer, for being my rock, my strength and constant support; and to my friend and mentor, Brian Baker, for helping me to shine.

I am grateful for all my colleagues in the academic community, particularly those of you who have read or heard versions of this manuscript in part or in full. Your feedback and support were invaluable. Thank you especially to my examiners, Adam Roberts and Andy Tate. Your encouragement gave me the motivation to turn the rough clay of my thesis into this publication. And finally, thank you to the editors and reviewers with Routledge for your enthusiasm with this project.

Introduction – Defining Heroic Epic Fantasy

This book explores elements of narrative in Fantasy novels published from 1990 to 2009 in the U.S.A. It examines plot, character, and setting of Fantasy fiction,[1] as, despite the growing commercial demand for the genre, these narrative elements have still not been investigated fully. As well, in spite of the number of Fantasy novels and films currently being produced, there is very little recent scholarship on contemporary productions of the genre. The purpose of this book is not to examine the validity of Fantasy fiction, but instead hopes to begin to address a gap in the field of scholarship: exploring the structure and forms of the Fantasy genre itself, specifically that of a common and popular Fantasy narrative, that of the Heroic Epic.

For the purposes of this book, the narrative structure of Heroic Epic Fantasy is one where the hero realises a messianic duty via a journey, one which results in a spiritual transcendence for the hero along with the salvation of the world by the act of healing or re-creating it, thereby fulfilling their destiny.[2] In "Evaporating Genres" (2002, 2011), Gary K. Wolfe suggests that: "it would be difficult for any critical approach based largely on narrative formula to accommodate the genres of the fantastic" as "formulas were never sufficient to be the defining characteristic of the genre" (23). However, I counter that while the Heroic Epic narrative structure is not embedded in *all* of the genres of the Fantastic, the Heroic Epic is a good example of a common narrative structure that is the skeletal frame of many Epic-derived Fantastika texts. The structures and form of this particular narrative arc can be found in many literatures that are not commonly thought of as Fantasy, although they may be most apparent in Fantasy. While much of existing criticism on Fantasy focuses on problems of definition or of finding the value of Fantasy, I propose that we move past these stagnant conversations and instead begin to examine the stories themselves. By exploring the structure of the Heroic Epic (a combination of plot, the Epic, with character, the Heroic), we can build the foundation for further research in similar narratives.

The Shape of Fantasy depicts these structural and narrative patterns of the Heroic Epic with models stemming from science, philosophy, and literary theory. Although Fantasy fiction is generally defined by its impossibility, Fantasy fiction is not an illogical form. It is, in fact, governed by a sense of rules and structure, one that reflects our current understanding of the world and cosmology. As I demonstrate throughout this book, these models are an integral part of the structure of Heroic Epic Fantasy. Accordingly, this book introduces new ways of reading current productions of the Fantasy genre. In doing so, it also explores how Fantasy fiction exhibits a conscious awareness of its own form.

The Current State of Fantasy Criticism

Before I turn to a detailed analysis of the Heroic Epic Fantasy form, I will first briefly outline current research in Fantasy fiction before then defining the Heroic Epic and the perimeters of this book. As other critics have discovered, establishing a definition of Fantasy is not as simple as it seems. What is Fantasy? There has been much debate regarding the definition of Fantasy – along with its sister genres of Science Fiction (SF) and other Fantastical texts, such as the Gothic and Weird. Let us take as a starting point a description offered by John Clute and John Grant in *The Encyclopedia of Fantasy* (1997): "A fantasy text is a self-coherent narrative. [...] it tells a story which is impossible in the world as we perceive it" (338). Fantasy is designated by the impossible, by the 'fantastical.'

In "Fantastika in the World Storm" (2007), Clute employs the term 'Fantastika' as an umbrella term to designate these genres as a whole: "I will start by defining fantastika in a way that may seem obvious, but is not: Fantastika consists of that wide range of fictional works whose contents are *understood* to be fantastic" (20, original emphasis). Clute advocates that the term Fantastika be employed in works that are conscious of their own form as a fantastical narrative. But where do we situate Fantasy within this 'Fantastika' umbrella term? How do we distinguish it from its sister genres? In *Strategies of Fantasy* (1992), Brian Attebery proposes a model of genre definition based on the concept of "fuzzy sets." This model suggests describing genres around a prototypical model, so that: "they [genres] are defined not by boundaries but by a center" (12). This is the model of Fantasy that will be utilised in this book; I will not set out to distinguish Fantasy from other Fantastika narratives, but instead will use my own "fuzzy set."

It should be noted that Attebery's approach to Fantasy, like Clute's to Fantastika, suggests that the genre's definition is dependent on the individual: on either the reader's reception or author's presentation of a particular literature as Fantasy. This is problematic in that, too often, a critical evaluation of Fantasy is arrested at the first hurdle of demarcating the borders of its study. For instance, the texts that I have selected for examination in this book are typical examples of Heroic Epic Fantasy. Yet another reader may argue for a wider or narrower remit of Fantasy or Heroic Epic than the scope under consideration. But genres evaporate (to borrow a phrase from Wolfe), as the boundaries constantly shift, and trying to separate texts into firm categorisations is a futile task. Many definitions of Fantasy (and indeed, definitions of SF and Gothic Horror as well) ultimately fail as a clear consensus of these terms are never reached.

Since the debate of definitions first offered by researchers of the Fantastic in the 1970s and '80s, there has been little recent scholarship on contemporary Fantasy fiction that has added to this conversation. These definitions evaluate Fantasy as separate or comparable to 'realistic' or 'mimetic' fictions and further add a commentary in how the genre compares to other 'non-realistic' fictions. Darko Suvin famously distinguishes SF from the Fantastic by the presence of "cognitive logic" in *Metamorphoses of Science Fiction* (1970): "*SF is distinguished by the narrative dominance or hegemony of a fictional 'novum' (novelty, innovation) validated by cognitive logic*" (63, original emphasis). SF is presented as a literature that is *different* from the real world, but one that is centred on the possible – "validated by cognitive logic" – while Fantasy is seen as the opposite, a genre or mode which contains the illogical:

> Anything is possible in a folktale, because a folktale is manifestly impossible. [...] Even less congenial to SF is the *fantasy* (ghost, horror, Gothic, weird) tale, a genre committed to the interposition of anti-cognitive laws into the empirical environment. Where the folktale is indifferent, the fantasy is inimical to the empirical world and its laws. (Suvin 8, original emphasis)

Suvin's definition groups all Fantastic narratives together as one: a collection of non-mimetic texts that he sees as antithesis to SF. He does not differentiate between these forms of the Fantastic. Furthermore, his definition conveys a dislike of fantastical narratives due to their irrationality. Other definitions of Fantasy imply similar hierarchies. For instance, C. N. Manlove in *Modern Fantasy* (1975) uses Frank Herbert's *Dune* (1965) and Isaac Asimov's *Foundation* trilogy (1951–1953) as examples of SF or: "possible worlds in that they are set in our universe" (3), counterpoising this model to Fantasy which is: "set in the empirically known world, but the world is either juxtaposed with or transfigured by the presence of the supernatural" (3). These definitions, of SF as "possible [...] in our universe" and Fantasy as "transfigured by the presence of the supernatural" is an attempt made by many scholars to differentiate the two genres. But it is illogical. *Dune*, for example, demonstrates a "presence of the supernatural" (through religion, prophecy, and the worms themselves) yet Manlove still describes it as a 'possible' text, defining it as SF rather than Fantasy.

When the critical evaluation of Fantasy fiction progress further than defining the perimeters of its field, much of the scholarship focuses on ascertaining why readers of Fantasy read Fantasy, or the *value* of Fantasy. Because of the focus on sociopolitical or psychological implications, the narrative value of the Fantasy genre has rarely been studied (except for when the study focuses on individual authors). In a later article, "Considering the Sense of 'Fantasy' on Fantastic Fiction: An Effusion" (2000), Suvin acknowledges a difference between Fantasy and Gothic. Yet, even here, Suvin's essay does not suggest that he has moved beyond his disparagement of Fantasy, and additionally, Suvin attempts to find the value and use of Fantasy by evaluating its allegorical functions. Other studies of Fantasy have also attempted to find the value of the genre for a post-Enlightenment audience, utilising tools of study which use psychoanalytic, archetypal, allegorical, or pedagogical readings of Fantasy; approaches that are used to defend or criticise the genre based on their own stance in regard to the reception of the Fantastic. For instance, in *A Rhetoric of the Unreal: Studies in Narrative and Structure, Especially of the Fantastic* (1981), Christine Brooke-Rose attempts to describe SF using methods of realism and suggests that the realistic procedures in Fantasy flattens the narrative: "Above all, the presence of a wholly invented and wholly unfamiliar (and magical) megatext makes a realistic narrative impossible. This invented megatext, however, combined with all the realistic techniques described, pushes the narrative into allegory, or very nearly" (254). Using J. R. R. Tolkien's *The Lord of the Rings* (1954–1955) as a model, Brooke-Rose dismisses Fantasy as near-allegory. But, unless these authors have deliberately intended an allegorical reading, one must be careful of forcing a reading onto a text. In "The Staring Eye" (1974), author Ursula K. Le Guin argues against reading Fantasy as allegory: "No ideologues, not even religious ones, are going to be happy with Tolkien, unless they manage it by misreading him" (175–176). Although Tolkien's *The Lord of the Rings* does have Christian significance, simplifying the books to a one-to-one allegorical reading has the effect of flattening the work, reducing the beauty and complexity of it in order to gain a meaning that is 'logical' to a 'rational' audience.

Instead, as many critics have identified (Michael Moorcock, *Wizardry and Wild Romance*, 1987; Richard Mathews, *Fantasy: The Liberation of Imagination*, 1997; Farah Mendlesohn and Edward James, *A Short History of Fantasy*, 2009, revised 2012; Brian Attebery, *Stories about Stories: Fantasy and the Remaking of Myth*, 2014), Fantasy is an inheritor of the evolutionary line of Mythology, Romance (Legends), and Folk and Fairy-Tales. I differentiate Fantasy from its sister genres accordingly. In Fantasy fiction, the language, structure, and affect of Myth, Romance, and Folk and Fairy Tale are embedded in the textual apparatus of the narrative. Attebery asserts that:

> If fantasy were only the denial of science, however, there would be no contest between them. But in affirming impossibility, fantasy opens the door to mythology, which is the name we give to cast-off

megatexts. Gods, fairies, ancestor spirits, charms, spells: a whole host of motifs no longer convey belief and yet retain their narrative momentum. (*Strategies of Fantasy* 108–109)

Thus, Fantasy is not a denial of science or rational law. Instead, Fantasy can be defined as a narrative that uses similar structures and language of Mythology, Legends, and Fairy-Tales in order to create a new world with its own rational laws.

As a result, Fantasy fiction *is* logical even when it is not possible. *In Defense of Fantasy* (1984), Ann Swinfen explores the world-building structures of Fantasy fiction from 1945 to 1984 in order to frame Fantasy as logical. Swinfen argues that: "What may at first sight seem to be a paradox lies, in fact, at the heart of the fantasy: that is, that to create an imaginative and imaginary world it is necessary to observe faithfully the rules of logic and inner consistency" (3). Fantasy must have internally consistent laws as a point of reference from which the reader can hope to understand the fiction. Accordingly, many Fantasy authors demonstrate a world-building that incorporates a sense of logic and understanding of real-world principles. In *The Magic Code* (1988), Maria Nikolajeva explores at length the idea that magic must be rational, using testimonies from authors such as George MacDonald, E. Nesbit, and Jane Yolen. Nikolajeva maintains: "One of the essential rules for writing fantasy seems to be the assumption that magic cannot be omnipotent and unlimited. Both critics and authors of fantasy are aware of this" (25). "Any minor inconsistency," she continues, "may shatter the whole construction" (26), and thus, using magic in a way that is irrational to the constructed logic of the Fantasy narrative is considered poor writing.

Accordingly, when Fantasy fiction breaks a scientific law, it must first understand how that law works, even if the comprehension does not take place on a conscious level. As this book will explore, the Fantasy genre, though often defined by the 'impossible,' still follows the *logic* of our current scientific and philosophical understanding of the world. As Attebery argues: "fantasy depends on mimesis for its effectiveness. We must have some solid ground to stand on, some point of contact" (*Strategies of Fantasy* 4). When world-building, authors must consider our world as points of comparison before they can manipulate and adapt known rules of the universe. As this book will demonstrate, the narrative structure of Heroic Epic Fantasy is heavily influenced by scientific and philosophical models that are embedded in our cultural awareness.

This study utilises a wide range of literary, philosophical, and scientific theories as models to explore the narrative structure of Heroic Epic Fantasy. N. Katherine Hayles sets the precedent for the approach of integrating scientific theory with literary analysis in *Chaos Bound*

(1990). As she argues in the introduction of the text, literature is a part of a feedback loop influenced by cultural context:

> The recurrent image I use to explain the complex interconnections of theory, technology, and culture is a feedback loop. [...] the feedback cycle connected theory with culture and culture with theory [...]. Literary texts and theories were also involved in this cycle, for they too were affected by technology at the same time that they were affecting it. (xiv)

Literature and the ideas that it conveys are a product of a cultural moment, which, in turn, is part of the feedback loop that influences other literatures and ideas in a continual open dialogue. It is my belief that models of world-building taken from classical philosophy and popular sciences have entered the feedback loop that Hayles describes, creating a set of ideas and assumptions on how the world works, which are then incorporated directly into the narrative structures of Fantasy fiction. Hayles' model does not indicate the idea "of science influencing literature but of literature and science as two mingled voices within the cacophonography that we call postmodern culture" (208). Similarly, this book does not argue the ways in theoretical models have influenced literary output; instead, in key places, it will use these models of science and philosophy as devices to further understand and evaluate the forms and structures of the Heroic Epic Fantasy genre. By using these models to describe narrative structures, I will demonstrate that the structure of Heroic Epic Fantasy not only reveals logical devices derived from real-world principles, but that these models themselves are an embedded facet of the narrative and essential to the way both story and character develops.

Defining the Heroic Epic Narrative Form[3]

For the purposes of this book, the narrative structure of Heroic Epic Fantasy is one where the hero realises a messianic duty via a journey (literal or metaphorical), one which results in a spiritual transcendence for the hero (the ascendance of the hero from human or superhuman to something closer to the divine) along with the salvation of the world by the act of healing or re-creating it, thereby fulfilling their destiny and the world's destiny. This is the basic structure of the 'Epic' or 'Heroic Epic' found in Mythology as many formalists have identified. James Frazer (1890), Otto Rank (1909), Lord Raglan (1936), and Joseph Campbell (1949) have all offered a comparative study of religion and mythologies in order to identify the basic structure of the hero's journey. Vladimir Propp's (1928; 1958 English translation) formalist approach to Folktales is also an important study in which Propp identifies formal functions of the Folktale. Yet, there are obvious problems with reducing the Heroic Epic to a simple pattern. I do not mean to dismiss those works or narrative patterns that do not follow my model of the Heroic Epic. It is simply the focus of this book. Additionally, I hope not to be reductive and ignore the depth and complexity of each work. While the texts that I study share common structural similarities, I attempt to acknowledge and make references to the differences between these texts. Though I expose the basic structure of Heroic Epic texts, I also point to how repetitive devices add complexity, a resonance, to the stories under investigation.

There are numerous and varied definitions of 'hero' which I discuss throughout this book, but as a starting point let us utilise the definition provided by Thomas Carlyle in *On Heroes, Hero-Worship, & the Heroic in History* (lectures 1835; published 1904): the hero is one (whether in fiction, mythologies, or the real world) who: "know[s] for certain, concerning [their] vital relations to this mysterious Universe and [their] duty and destiny there" (2–3). The hero is defined by the manner in which they come to identify their place in the universe and fulfil their destiny, taking on this duty of their own free will. Accordingly, the Epic is a journey which results in fulfilling a world destiny; the Heroic journey is one where the hero achieves spiritual transcendence; and the Heroic Epic is where the two meet.

If there is no journey (literal or metaphorical) through which the hero achieves spiritual transcendence and fulfils a world destiny, then the book or series is not part of the Heroic Epic subgenre of Fantasy. The 'journey' of the hero does not indicate the hero's life from birth to death, but the path through which they come to save the world. The Epic Hero is a messianic hero, one who saves the world through a sacrifice, usually associated with some literal or metaphorical connection to death as part of their journey. In *The Epic Hero* (2000), an analysis of Greco-Roman Mythological heroes, Dean A. Miller identifies that: "the heroic individual comes from his voluntary submission to death: the hero wills himself to accept and even to welcome the danger of death" (121). Like the Mythological hero, the Epic Fantasy hero's power comes from their "voluntary submission to death." Through this sacrifice, the hero achieves transcendence; that is, the hero ascends spiritually and achieves a connection with the divine.

Transcendence indicates that some conception of a higher power – a divinity or fate or a metaphysical entity – *must* be present in the work in order for it to be defined as the Epic Fantasy genre. In all of the Epic case studies examined in this book, there is some awareness of a higher power that orders the world. However, this power can be expressed either implicitly or explicitly. Tolkien's *The Lord of the Rings*, for example, is a foundational text for this Heroic Epic pattern, but the Epic motifs are largely in the background as the conceptions of divinity are presented as less concrete in the trilogy itself. There are also many examples of texts where the narration may lack any explicit presence of divinity, but the structures of fate and prophecy are essential to the narrative plot. For instance, J. K. Rowling's *Harry Potter* series (1997–2007) does not evoke a clear sense of divinity. However, despite that absence, Harry is still linked to the idea of prophecy. Thus, fate can be a stand in for divinity, as there is still some idea of a higher power that guides the characters and narrative. These works may be defined as 'Epic Fantasy' as well.

While the nomenclature of the genre of 'Epic Fantasy' already exists, this term often seems to refer to the length of the texts and/or the details of the imagined histories contained within, rather than indicating an awareness of the development of the Epic from Mythology. The Epic connection with Mythology is important to remember when considering this nomenclature as it directly impacts on that essential structure of fate or divine order. The category of 'High Fantasy' has also been employed, but both 'High Fantasy' and 'Epic Fantasy' are often used to encompass 'Heroic Fantasy' (for example, Tolkien's *The Lord of the Rings*) as well as 'Sword and Sorcery' (for instance, Robert Howard's *Conan the Barbarian*, 1932–1969). For this reason, in "The Demarcation of Sword and Sorcery" (2011), Joseph A. McCullough suggests that the major distinction between 'Heroic Fantasy' and 'Sword and Sorcery' is one of scale:

> [T]he definitive aspect of the idea of scope or scale lies in the idea that something exists that is bigger and stronger than the heroes. This can be God, gods, fate, destiny, good and evil, law and chaos. But these must be more than mere concepts. *They must be tangible driving forces at work in the world.* (n.p., my emphasis)

To expand on McCullough's argument, in Heroic Epic Fantasy the narrative results in a world-salvation, usually as a result of the interactions of divinity and fate. Sword and Sorcery, in contrast, while still incorporating the idea of overcoming an obstacle or villain, is less grand in scale, lacking the motifs that suggests a hero's connection to divinity.

That is the distinction, I argue, between different labels of genre Fantasies; between the Epic and 'Urban Fantasy,' or between the Epic and 'Sword and Sorcery,' or between the Epic and what I call the 'Localised Fantasy.' The distinction is not so much the distinction between countryside and city, or the literal movement between the two, but instead the distinction is the sense of a profound scale; a scale that includes the entire cosmos, dimensions, depths and heights of heaven and hell; a scale that indicates a divine order to the world which *impacts* on the plot or narrative arc. Epic Fantasy must culminate in the hero transforming and remaking the world or land as a whole, and not just a city or village.

Accordingly, I identify Heroic Epic at one corner of a two-dimensional scale (Figure 0.1). One end of the horizontal axis – the character axis – is the Heroic. The Heroic is a unified group who, along with the prophesised

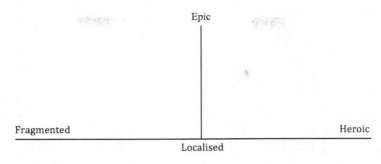

Figure 0.1 The Heroic/Epic Graph of Fantasy.

hero(es), bring about the resolution of the plot. Even if the group is divided or broken – as happens in Tolkien's *The Lord of the Rings* or Robert Jordan's *The Wheel of Time* (1990–2012) – the divided group has a common goal. The resolution is brought about through the actions of all the protagonists as a unified whole. On the other end is what I call the 'Fragmented Hero.' In this end of the axis, the protagonists are so numerous and disintegrated, each with their own individual contradictory goals, that it is often difficult to determine who is the primary hero of the novel or series. George R. R. Martin's *A Song of Ice and Fire* series (1996–present) and Steven Erikson's *Gardens of the Moon* (1999) are such examples, where it may be difficult to predict which characters are the 'good' characters that will save the world. Note, however, that there still exists the potential for the characters to develop heroic qualities as these series progress, as the authors may suggest some hint of destiny earlier in the narrative. The 'prophesised hero' is the intersection where the Hero and the Epic axis meet, combining the chosen hero with the Epic axis through the idea of destiny.

The vertical axis – setting – I have outlined above, with Epic on one end and the Local or regional on the other. The Localised Fantasy differs from Epic in two major ways. First, the plot and resolution of Localised Fantasy takes place in a central area, rather than on the world or multi-universe scale. However, it is possible that characters may move from region to region on a series of adventures, as is the case with Howard's *Conan the Barbarian* series or Michael Moorcock's *Elric* series (1961–1977). For this reason, there is perhaps a further distinction between 'Localised Fantasy' and 'Adventure Fantasy.' It is also possible for Localised or Adventure Fantasy to become gradually more Epic, as Moorcock's *Elric* does. The identification of these Fantastika texts along the horizontal and vertical scales are not always static (Figure 0.2).

For instance, Scott Lynch's *Gentleman Bastard* series (2006–present) moves gradually from Localised to Epic, as by the third book of the

10 Introduction

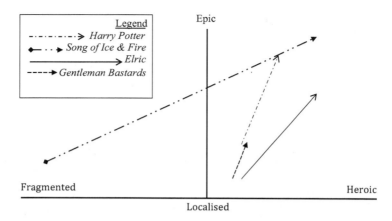

Figure 0.2 Textual Examples on the Heroic/Epic Graph of Fantasy.

unfinished series a hint of destiny starts to emerge. Here the underlying markers of 'hero' found in the protagonist (initially present in the first two books) begin to manifest more overtly as the protagonist Locke Lamora gradually moves from antihero to hero. As such, Epic and Local do not operate as distinct binaries, but rather as a spectrum. In this light, Rowling's *Harry Potter* series may be seen as halfway between the Epic and Localised Fantasy scale: although the hero has a destiny to fulfil, the story is largely contained to a hidden society in Britain and rarely moves beyond those regional borders. However, the hero crosses a metaphysical boundary through death, and thus the final book leans towards the Epic scale.

Accordingly, second, as I identified above, the true Epic often contains and conveys a cosmic destiny; that is, the universe of the Epic includes some hint of metaphysical worlds and an idea of a higher power (whether a benign or malignant anthropomorphic god or a numinous fate) influencing the events of the narrative. As suggested above, in some Epic Fantasies, this hint of divinity is often an overt and explicit motivator of the plot, whereas in others, the divine intervention, while not as visibly noticeable, may still be present in the background. Note that there is also a difference between practiced religions and divine entities that actually influence the world. For example, Brandon Sanderson's *Mistborn* trilogy (2006–2008) has many ancient religions which are localised. Yet the world itself was created by two spirits. While neither of these entities have a religious following, both entities directly impact on the narrative and I classify it as an Epic accordingly.

The Heroic Epic graph can be utilised in a number of Fantastika genres. For instance, many Superhero adventures may be set in a specific locale, such as stories of Batman that focus on Gotham City, whereas the recent Marvel franchises have expanded their perimeters to narratives that effect the entire universe. Fairy-Tale revisions (which, it should be noted, are often published as Fantasy) may fall into either end of the graph depending on plot and character. For example, Mercedes Lackey's *Five Hundred Kingdom* series (2004–2012) leans more towards the Epic: although each novel takes place in one or two kingdoms, the books are motivated by fate and destiny. Lackey's *The Fire Rose* (1995), in contrast, is more Localised, a "Beauty and the Beast" retelling set in the city of San Francisco. These examples illustrate how texts can be categorised by narrative structure, rather than setting, motifs, or effect. Thus, while critics may disagree over whether texts such as Herbert's *Dune* or George Lucas's *Star Wars* films (1977–present) are best classified as SF or Fantasy based on their perception and reception of 'impossible' elements, I would emphasise the need to identify the text in terms of narrative structures first. *Dune* and *Star Wars* are both 'Heroic Epics' in this sense, and whether they are SF or Fantasy are secondary considerations.

The Textual Boundaries of This Study

The evaluation of Fantasy as a text that is perceived as 'impossible' in the real world is dependent on both the audience's and author's reception of these elements *as* fantastical or realistic. Consequently, I have selected defined perimeters for this investigation in order to control variables that may influence the presentation and development of Fantasy. The case studies in this book are all Heroic Epic novelisation forms of Fantasy produced in the English language by (predominantly[4]) white authors for an adult audience from 1990 to 2009 in the U.S.A. Wherever possible, I have bolstered these examinations by close reading comparisons of the other works under discussion or texts from outside of this defined range.

This book focuses on texts that are produced for an adult audience for two reasons. First, the definition of Fantasy in children's literature may be nebulous. For instance, are anthropomorphised creatures considered fantastical? Here, structure may add a nuance to the genre demarcation, so that while a talking animal who attends primary school may not be considered Fantastic, one that engages in a quest or journey might very well be. However, for practical reasons, children's Fantasy may not be suited for the Heroic Epic Fantasy form as the necessity of a journey indicates some form of independence. Of course, there are still good examples of Epic journeys found in children's literature. C. S. Lewis's *The Lion, the Witch and the Wardrobe* (1950) is one such early example. Lyra and Will in Philip Pullman's *His Dark Materials* trilogy (1995–2000) also undertake an Epic journey, as does the mouse Matthias in Brian Jacques's *Redwall* (1986). But in these cases, parental guidance must be removed in some way, and thus, second, it is possible that this variation in the form may impact on the rest of the structure. This is not because children's or young adult Fantasy does not have the depth and beauty of adult Fantasy – far from it! – but I hope to be careful of the claims I make towards the genre as a whole when considering differences in audiences. For instance, Farah Mendlesohn in *Rhetorics of Fantasy* (2008) begins her chapter on the portal-quest Fantasy (a taxonomy comparable to the Heroic Epic) with the suggestion that: "Although I hesitate to describe the position constructed in the portal-quest fantasy as infantilizing [...] it is perhaps not coincidental that the classic portal tale is more common in children's fantasy than in that ostensibly written for the adult market" (1). Yet, as Paul Kincaid notes in his review of her book (2009), Mendlesohn: "includes many books published for children, perhaps fifty percent or more of the books that received extended attention" (266), and thus her choice of texts may lead to her criticism of the form.

Similarly, the texts under investigation in this monograph are all published in the English language in the U.S.A in order to limit the variations that may occur from texts published in other languages or cultures. For instance, there is a world of difference between the formula-driven Heroic Epic which is discussed in this book and modes of Magic Realism that has abounded in other parts of the world; each development may differ based on the reception of the fantastical and mythologies within the culture that produces it. However, critics may take little notice of these differences when discussing Fantasy as a whole. To avoid making similar conflations between different cultural productions of Fantasy, I have selected defined perimeters accordingly.[5]

As Helen Young notes in *Race and Popular Fantasy Literature* (2016): "Given that the foundations of the [modern Fantasy] genre were laid in the first half of the twentieth century, it is perhaps not surprising that the authors who were most visibly influential were White men" (15). Young also asserts that the genre: "is stereotypically – if increasingly inaccurately – White, middle-class, and male" (6), although the genre in recent years is "struggling to break" free of these stereotypes (10). While there are numerous voices producing Fantasy fiction, attempting to include the vast range of authorial identities would undermine the investigation of this book as it would bring in multiple variables that may influence the structure. While I have made some attempt to address the uneven dominance of patriarchal authorial voices by utilising case studies that are written by men and women, I have not attempted to examine productions from authors from a wide range of classes, races, religions, genders, or sexualities, or examine how these variables may influence or subvert the structure or representation of the hero. These limitations should demonstrate the number of areas that still require further research in the genre as a whole.

Finally, I have selected the two decades of the 1990s and 2000s as areas of focus in order to address the lack of scholarship on recent productions of the genre. Many studies of Fantasy fiction have become dated: published in the '80s and '90s, they are unable to take into account the recent explosion of Fantasy literature. As well, many of the recent studies of Fantasy (those produced in this millennium) continue to centre on earlier forms of Fantasy with little discussion of Fantasy produced in the last three decades. As author Steven Erikson laments in "Not Your Grandmother's Epic Fantasy" (2012), a review of the *Cambridge Companion to Fantasy Literature* (edited by Mendlesohn and Edward James, 2012):

> If I am to conclude that the work is representative of the present state of scholarship in the field of fantasy, then as a producer of fantasy fiction, I was naturally curious about my place in the genre, and not just mine, but that of a whole host of best-selling, award-winning fantasy authors who write epic fantasy [...]. Imagine my bemused state, then, to find that we pretty much don't exist. (4)

It is notable that, in the exploding field of Fantasy fiction, critical works that attempt to engage with a wide remit of the genre may leave out or minimalise the importance of recent productions.[6] This study hopes to address that gap.

That being said, I have not utilised as case studies novels published in *this* decade. As this book focuses on form and structure, some of the post-2010 productions of Fantasy have already begun to evolve past the Heroic Epic patterns identified in this book. Consequently, I have selected texts published from 1990 to 2009 in order to keep this discussion of structure contained. The 2010s has seen a major shift in market as independent or smaller publishers have become more accessible. This, in turn, has led to an explosion in productions from authors from a wide range of non-hegemonic racial, gender, and sexual backgrounds, each who bring global awareness and an assortment of their own unique histories into the Heroic Epic Fantasy structure. These authors begin to shift the Heroic Epic structure so that nuances in the presentation of character and plot lead to a slight departure from the structure identified in this book. In contrast, I believe the output of American Fantasy fiction in the '90s and '00s are comparable to each other, with very little differentiation. There is perhaps a slight demarcation between pre- and post-9/11 texts which has led to a collapsing of a rigid understanding of the good/evil binary, but it is possible that this collapse may have begun at a much earlier date (perhaps even reaching back into the '60s Cold War era, which such characters as Moorcock's Elric) and only begins to fully coalesce recently. While this book serves as a foundation to discuss the development of the genre over several decades, that is a study for another day.

Each of the following chapters focuses on a case study to investigate the structures under discussion. Each novel was carefully selected as overt examples of the structures under consideration. As Attebery asserts in "Structuralism" (2012): "fantasy typically displays and even celebrates its structure" (83). Often, the texts themselves seem conscious of their own form and I have deliberately chosen these texts for study as they offer more material for discussion. In some cases, I have avoided authors for practical reasons. For instance, as many of these series are still in publication or being released, there are times when it is necessary to discuss the text as a finished product. For example, Martin's *A Song of Ice and Fire* series moves back and forth on the Epic spectrum in the HBO television adaptation, but this development is only hinted at in the currently published novels. Other authors have been excluded because of the focus on the Heroic Epic Pattern. Again, this is not to dismiss the importance of these authors and other Fantasy patterns. Instead, I focus on a pattern that is one of the most common. There are also a number of Fantasy authors that are important and integral to the Heroic Epic which may have been left out in this study, as it is difficult to touch on all of these in a meaningful way. This is one of the limitations of the case studies approach. While there are a number of texts that would fit the arguments under discussion, I have chosen examples that I feel give the greatest material to investigate and analyse. Yet it is inevitable that I have missed a favourite author that a reader may feel would have fit the argument better. Indeed, that may be the case and, if so, I invite you to extend my analysis to your own reading of these authors.

It is not necessary for you, the reader, to have read the case studies in order to follow the arguments of this book. These studies are presented in such a way that a reader who is familiar with Fantasy fiction should be able to understand this investigation of Fantasy. I also caution that while this book should be a useful tool for both readers of Fantasy as well as prospective writers, I do not intend it as a step-by-step guide to writing Heroic Epic Fantasy. While I believe that authors should be inspired by others in the fields and in this way attempt to recreate those aspects that are particularly simulating, a simple repetition of the formula of Heroic Epic Fantasy will lead to a flat, unimaginative production. Instead, I urge writers in the field to utilise this book to help examine and interrogate their own ideas when they build a new world or story. As is often the case, whenever a critic declares that a text must have x and y features in order to be defined as a certain genre, mode, or structure, authors will unsurprisingly begin to play with these boundaries, pushing past the known, to create something new and original. I certainly hope this holds true with my own work.

The chapters in this book will analyse key components of the Heroic and Epic structure, focusing on close readings of a case study for each chapter. Chapter 1 examines the motif of fate and prophecy, exploring whether the conception of destiny limits the free will of the character. I argue that while the shape of the hero's nature is pre-determined, it remains up to the hero's free will whether to fulfil the functions of their design. Chapter 2 expands on this premise of how to resolve the paradox of a fixed future with the freedom of choice. I propose that the expression of prophecy does not indicate a single fixed future, but instead demonstrates the possibility of a number of different possible outcomes. Chapter 3 furthers this discussion with an examination of how recursive structures exhibit how the hero is constructed by the text, and, reciprocally, also reveal how the hero constructs the text. In this way, the characters themselves come to understand their purpose in the world, almost recognising themselves as heroes of the story. Chapter 4 then examines the structure of another character-type: what I refer to as the 'ou-hero.' The ou-hero is a character that fails to fulfil their potential as hero. Moreover, each hero also has the possibility of turning into an ou-hero themselves. Chapter 5 focuses on the hero's function as a messianic hero. The hero's success or consequent failure as an ou-hero is dependent on the realisation of this messianic function and their comprehension of the underlying balance of the world.

After exploring the role of character in the first half of the book, the latter half then expands the discussion to consider the plot. Chapter 6 examines how the plot is triggered or motivated by the impact of entropy on Fantasyland.[7] Chapter 7 extends this argument further, contending that the hero's role is to reverse the system of entropy, restoring the balance, while simultaneously re-establishing a closed system, making the broken Fantasyland whole again. Chapter 8 investigates how this new state is triggered by far-from-equilibrium conditions. The hero acts as an agent of change, forcing a break in the cycle and thereby resolving the major conflict of the narrative. Chapter 9 then concludes the book with a discussion of sequels and long-running series, exploring the continuation of the narrative once the conflict is resolved. Heroic Epic Fantasy fictions are rarely published as individual stand-alone novels. Accordingly, the resolution of the conflict at the end of the novel is ephemeral, as Fantasyland will begin to deteriorate again, leading to a new cycle, a new series.

In the following chapters, I identify and analyse these key narrative structures, structures that are deliberately exposed and repeated. Far from being simplistic or reductive, the repetition of these devices adds to the nuances of readings, building layers of text that resonate with each repetition. Using scientific, philosophical, and literary models as analogies to explore narrative devices, I will reveal that the logic of Heroic Epic Fantasy is codified by a real-world understanding of the world. Thus, this book will demonstrate that although Fantasy is often defined because of its qualities of impossibility – often undervalued by a rational audience – Heroic Epic Fantasy *is* a rational literature.

Notes

1 I have capitalised genres or groups of literature in order to differentiate from the common usage of the word (for example, 'Fantasy' as a genre, and 'fantasy' as an adjective, noun, or verb indicating fancy or to fantasise).
2 Note that throughout this book I use 'hero' to designate the character that fully realises and fulfils their role as hero. However, there may be many protagonist characters, all who work together as a collective group. Chapters 4, 5, and 6 will discuss further complications of this nomenclature.
3 An earlier version of this section is published in editorial form as "Excavations of Genre Barriers: Breaking New Ground with *Fantastika Journal*" in *Fantastika Journal* 1.1 (2017).
4 Although all the authors utilised for case studies are visibly white, there may be some genetic inheritance from other cultures or ethnicities.
5 The Epic tradition not only concerns the Heroic Epic, but the National Epic. However, this book, focusing as it does on form, does not examine the cultural influences and evolution of the texts within a nation. A study in how Heroic Epic Fantasy differs in a range of English-speaking countries to produce its own National Epic may be an avenue of further research. Brian Attebery sets the groundwork for this research with *The Fantasy Tradition in American Literature: From Irving to Le Guin* (1980) which explores the history and influence of American folklore on key Fantasy authors.
6 It should be noted that there *are* numerous criticisms that focus on single-author studies, but few regarding the genre as a whole.
7 The term "fantasyland" is common in the critical field of Fantasy research to specify the world of Fantasy, as can be evidenced in the title of Diana Wynne Jones' *The Tough Guide to Fantasyland* (1996), a satirical encyclopaedia of tropes of Fantasy.

Bibliography

Asimov, Isaac. *Foundation Trilogy*. Gnome Press, 1951–1953. Foundation 1–3.
Attebery, Brian. *The Fantasy Tradition in American Literature: From Irving to Le Guin*. Indiana University Press, 1980.
———. *Strategies of Fantasy*. Indiana University Press. 1992.
———. "Structuralism." *A Cambridge Companion to Fantasy Literature*. Eds. Edward James and Farah Mendlesohn. Cambridge University Press, 2012. pp. 81–90.
———. *Stories about Stories: Fantasy and the Remaking of Myth*. Oxford University Press, 2014.
Brooke-Rose, Christine. *A Rhetoric of the Unreal: Studies in Narrative and Structure, Especially of the Fantastic*. 1981. Cambridge University Press, 1988. Print.
Campbell, Joseph. *The Hero with a Thousand Faces*. 1949. New World Library, 2008.
Carlyle, Thomas. *On Heroes, Hero-Worship, & the Heroic in History*. 1841. Chapman and Hall Limited, 1904.
Clute, John. "Fantastika in the World Storm." 2007. *Pardon this Intrusion: Fantastika in the World Storm*. Beccon Publications, 2011. pp. 19–31.

Clute, John and John Grant. "Fantasy." 1997. *The Encyclopedia of Fantasy*. Orbit, 1999. pp. 337–339.
Erikson, Steven. *Gardens of the Moon*. 1999. Bantam Books, 2007. Malazan Book of the Fallen 1.
———. "Not Your Grandmother's Epic Fantasy: A Fantasy Author's Thoughts upon Reading *The Cambridge Companion to Fantasy Literature*." *The New York Review of Science Fiction*, vol. 24, no. 9, 2012, pp. 1, 4–5.
Frazer, Sir James George. *The Golden Bough: The Roots of Religion and Folklore*. 1890. Project Gutenberg. 23 March 2003. Ebook.
Hayles, N. Katherine. *Chaos Bound: Orderly Disorder in Contemporary Literature and Science*. 1990. Cornell University Press, 1994.
Herbert, Frank. *Dune*. 1965. Gollancz, 2010. Dune Saga 1.
Howard, Robert E. *The 'Conan' Stories*. 1932–1938. eBooks@Adelaide. 2014. Web. Accessed 4 November 2018. https://ebooks.adelaide.edu.au/h/howard/robert_e/index.html
Jacques, Brian. *Redwall*. Hutchinson, 1986. Redwall 1.
Jordan, Robert. *The Wheel of Time*. Tor, 1990–2005. The Wheel of Time 1–11.
Jordan, Robert and Brandon Sanderson. *The Wheel of Time*. Tor, 2009–2012. The Wheel of Time 12–14.
Kincaid, Paul. "Review Essay: Starting the Conversation." *Journal of the Fantastic in the Arts*, vol. 20, no. 1, 2009, pp. 262–269.
Lackey, Mercedes. *The Fire Rose*. 1995. Baen, 2006. Elemental Masters 1.
———. *Five Hundred Kingdoms*. Luna Books, 2004–2011. Five Hundred Kingdoms 1–6.
Le Guin, Ursula K. "The Staring Eye." 1974. *The Language of the Night*. 1979. Rev. ed. 1989. HarperCollins, 1992. pp. 173–176.
Lewis, C. S. *The Lion, the Witch and the Wardrobe*. 1950. HarperTrophy, 1978. The Chronicles of Narnia 2.
Lynch, Scott. *Gentleman Bastard*. Bantam, 2006–2013. Gentleman Bastard 1–3.
Manlove, C. N. *Modern Fantasy: Five Studies*. Cambridge University Press, 1975.
Martin, George R. R. *A Song of Ice and Fire*. Bantam Books, 1996–2011. A Song of Ice and Fire 1–5.
Mathews, Richard. *Fantasy: The Liberation of Imagination*. 1997. Routledge, 2002.
McCullough, Joseph A. "The Demarcation of Sword and Sorcery." 2011. Web. Accessed 25 June 2014. www.blackgate.com/the-demarcation-of-sword-and-sorcery/#3
Mendlesohn, Farah. *Rhetorics of Fantasy*. Wesleyan University Press, 2008.
Mendlesohn, Farah and Edward James. *A Short History of Fantasy*. 2009. Rev. ed. Libri Publishing, 2012.
———., editors. *A Cambridge Companion to Fantasy Literature*. Cambridge University Press, 2012.
Miller, Dean A. *The Epic Hero*. 2000. John Hopkins University Press, 2002.
Moorcock, Michael. 1957–1967. *Elric: The Stealer of Souls*. Del Rey, 2008.
———. *Wizardry and Wild Romance: A Study of Epic Fantasy*. 1987. MonkeyBrain Publication, 2004.

Nikolajeva, Maria. *The Magic Code: The Use of Magical Patterns in Fantasy for Children*. Almqvist & Wiksell International, 1988.

Palmer-Patel, C. "Excavations of Genre Barriers: Breaking New Ground with *Fantastika Journal*." *Fantastika Journal*, vol. 1, no. 1, 2017, pp. 21–35.

Propp. Vladimir. *Morphology of the Folktale*. 1928. Ed. Louis A. Wagner. Trans. Laurence Scott. 1968. University of Texas Press, 2009.

Pullman, Philip. *His Dark Materials*. Scholastic, 1995–2000. His Dark Materials 1–3.

Rank, Otto. *The Myth of the Hero: A Psychological Exploration of Myth*. 1922. Trans. Gregory C. Richter and E. James Lieberman. John Hopkins University Press, 2004.

Raglan, Lord. *The Hero*. 1936. New American Library, 1979.

Rowling, J. K. *Harry Potter*. Bloomsbury, 1997–2007. Harry Potter 1–7.

Sanderson, Brandon. *Mistborn Trilogy*. Tor, 2006–2010. Mistborn 1–3.

Star Wars. Lucasfilm, 1977–2017. Star Wars 1–8.

Suvin, Darko. "Considering the Sense of 'Fantasy' or 'Fantastic Fiction': An Effusion." *Extrapolation*, vol. 41, no. 3, 2000, pp. 209–247.

———. *Metamorphoses of Science Fiction*. 1979. Yale University Press, 1980.

Swinfen, Ann. *In Defense of Fantasy: A Study of the Genre in English and American Literature Since 1945*. Routledge & Kegan Paul, 1984.

Tolkien, J. R. R. *The Lords of the Rings*. Allen & Unwin, 1954–1955. The Lord of the Rings 1–3.

Wolfe, Gary K. "Evaporating Genres." 2002. *Evaporating Genres: Essays on Fantastic Literature*. Wesleyan University Press, 2011. pp. 18–53.

Young, Helen. *Race and Popular Fantasy Literature: Habits of Whiteness*. Routledge, 2016.

1 The Shape of a Hero's Soul
Interrogating the Destiny of the Hero in Lois McMaster Bujold's *The Curse of Chalion* (2001)

Prophecy or the idea of the 'destined hero' are essential motifs in Heroic Epic Fantasy fiction. Customarily, a seer will predict some outcome of the future where a hero will arise who is capable of 'saving the world.' As the declaration of a prophecy seems to imply that a hero must live according to their destiny, does this then mean that heroes are incapable of acting of their own free will? Certainly, C. N. Manlove in *Modern Fantasy* (1975) argues that:

> Kingsley, MacDonald, Lewis and Tolkien (and Charles Williams) all limit the free choice of their protagonists in order to get them where they want to go; though the degree to which they do it varies, they are all 'benign determinists' who do not allow evil or free will full scope. (260)

Influenced by a Christian theology, Manlove views fate and free will as mutually exclusive terms, taking the stance that a figure of destiny is not a 'free' character and that all actions made by the protagonist are determined as a result of fate. In *Rhetorics of Fantasy* (2008), Farah Mendlesohn likewise asserts that the Fantasy hero is not free due to the motif of prophecy: "Prophecies allow knowledge to be imparted, so that in fact the goal is 'known' even though its meaning is not understood [...]. The hero does not have free will in a narrative driven by prophecy" (42). While these critics maintain that prophecy and fate limits the free will of the characters, I counter that, while prophecy may motivate or 'drive' characters and events in a narrative, the hero's free will is not limited, and, is, in fact, a crucial component of the Heroic Epic Fantasy structure.

In this chapter, I demonstrate how the genre of Heroic Epic Fantasy effectively combines a paradox of fate and free will in order to create a narrative with open possibilities. I argue that this paradox is an essential part of the genre itself as the author must blend the idea of the destined hero with a free character who is allowed to make choices. I examine this argument through a conception of the hero as a pre-determined shape. Drawing from a tradition of Stoic philosophy, I assert that, while the shape of the hero's nature is pre-determined, it remains up to the hero's free will to determine whether to fulfil the functions of their design.

This chapter utilises Lois McMaster Bujold's *The Curse of Chalion* (2001) as a case study. While other Heroic Epic Fantasy authors also briefly describe the shape of the hero as a vessel, this conception of shape is an essential theme in *The Curse of Chalion* and I have selected it as a case study accordingly. In *The Curse of Chalion*, Lady Ista informs the hero Lupe dy Cazaril of the following prophecy: "the gods might draw the curse back to them only through the will of a man who would lay down his life three times for the House of Chalion" (360–361). At this time, neither he or Lady Ista is certain whether Cazaril is the man spoken about in the prophecy, or, indeed, even though they are explicitly told how to break the curse of Chalion, they cannot comprehend how to bring it about. Using the novel as a model of Heroic Epic Fantasy, I demonstrate that in a narrative with prophecy and fate, the hero interacts with these devices through an assertion of free will.

The Hero as Pawn or Avatar

Before we examine the paradox of fate and free will, it is important to note that the hero of a Heroic Epic Fantasy often acts as an agent of a metaphysical entity in the physical world. In his book *Lois McMaster Bujold* (2015), Edward James argues that: "The centrality of religion in Bujold's presentation of the world – the action of all three novels is directed at a crucial stage by the intervention of a god – is refreshingly different from the bulk of modern fantasy" (54). However, as I outlined in this introduction, the concept of a higher power that directly impacts on the narrative is an essential part of the structure of the Heroic Epic. Bujold's text is not notable in this regard but is instead representative of the genre. Inspired by or deriving from Mythology, a presence of divinity or a metaphysical power is seen in both modern and early Epic Fantasy. When a divine presence is explicitly noted in the narrative, an idea of positive and negative dualism may emerge, as the hero's perception of the god as 'good' or 'evil' may initially be taken at face value by the reader. Regardless of whether this moral coding is correct, a central structure of Heroic Epic Fantasy is that the hero *chooses* to align themselves to a higher power and accept or reject a responsibility as their agent.

The idea of fate being an absolute determined future may have come about because of this association between heroes and divinity. In Thomas Carlyle's evaluation of different types of heroes in *On Heroes, Hero-Worship, & the Heroic in History* (lectures 1835; published 1904), Carlyle suggests that the first phase of hero is where the hero *is* divine. Such examples would include Heracles in Greek Mythology and Ramayana in Hindu Mythology, where Heracles has divine blood and

Ramayana is a god reborn in mortal form. The next phase in Carlyle's assessment is hero as prophet: "The Hero is not now regarded as a God among his fellowmen; but as one God-inspired, as a Prophet" (42). The hero as prophet is one who is inspired by the words of god and acts or speaks accordingly. This phase leads to the third, of the hero as poet. In *Anatomy of Criticism* (1957), Northrop Frye likewise describes how the poet is god-touched:

> [I]t is clear that the poet who sings about gods is often considered to be singing as one, or an instrument of one. His social function is that of an inspired oracle; [...] The poet's visionary function, his proper work as a poet, is on this plane to reveal the god for whom he speaks. This usually means that he reveals the god's will in connection with a specific occasion, when he is consulted as an oracle in a state of "enthusiasm" or divine possession. (55)

Frye describes a process where the prophet and poet are one, speaking out loud the words of the gods in a state of "divine possession." Like Carlyle's categories of heroes, Frye makes a direct connection between divinity, the prophet, and the poet, through the act of speaking. In Heroic Epic Fantasy Fiction, this connection is often revealed through the device of prophecy and fate.

The word 'fate' itself may be connected to the 'word of god.' In *Religion in Virgil* (1935), Cyril Bailey argues that the word fate (*fatum*):

> is connected with the verb *fari*, "to speak," and that it is in fact its passive participle, meaning "the spoken word." [...] To Virgil himself it seems to have implied primarily the notion of the "spoken word" of divine beings and in particular of Iuppiter, which was the expression of his will and so of the destiny of mankind. (205)

Thus, accepting fate means accepting the spoken words of the gods. In Virgil's *The Aeneid* (19 BCE), 'fate' conveys the idea that the action is not something that one wants to do, but it is the best possible action to do at the time. Accordingly, the hero – Virgil in Bailey's examination or Cazaril in our example of Heroic Epic Fantasy – agrees to become a pawn of the gods and follow the "spoken word" of these divine beings.

The necessity of having a hero as an agent of divinity is imposed by the limitations of the universe where the gods are unable to directly act in the physical world. Many Epic Fantasy writers create an origin story for the setting of their world that is reminiscent of Mythology. Lord Dunsany's *The Gods of Pegāna* (1905) is one of the earliest modern Fantasy texts which invents a new pantheon of gods where the chief of the gods Mana-Yood-Sushai creates lesser gods who in turn create humanity.

Likewise, in the stand-alone sequel to *The Curse of Chalion*, *Paladin of Souls* (2003), the origin story of the world is depicted as follows:

> The world was first and the world was flame, fluid and fearsome. As the flame cooled, matter formed and gained vast strength and endurance, a great globe with fire at its heart. From the fire at the heart of the world slowly grew the World-Soul. [...] But the eye cannot see itself, not even the Eye of the World-Soul. So the World-Soul split in two, that it might so perceive itself; and so the Father and the Mother came into being [...]. (*Paladin of Souls* 41)

This creation story in Bujold's *Chalion* universe is similar to many Mythologies in that the world and god(s) are created from chaos first and then the created gods or world create humankind in turn. After creating humans, the gods are made to depart the physical plane as James Campbell notes in *The Hero with a Thousand Faces* (1949): "The cosmogonic cycle is now to be carried forward, therefore, not by the gods, who have become invisible, but by the heroes, more or less human in character, through whom the world destiny is realized" (271). There is first a 'Golden Age' where the gods are visible and actively present, interacting directly with humankind. But, due to a 'Fall,' this Golden Age where the gods are on Earth soon passes and the gods leave the Earthly dimension for another one. Following the creation of the world, the gods are not allowed or capable of returning to Earth and must then operate through other means. In *The Epic Hero* (2000), Dean A. Miller likewise concludes for the Mythological hero that:

> Strictly speaking this hero is a representative, even a pawn, of the vast inhuman potencies, and his destiny is constrained (and may be formed) by the whim of divine cosmogonies and supernatural arbitrators. [...] The mythological epic and its archetypical thematic elevates the hero, who is made the shadow partner or the earthly avatar of divinity, to an awesome height. (31)

In Mythology, as the gods have become "invisible" (Campbell 271) or are incapable of carrying out these actions on their own, a god must designate a hero as an agent. In Heroic Epic Fantasy, as gods are removed from the physical material world of humans, they must operate through a hero who has allowed a benevolent or malevolent divine force to guide their actions. The Heroic Epic Fantasy hero fulfils the same function as the Mythological hero, as a god's pawn or avatar, and in doing so, transcends in some way "to an awesome height" (Miller 31) – a notion that will be expanded on further below.

Note that the hero's position as agent of divinity may be depicted as either pawn, knight, or avatar, dependent on the text. Thus, throughout this book, I use these words not interchangeably, but as the language of the text require it. For instance, Bujold uses this word 'avatar' in a ceremonial circumstance, where, in a spring rite, a person is chosen to fill the role of the goddess. This person is in no way actually possessed by the spirit of a god as the ceremony is only representational. Yet this symbolic event foreshadows the conclusion of the novel, when the body of the hero Cazaril *does*, in fact, become a temporary vessel for the spirit of a god. The use of the word 'avatar' is an interesting word choice, as it would derive from the Sanskrit word. In the Hindu Epic Mythologies *Ramayana* and *Mahabharata*, the gods literally descend down to earth in mortal forms to correct the evils of the world. In *The Curse of Chalion*, the gods can only modify blunders in the world by possessing the body of a mortal person; since they are removed from the physical world, they must operate through the body of the hero.

The narration in *The Curse of Chalion* indicates that the gods are unable to *comprehend* the physical world, which may be the reason why, in Bujold's *Chalion* universe at least, the gods are unable to cross into the physical world:

> If the gods saw people's souls but not their bodies, in mirror to the way people saw bodies but not souls, [...] Perhaps heaven was not a place, but merely an angle of view, a vantage, a perspective.
>   *And at the moment of death, we slide through altogether.* [...] Death ripped a hole between the worlds. (*Curse of Chalion* 457–458, original emphasis)

A motif of crossing borders occurs here, with very violent imagery indicated in this transgression: "Death ripped a hole between the worlds." As an agent of the divine, the Heroic Epic Fantasy hero operates as a figure of transgression, of fluidity, in order to cross borders where no human – and not even the gods – can cross. Miller likewise contends that: "Beneath the literary constructions persists a widely accepted common notion of the 'hero' as a mediator, a conduit between the living world and whatever nonhuman powers and zones exist" (4). As this book will explore, like the Mythological hero, the ability to cross borders and to act as mediator between humanity and metaphysical forces is a significant role of the Heroic Epic Fantasy hero as well.

In *The Curse of Chalion*, the prophecy that Cazaril must fulfil involves removing a curse that has affected the land of Chalion. This curse is, in fact, "a drop of the Father's blood" – a god of Chalion – that was improperly "spilled, soiled" into the physical world of humans (477, 466). Bujold expresses a recurrent motif of spilling, pouring, and fluidity, which seems to indicate a transgression or a crossing of borders and boundaries. As I expand on throughout this book, similar motifs of crossing borders are also apparent in other works of Heroic Epic Fantasy. That only a *drop* of a god's blood results in a generational curse across the whole land of Chalion seems indicative of the gods' inability to cross the boundary into the physical world. As a result, they are only able to influence the physical world through the actions of a hero: "The gods [...] worked [...] through the world, not in it. [...] – men's free will must open a channel for good or evil to enter waking life" (66). Note that while above Manlove argued that fate does not "allow evil or free will full scope" (260), here the narration indicates that free will allows for the possibility of good *or* evil. As the gods are removed from the physical world, the Heroic Epic Fantasy hero acts as an agent or a 'channel' that allows a metaphysical entity – benevolent *or* malevolent – to enter into the world.

Does Fate Deny Freedom?

While the gods may not be able to cross into or comprehend the physical world, they still seem to be omniscient, as indicated by the act of prophecy itself. The Mother of Summer, one of the five gods of Chalion, is the one that informs Lady Ista of the prophecy. Do the gods then, by being able to see into the future, prompt the hero onto their adventure? Or is the hero's journey motivated by internal factors? Campbell describes the first step of the journey as a "call for adventure," where the Mythological hero encounters the supernatural world. This encounter can be met accidentally:

> A blunder – apparently the merest chance – reveals an unsuspected world, and the individual is drawn into a relationship with forces that are not rightly understood. As Freud has shown, blunders are not the merest chance. They are the result of suppressed desires and conflicts. (42)

Campbell's psychoanalytical approach suggests that acts that seem to be accidental are a result of suppressed desires. While Cazaril in *The Curse of Chalion* appears to encounter similar chance events, I assert that this is not a result of suppressed desires, but instead an active declaration of free will. While gods or fate may prompt the hero on their journey, it remains up to the hero to choose whether to follow this path.

In *The Curse of Chalion*, Cazaril only encounters the prophecy in the latter half of the novel. Lady Ista tells him how the Mother of Summer had come to her in a dream:

> She said that the gods sought to take the curse back, that it did not belong in this world, that it was a gift [... that was] spilt improperly. She said that the gods might draw the curse back to them only through the will of a man who would lay down his life three times for the House of Chalion. (361)

It is up to the hero of the prophecy to repair the damage that has been done through an act of transgression, of spilling into this world a "gift" or "curse" that does not belong there. It is up to this hero to return this spillage to its proper place. However, it is evident that, at this time, Cazaril and Ista do not understand how to fulfil the prophecy as it is incomprehensible how a man could literally die three times.

When Cazaril comes across the prophecy three-quarters of the way through the book, he is already well on his way to fulfilling the prophecy without realising that he has done so. Cazaril discovers that his journey to his present moment began even earlier than he had supposed: "*How long have I been walking down this road?* [...] Was he nothing but a puppet on a string? Or was that, a mule on the rope, balky and stubborn, to be whipped along?" (392, original emphasis). Cazaril determines that all the hardships that he has suffered are a required part of his journey in order to bring him to the time and place where he can fulfil the prophecy.

This may seem to indicate that Cazaril followed a pre-determined path blindly. And yet, at the same time, Cazaril recognises that *each* event was determined through *his own choice*. Cazaril remembers submitting himself to the mercy of the gods, any god, and praying for deliverance for his men: "And he'd [...] sworn that any other god could pick him up who willed, or none, so long as the men who had trusted him were let out of this trap" (394–395). This moment of self-recognition is profound for Cazaril. It is only towards the end of the novel that Cazaril recognises the consequences of each 'trivial' action, that with every choice he had made, he had chosen and reaffirmed that he had accepted divine ordinance. Cazaril's "call to adventure" was not a result of suppressed desires, but a conscious decision to save his men. Although he did not understand the full implications of his actions at the time, it is enough that Cazaril did choose to submit.

The choice itself demonstrates his free will. In an earlier conversation with Umegat, a priest, the characters in *The Curse of Chalion* contemplate whether Cazaril's entire life is fated. Umegat suggests a scenario to Cazaril that allows them to combine both fate and free will: "Perhaps, instead of controlling every step, the gods have started a hundred or a thousand Cazarils and Umegats down this road. And only those arrive *who choose to*" (257, my emphasis). Thus, Cazaril and Umegat determine that fate does not deny one's free will. A god or fate might propose a path for ordinary humans, but the choice to follow that path comes from within. Note that the characters themselves explicitly expose these mechanics. Moreover, Cazaril later considers that this choice must be re-affirmed repeatedly: "did one have to choose and choose and choose again, every day?" (394). The moment of choice comes frequently and is not dependent on a single act of choosing or a mere blunder.

Similar choices and discussions of free will occur in other works of Heroic Epic Fantasy. For instance, Jonmarc in Gail Z. Martin's *Dark*

Lady's Chosen (2009) has a near-identical conversation with his companion Gabriel:

> What Gabriel called "choice" Jonmarc has seen as a series of practical steps, each following one from the one before it. [...]
> An awful thought chilled him. "How long have I been Her chosen?" [...] *Have I been nothing but a pawn?* [...]
> [Gabriel replies] "We're not puppets, Jonmarc. [...] Always, it was your choice." (296–297)

Note the similarities in their discussion with that of Cazaril and Umegat. Both narratives exhibit characters which consider their life as a journey or path with the steps being pre-determined; the characters also reflect on whether they are "pawns" and "puppets." Similarly, in Mercedes Lackey's *The Fairy Godmother* (2004), when fate tries to force the hero onto a pre-determined path, she vocally resists it, proclaiming: "I am [...] no puppet to be danced about on a path you choose!" (303). These discussions or declarations demonstrate an awareness and conscious self-reflection of the character's position in the narrative (an idea that will be expanded in Chapter 3). Notably, the characters must accept *or* refute their position in the narrative. In Lackey's *The Fairy Godmothers*, the character's refusal of her destiny allows her to create a new path. In contrast, in Terry Goodkind's *Wizard's First Rule* (1994), the characters refuse to accept the command of prophecy, but, as will be discussed further in Chapter 6, an attempt to avoid fate results in the prophecies being fulfilled. Despite this, the protagonists still exhibit the ability to make free choices as the prophecy is fulfilled because of their lack of comprehension in the consequences of their actions; as with Cazaril, it is not knowledge of prophecy that leads to fulfilment of fate, but the conscious declaration of free choice.

As the next two chapters will explore, the character's struggle to interpret and comprehend prophecy is an essential part of these stories and directly influences the free choices they make. In Heroic Epic Fantasy fiction, as in many literatures, the hero must always begin the journey as a naïve character, the tarot Fool, completely ignorant to where the path might take them. But, as the narration reveals in Philip Pullman's *His Dark Materials* trilogy (1995–2000), the hero "must be free to make mistakes" (*Northern Lights* 176). It is through the free choices of the characters that the events of prophecy are fulfilled (or not fulfilled). While the gods prefer a particular event to occur, they cannot force anyone in any one direction. As Umegat clearly states: "Men's will is free. The Gods may not invade it" (*Curse of Chalion* 224).

Of course, the debate of whether fate denies free will has been a long philosophical discussion lasting millennia; this debate continues in literary criticism as identified above with the examples of Manlove and Mendlesohn. In her analysis of J. R. R. Tolkien's *The Lord of the Rings*

(1954–1955), Mendlesohn argues that the text is closed and fixed as a result of imparted knowledge:

> [H]istory or analysis is often provided by the storyteller who is drawn in the role of sage, magician, or guide. While this casting apparently opens up the text, in fact it seeks to close it down further by denying not only reader interpretation, but also that of the hero/protagonist. (*Rhetorics of Fantasy* 7)

In contrast, Richard Mathews in his examination of Tolkien's trilogy in *Fantasy: The Liberation of Imagination* (1997) indicates that knowledge leads to freedom: "Free will is of great importance in Tolkien's moral scheme [...]. Freedom of choice is only possible through knowledge and it is partly for this reason that Gandalf relates the Ring's history to Frodo" (66). Mathews here suggests that knowledge *opens up* the text so that the hero is enabled to make free choices. Rather than closing the text, by providing knowledge, heroes are able to make informed decisions.

Likewise, in *Our Knowledge of the External World* (1914), Bertrand Russell counters the idea that knowledge of the future denies free will:

> Everything else is confusion of time, due to the feeling that knowledge *compels* the happening of what it knows when this is future, though it is at once obvious that knowledge has no such power in regard to the past. (191, original emphasis)

He comes to this deduction by arguing:

> It must be remembered that the supposed prevision would not create the future any more than memory creates the past. We do not think we were necessarily not free in the past, merely because we can now remember our past volitions. Similarly, we might be free in the future, even if we could now see what our future volitions were going to be. (190–191)

Russell pragmatically suggests that knowledge of the future does not necessarily indicate that humans are required to follow the actions of their pre-vision. Knowledge of the future may guide actions but does not mean that one is required to abide by them.

As Stoic philosophy has argued,[1] the idea that knowledge of the future denies free will is a sophism. In *Determinism and Freedom in Stoic Philosophy* (1998), Susanne Bobzien outlines this argument, known as the Idle Argument:

> (1) If it is fated that you will recover from this illness, then, regardless of whether you consult a doctor or you do not consult <a doctor>

you will recover. (2) But also: if it is fated that you won't recover from this illness, then, regardless of whether you consult a doctor or you do not consult <a doctor> you won't recover. [...] (4) Therefore it is futile to consult a doctor. (Origen, translated in Bobzien 182)

The Idle Argument suggests that, if every action is fated or determined, then it is futile to take any action at all. Consequently, the Idle Argument results in total passivity or inertia. But as Bobzien explains, the Stoic philosophers Origen and Cicero argued that this argument was a sophism:

First, [...] even though someone may have been theoretically convinced by the Idle Argument [...] this does not preclude that, when it comes to acting, they cannot help but believe that their actions are relevant to the outcomes, even if the Idle Argument proved otherwise. [...] Second, the Idle Argument allows us to infer the futility of not ϕ-ing in the same way as that of ϕ-ing. (Bobzien 192)

As Origen and Cicero assert, the argument that a person or character is denied free will because of the presence of fate is not logical, as one would still need to make a choice between doing and not-doing.

This philosophy provides a conception of fate and free will that is similar to the notions encoded within the Heroic Epic Fantasy genre. Though they may be omniscient, the gods are not omnipotent:

[H]ave you really understood how powerless the gods are, [...]? [...] If the gods could seize passage from anyone they wished, then men would be mere puppets. Only if they borrow or are given will from a willing creature, do they have a little channel through which to act. (*Curse of Chalion* 225)

In this passage, Umegat describes how the gods of Chalion are limited. His depiction of the soul incorporates the motif of pouring and fluidity again: "sometimes, a man may open himself to them, and let them pour through him into the world" (225). Using a cup and a jug of wine to act out a physical demonstration, "the sermon of the cup" (225), Umegat exhibits how a hero allows himself to be made into a channel or a cup in order for the spirit of god to pour through them and cross into the physical world.

The imagery of the cup that occurs in the text evokes a Stoic metaphor, where a similar conception of shape is used to illustrate the combination of determinism and free will. This model is described by Marcia L. Colish in *The Stoic Tradition from Antiquity to the Early Middle Ages* (1990):

The Stoics, following Chrysippus, illustrate this argument with one of their most famous metaphors: A cylinder is at rest. If it is set in motion it will move necessarily in a circular manner, in obedience to its given shape. But whether it is set in motion or not lies within the realm of possibility. So, the Stoics conclude, man is determined by his given nature, but he is free to act in terms of it. (35)

The shape of the hero's nature is determined – a cup (in Bujold) or a cylinder (Chrysippus) – but it remains up to the hero's free will whether to fulfil the functions of this design. That is, a divine entity may determine a 'fate' for a hero, shaping their nature in the hopes that the hero will choose to act as their agent on Earth, but it remains up to the hero to choose to live according to this given nature.

While it is difficult to determine whether Bujold consciously evokes this Stoic imagery, it is evident that the Stoic philosophy of life *is* encoded within Heroic Epic Fantasy. For instance, Madeline L'Engle conveys a similar analogy in the children's novel *A Wrinkle in Time* (1962). Using the metaphor of the rigid structures of a sonnet, the characters conclude:

> "You mean you're comparing our lives to a sonnet? A strict form, but freedom within it?"
>
> "Yes," Mrs. Whatsis said. "You're given the form, but you have to write the sonnet yourself. What you say is completely up to you." (186)

The exchange demonstrates how embedded the concept of 'freedom in a fixed form' is even in early Science Fiction and Fantasy. Other Fantasy authors explicitly use the shape of vessels and containers to convey the combination of fate and free will. In L. E. Modesitt Jr.'s *The Magic of Recluce* (1991), the narration uses the metaphor of a potter when discussing the purpose of the hero: "A potter may use his skill for producing containers. Those containers may be used for good or evil purposes. Most are used for purposes without much real good or evil" (21). The potter may create a vase, but the potter's intent does not factor into how the vase is used. Similarly, the hero Gaborn in David Farland's *The Lair of Bones* (2003) contemplates: "What if … a man is like a vessel […]. And what if that vessel can be filled with light, or it can be filled with darkness?" (315). The conception of a vessel is used frequently to describe the connection or disconnection between the creator's intent and consequent usage. In Saladin Ahmed's *Throne of the Crescent Moon* (2012, an American author first published in the U.K.), the description of being 'filled' pertains not to a god or benevolent creator, but to a devil-like creature, the Traitorous Angel:

> There's an old tale of a man called the ghul of ghuls […] A man who'd cut out his own tongue to better let the Traitorous Angel speak through him. Who had his soul emptied, then filled with the will of the Traitorous Angel. (182)

The passage here conveys the idea that there exists a man who is completely subservient, to the point that he deforms himself in order to let the "Traitorous Angel speak through him." In this more recent text, the idea of a "soul emptied" and "then filled with the will" of a divine entity is subverted and transforms the traditional depiction of a Heroic Epic Fantasy hero as a pawn or avatar of god into an avatar of a devil-like figure instead.

The motif of a hero as a vessel or container indicates the use of the hero as a tool of the gods. Burton Scott Easton indicates that, in the Bible, the word 'vessel': "[i]s used freely in English Versions of the Bible to translate *keli*, the Aramaic *ma'n*, and *skeuos*, words all meaning 'an implement or utensil' of any kind, when the context shows that a hollow utensil is meant" (*International Standard Bible Encyclopedia* n.p.). Thus, in religious texts, the idea of cup, chalice, or similar hollow device indicates that the character functions as a utensil, a tool of god. This connection is also made in *The Curse of Chalion*: "you are the tool. You are not the work. Expect to be valued accordingly" (*Curse of Chalion* 232). Although a god may provide the shape of a hero, it is up to the character whether they are to fulfil the function of this shape and perform as a tool of the gods.

Although the hero of the Heroic Epic Fantasy acts as an agent of divinity and follows their 'spoken word,' I conclude that there is perhaps some ambiguity with the word 'fate.' The word here does not indicate a deterministic future. Instead, the word 'fate' seems to imply that a person has a *purpose* in life and choosing this path will provide a reward. For instance, in David and Leigh Eddings' *Demon Lord of Karanda* (1988), the characters discuss how: "you've come to that crossroads in your life that Cyradis mentioned, [...]. You're being rewarded because you've chosen the right fork" (98). The next chapter will return to the idea of crossroads and forks in the road, but the important thing to note here is the idea that free choice can lead to personal or spiritual fulfilment.

In *The Curse of Chalion*, Cazaril suffers horribly in his journey as he physically dies three times. However, it is the act of death itself that allows Cazaril to be rewarded, as in the third death he is temporarily unified with the divine. Accordingly, by accepting his purpose as a vessel of god, Cazaril is granted a reward by fulfilling that purpose: functioning as a vessel of god gives Cazaril a sublime experience. Similarly, in the stand-alone sequel to *The Curse of Chalion*, *Paladin of Souls*, the hero Lady Ista initially refuses the commands of divinity as she has been expected to follow a prescribed path all of her life as a dutiful daughter, wife, and mother. Repeated refusals demonstrate that when Ista eventually accepts divinity's commands, she does so out of her own free will. In accepting her purpose as an agent of god, Ista is granted a reward by fulfilling that purpose: functioning as an agent of god gives Ista more freedoms than her previously confined life. Thus, by choosing to follow their fates – the word of god – both Cazaril and Ista are rewarded. Simply by choosing to accept the shape of their characters, Cazaril and Ista find fulfilment.[2]

The Transcendent Hero

The potential of the Heroic Epic Fantasy hero is demonstrated through the words of prophecy and fate. In *Scientific Thought* (1923), C. D. Broad discusses how when the present meets the future, a "change" occurs: "Let us call the third kind of change *Becoming*" (67, original emphasis). Applying this idea to Heroic Epic Fantasy, when a character chooses to accept the words of prophecy and fate, they move from the present to the future, from a potential state of hero to becoming an *actualised* hero. In *The Dialogic Imagination* (1975, translated 1981), M. M. Bakhtin argues that the characters in a story of fate are essentially unchanged: "people and things have gone through something, something that did not, indeed, change them but that did (in a manner of speaking) [...] verify and establish their identity" (106–107); the hero simply reaffirms their character with an "identity absolutely unchanged" (105). However, I argue that in a story of fate, the act of transcendence, while affirming the potential of the character, also *changes* the character from potential hero into actualised hero.

In *The Curse of Chalion*, the act of dying grants Cazaril an indescribable euphoric experience where he is temporarily made one with the divine spirit of a god: "'I don't know how to open my mouth and push out the universe in words. It won't fit. [...].' He was shivering, suddenly, his eyes blurred with tears" (476). For a brief moment, Cazaril is one with god, intrinsically connected body and soul. This experience affects the hero deeply. While the experience is ephemeral – as Cazaril's movement from potential hero to actualised hero is only possible at the *moment* of death, and thus, only temporary – the experience still leaves his character changed. To use Broad's conception of becoming: "the sum total of the existent is continually augmented by becoming" (69); this is true for the characters in Heroic Epic Fantasy as well. Cazaril has been profoundly affected by his moment as hero and is *changed*. Though his moment as actualised hero may be over, he is no longer the man that he once was.

After the moment of transcendence has passed, Cazaril attempts to recapture the moment through poetry. This is a notable change in his behaviour and is commented on by the other characters as well. Recall that Carlyle's third phase of the hero is the hero as poet:

> In some old languages, again, the titles are synonymous; *Vates* means both Prophet and Poet: and indeed at all times, Prophet and Poet, well understood, have much kindred of meaning. Fundamentally

indeed they are still the same; in this most important respect especially, that they have penetrated both of them into the sacred mystery of the universe. (Carlyle 80)

Like the prophet, the hero as poet is god-inspired, as the hero desires to cross back into the boundary of the gods. The god-touched hero is momentarily able to see the universe from the god's perspective. This knowledge leaves a sacred mark on the hero, even as they return to their own vantage point. As such, the characters of a story with fate do not simply have their identities as heroes reaffirmed, but instead are profoundly altered.

All of the case studies of Heroic Epic Fantasy discussed in this book depict a hero that *becomes* something more, the transcendent hero, but this moment may be temporary, and the hero may diminish into something less than a hero but greater than they once were. Consider, for example, the discussion between Frodo and Sam at the end of Tolkien's *The Lord of the Rings*, as Frodo departs Middle Earth:

"Where are you going, Master?" cried Sam, [...]
"To the Havens, Sam," said Frodo.
"And I can't come."
"No, Sam. Not yet anyway, not further than the Havens. Though you too were a Ring-bearer, if only for a little while. Your time may come." (*The Return of the King* 375)

Frodo's status as Ring-bearer, a fulfilled and actualised hero that has carried through his destiny, indicates that he is something different from the rest of the Fellowship. The Heroic Epic Fantasy Hero, then, is similar to Bakhtin's description of the adventure hero of everyday life instead of the adventure hero of fate: "The series of adventures that the hero [of everyday life] undergoes does not result in a simple affirmation of his identity, but rather in the construction of a new image of the hero, a man who is purified and reborn" (Bakhtin 117). Similar to the adventure hero of the everyday life, Cazaril and Frodo are quite literally "purified and reborn" as they are transformed by their experiences.

As this chapter has demonstrated, in Heroic Epic Fantasy, fate does not limit the hero's free will: while the shape of the hero may be predetermined, it is up to the hero to decide whether to fulfil the function of that shape. In doing so, the hero transcends and is transformed from a position of potential hero to becoming an actualised hero. Note, however, that though the Hero of *The Curse of Chalion* has a shape of the cup, this does not signify that *all* heroes must be cups or containers. Indeed, Cazaril describes the hero of the sequel, Lady Ista, as a sword. In *Paladin of Souls*, Ista acts a porter for a god, carrying spirits across a doorway between the worlds through her own body as a portal. Unlike a cup, which contains and retains the divine spirit by being passive, Ista enables the fluidity and transmission of spirits from one border to the other by actively 'cutting' through the worlds. The next two chapters will contrast the more passive vessel shape of the hero as demonstrated by Cazaril to the model of the heroes in Mercedes Lackey's *Five Hundred Kingdom* series (2004–2012) and Robert Jordan's *The Wheel of Time* series (1990–2012). Here, instead of allowing the workings of fate to flow *through* them, the heroes actively manipulate events and prophecy itself as they negotiate the demands of fate.

Notes

1 Note that Stoic philosophy is not unified in thought, especially as it spans several centuries.
2 For a more detailed comparative discussion of fate and purpose with Cazaril and Ista, see "The Shape of a Hero's Soul: Exploring the Paradox of Fate and Free Will in *The Curse of Chalion* and *Paladin of Souls*," a more focused variation of this chapter in *Biology and Manners: The Worlds of Lois McMaster Bujold*.

Bibliography

Ahmed, Saladin. *Throne of the Crescent Moon*. 2012. Daw, 2013. Crescent Moon Kingdoms 1.
Bailey, Cyril. *Religion in Virgil*. 1935. Barnes and Nobles, 1969.
Bakhtin, Mikhail Mikhaïlovich. *The Dialogic Imagination*. 1975. Ed. Michael Holquist. Trans. Caryl Emerson and Michael Holquist. University of Texas Press, 1981.
Bobzien, Susanne. *Determinism and Freedom in Stoic Philosophy*. Clarendon Press, 1998.
Broad, Charlie Dunbar. "The General Problem of Time and Change." *Scientific Thought*. 1923. Routledge, 1952. pp. 53–84.
Bujold, Lois McMaster. *The Curse of Chalion*. 2000. HarperCollins, 2011. Chalion 1.
———. *Paladin of Souls*. HarperTorch, 2003. Chalion 2.
Campbell, Joseph. *The Hero with a Thousand Faces*. 1949. New World Library, 2008.
Carlyle, Thomas. *On Heroes, Hero-Worship, & the Heroic in History*. 1841. Chapman and Hall Limited, 1904.
Colish, Marcia L. *The Stoic Tradition from Antiquity to the Early Middle Ages*. E. J. Brill, 1990.
Easton, Burton Scott. "Vessel." *International Standard Bible Encyclopedia*. 1915. Ed. James Orr. Accessed 6 August 2017. www.biblestudytools.com/dictionary/vessel/
Eddings, David and Leigh Eddings. *Demon Lord of Karanda*. Del Ray, 1988. Malloreon 3.
Farland, David. *The Lair of Bones*. 2003. Tom Doherty, 2005. The Runelords 4.
Frye, Northrop. *Anatomy of Criticism*. 1957. Princeton University Press, 1973.

Goodkind, Terry. *Wizard's First Rule*. 1994. Tom Doherty, 1995. The Sword of Truth 1.
James, Edward. *Lois McMaster Bujold*. University of Illinois Press, 2015.
Lackey, Mercedes. *The Fairy Godmother*. Luna Books, 2004. Five Hundred Kingdoms 1.
L'Engle, Madeline. *A Wrinkle in Time*. 1962. Bantam Doubleday Dell Books, 1976. Time 1.
Lord Dunsany. *The Gods of Pegāna*. 1905. Project Gutenberg. 19 October 2012. Web. Accessed 9 May 2016.
Manlove, Colin N. *Modern Fantasy: Five Studies*. Cambridge University Press, 1975.
Martin, Gail Z. *Dark Lady's Chosen*. Solaris, 2009. Chronicles of the Necromancer 4.
Mathews, Richard. *Fantasy: The Liberation of Imagination*. 1997. Routledge, 2002.
Mendlesohn, Farah. *Rhetorics of Fantasy*. Wesleyan University Press, 2008.
Miller, Dean A. *The Epic Hero*. 2000. John Hopkins University Press, 2002.
Modesitt, Leland E., Jr. *The Magic of Recluce*. 1991. Tor, 1992. The Saga of Recluce 1.
Palmer-Patel, Charul. "The Shape of a Hero's Soul: Exploring the Paradox of Fate and Free Will in *The Curse of Chalion* and *Paladin of Souls*." *Biology and Manners: The Worlds of Lois McMaster Bujold*. Eds. Una McCormack and Regina Yung Lee. Liverpool University Press, 2020.
Pullman, Philip. *The Northern Lights*. 1995. *His Dark Materials*. Everyman's Library. 3–350. His Dark Materials 1.
Russell, Bertrand. "On the Notion of Cause, with Application to the Free-Will Problem." *Our Knowledge of the External World*. 1914. Routledge, 2009. pp. 169–196.
Tolkien, John Ronald Reuel. *The Return of the King*. 1955. HarperCollins, 1994. The Lord of the Rings 3.
Valmiki. *Ramayana*. Trans. Kamala Subramaniam. Mumbai: Bharatiya Vidya Bhavan, 2009.
Vyāsa. *Mahābhārata*. Trans. Kisari Mohan Ganguli. 1896. *Internet Sacred Text Archive*. 2010. Web. Accessed 4 November 2018. www.sacred-texts.com/hin/maha/index.htm
Virgil. *The Aeneid*. 19 BCE. Trans. Robert Fitzgerald. Vintage Classics, 1983.

2 Forks in the Road

Assessing the Paradoxical Nature of Fixed and Fluid Time in Mercedes Lackey's *The Fairy Godmother* (2004)

Through its paradoxical structure of fate and free will, Heroic Epic Fantasy fiction captures and rearticulates current theories of time. In tenseless time, all time – past, present, future – are 'real' or fixed. The future is just as actualised and unchangeable as the past. Points of time can be described in relation to one's own perspective, like events on a map. In contrast, in tensed time, time 'flows' from the past to the future with the present as the mediator; there is movement from one to the other. In Heroic Epic Fantasy fiction, theorising the conceptions of time becomes important when considering the motif of fate. Is time depicted as fixed and unchangeable; a tenseless time? If the future is predictable through the device of prophecy, this seems to indicate so. Yet, the free will of a character as determined in the previous chapter seems to indicate that the future is changeable, a fluid tensed time. How do we as readers resolve this paradox?

In this chapter, I argue that the events in a Heroic Epic Fantasy can be articulated by a tensed theory of time, by either branching-futurism or no-futurism. This approach considers a conception of time that focuses on its possibilities. Using excerpts from Stephen Hawking's *A Brief History of Time* (1988), I propose that the narrative structure of Heroic Epic Fantasy has embedded within it principles of quantum mechanics: "quantum mechanics does not predict a single definite result for an observation. Instead, it predicts a number of different possible outcomes and tells us how likely each of these is" (Hawking 64). In this way, Heroic Epic Fantasy fiction effectively combines a fixed path of destiny with the fluid paths that arise from the hero's free choices.

This is the manner in which Mercedes Lackey presents her hero Elena in *The Fairy Godmother* (2004), the first stand-alone novel in the *Tales of the Five Hundred Kingdoms* series (2004–2012). In the series, Lackey manipulates familiar Fairy-Tale stories in order to deliver a new Fantasy narrative. The characters in the series demonstrate a conscious awareness of these stock Fairy-Tale structures which allows a detailed discussion of the interactions of fate and freedom of choice. The idea of fate is represented through Lackey's conception of "The Tradition":

> [W]e call that, *The Tradition*. The way that magic tries to set things on a particular course, you see. And there are dozens and dozens

of other tales that The Tradition is trying to recreate, all the time, and perhaps one in a hundred actually becomes a tale. (58, original emphasis)

The Tradition is a magical force that attempts to influence events so as to occur as in Fairy-Tales. With each repetition of the tale, the motifs and events become stronger as they are reaffirmed. However, note that The Tradition rarely succeeds in its attempt to sway events. For instance, in the beginning of *The Fairy Godmother*, Elena is meant to fulfil a set path, a Cinderella story, but chooses to become a fairy godmother instead. Thus, Lackey makes explicit the idea embedded in Heroic Epic Fantasy fiction that the 'fate' of a character is simply one possible path in "a number of different possible outcomes" (Hawking 64). Utilising *The Fairy Godmother* as an example, I argue that Heroic Epic Fantasy portrays the idea that the future has many possible outcomes and the act of prophecy or workings of fate simply demonstrates the possibility of fulfilling one of these potentials.

Potential States

The ability to perceive possible events of the future may come about because the experience of space-time is relative. As Hawking describes in *A Brief History of Time*:

> The lack of an absolute standard of rest meant that one could not determine whether two events that took place at different times occurred in the same position in space. For example, suppose [a] ping-pong ball on [a] train bounces straight up and down, hitting the table twice on the same spot one second apart. To someone on the track, the two bounces would seem to take place about forty metres apart, because the train would have travelled that far down the track between the bounces. [...] The positions of events and the distances between them would be different for a person on the train and one on the track, and there would be no reason to prefer one person's positions to the other's. (20)

If a person or metaphysical entity is at a different vantage point from humanity, one where they see human life pass them by as if a train is moving pass them on the tracks, then they would view events at a different perspective from the passenger on the train. Such a scenario may explain why the entity is able to see forward into the future in order to predict a hero's fate. Elizabeth Haydon's *Rhapsody* (1999) makes this idea explicit by creating a frame story where the character Meridion views the contents of the story (the novel) through a Time Editor: a device similar to a microfilm in which Meridion can move back and forth between viewing different historical points in time. The character of Meridion is thus presented as one outside of the narrative time of the story and is able to view multiple events in time accordingly. Fairyland and dreamscape are two other common examples in Fantasy fiction where locations or events are presented as set outside of the space-time of the narrative. Characters who interact with or originate from these alternate worlds may receive images of foretelling or demonstrate prophetic abilities accordingly.

Hawking describes the concept of perceiving the future in the following way:

> It will be like the ripples that spread out on the surface of a pond when a stone is thrown in. The ripples spread out as a circle that gets bigger as time goes on. [...] the expanding circle of ripples will mark out a cone whose tip is at the place and time at which the stone hit the water. (29)

Like a stone thrown into a pond, an event creates ripples around itself spreading out in a circle. An observer may see the pattern of ripples and be able to predict where the stone hit the water. Hawking extends this analogy to illustrate his conception of a "future light cone." Just as the ripples made by a stone in a pond spread out in bigger and bigger circles, so do events in space-time:

> Similarly, the light spreading out from an event forms a three-dimensional cone in the four-dimensional space-time. This cone is called the future light cone of the event. In the same way we can draw another cone, called the past light cone, which is the set of events from which a pulse of light is able to reach the given event. (29–31)

Hawking visually represents this idea with a diagram of two cones joined together at the apexes (30). The top cone is the future light cone, the bottom cone is the past light cone, and the apex where the cones are joined is the present, or event P. Only events inside the light cones can affect or be affected by events that happen at point P:

> The absolute future of the event is the region inside the future light cone of P. It is the set of all events that can possibly be affected by what happens at P. Events outside the light cone of P cannot be reached by signals from P because nothing can travel faster than light. They cannot therefore be influenced by what happens at P. [...] If one knows what is happening at some particular time everywhere in the region of space that lies within the past light cone of P one can predict what will happen at P. (31)

If an observer is able to see all the events in the future light cone (the ripples from a stone) that forms starting from event P (the stone hitting the water), then they would be able to predict a number of possible events that can occur as a result of P.

This depiction of visualising the future can also be utilised to examine fate and time in Heroic Epic Fantasy. From the pattern of future light cones or ripples in the water, it is possible to predict: "a number of different possible outcomes and tells us how likely each of these is" (Hawking 64). Accordingly, while the future may be visible, these future events can only be seen as a series of possible outcomes that are possible at P.

In Lackey's *The Fairy Godmother*, the characters demonstrate their awareness of different possibilities of the future. For example, in one event, Godmothers Bella and Elena divert the pre-set narrative of the Sleeping Beauty story. Bella distracts the Evil Sorceress with a romantic interest so that the Sorceress places a gentler curse on the infant, causing Sleeping Beauty's hair to become tangled rather than falling into a deathly sleep. And yet, despite Bella's manipulation, "the *potential* of the curse" still remained (140, original emphasis). Note the character's conscious awareness of the potential of different paths of the future. The fairy godmothers recognise that it is possible for the curse to manifest in a way that the tangled hair would lead to strangulation. Because of this, when Elena attempts to divert The Traditional path further, certain motifs and key phrasings still have to be followed: "The poor little Princess would have to endure *something*, and at the same time, the end of the tale had to provide something for another person" (140, original emphasis). While re-directing the path, the basic structure of the curse must still be followed. And consequently, Elena must select another potential path for a hero character to step forward to resolve the problem. She devises a solution where the princess's rescuer is a 'low-born girl' who wins the princess's friendship. Elena changes the curse and sets it along another potential path, but utilises the tools, weapons, and very language of The Tradition itself to do so. By doing so, Elena is able to explore the possibilities of the narrative path and manipulate the set version of the story into a different possible route. While fate or prophecy suggests a potential path that Sleeping Beauty is to follow, Elena is able to manipulate these potentials into selecting a more preferable one.

Forks in the Road

The previous chapter considered that while Heroic Epic Fantasy heroes have a 'fated' path, a path that the gods' wish that they take, they must choose it through their own free wills. Madame Bella, the Fairy Godmother that has taken Elena as her apprentice, explicitly states this idea herself: "no outcome is *certain*, not even with The Tradition pushing it along" (123, original emphasis). Bella demonstrates this concept in practice through her help in aiding Rosalie, a young woman who attempts to resist the Rapunzel story:

> [The Tradition] bent its power towards making her into that something. It was like an enormous, blind, insensate beast, *pushing* her towards that end, and it did not want to let her go down some other path.
> But Rosalie did not want to go there. [...] The more The Tradition pushed her, the more she pushed back, [...]. (161, original emphasis)

Here, Lackey utilises a conscious metaphor of the path and the concept of being able to divert it. The character Rosalie actively chooses a different path from the one that The Tradition pushes her towards.

This choice to redirect the path requires intense energy, but it *is* possible. Elena and Bella gather this energy of The Tradition, the power of a "coiled spring" (40). The metaphor conveys the idea of potential energy. They redirect this energy from Rosalie into themselves to use for further magic: "she [Elena...] felt it join her power, as if she was a vessel, and it was water flowing in from some outside source" (162). Notice the use of the language of "vessel" combined with the motif of "flowing," as in the previous chapter, to express the idea that The Tradition flows through the hero as a vessel of power through which The Tradition operates. The Tradition attempts to force the characters onto a pre-determined path, but the characters actively resist, redirecting the flow of power into selecting a different route.

In *A Future for Presentism* (2006), Craig Bourne describes several variations of the tensed theory of time. Bourne argues for the theory of "presentism," where time flows but: "only the present exists, the future is that which will come to exist, and the past is that which did exist" (13). In presentism, only the present is 'real.' Another variation of the tensed theory includes branching-futurism, where "time's flow amounts to the dropping out of existence of the many real possibilities" as the branches of future times become actualised (12). A third variation is no-futurism theory, where "only the past and present exist" (13), as the future is unreal. Bourne explains that: "[n]o-futurism conceives of reality growing, whereas branching-futurism conceives of reality shedding, but both conceive of time's flow as a change in what exists" (13). Note that in either analogy, Bourne uses the metaphor of a tree branching, with time – indicated by 'reality' – shedding or growing as the possible becomes actualised.[1]

Combining Bourne's model of branching-futurism with an extrapolation of Hawking's analogy of a stone in a pond, I propose the following model of the hero's journey in Heroic Epic Fantasy: The heroes themselves functions much like the stone thrown into a pond which creates ripples on the surface. That is, it is possible to predict the likelihood of

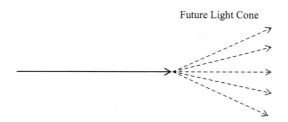

Figure 2.1 The Hero's Path, Before Choice.

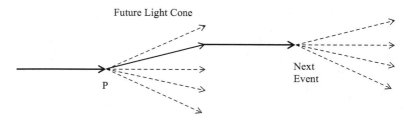

Figure 2.2 The Hero's Path, After Choice.

the hero fulfilling a prophecy but only as a possible outcome. It is as if the hero is walking down a literal path until they come to a branch in the road, event P (Figure 2.1).

By making a choice through their free will, the hero's future is assured (visible) until the next branch in the road, the next event P (Figure 2.2). At this next branch, the protagonist's journey is undetermined or open, and it is left up to the hero's choice on which way to proceed.

In this way, the Heroic Epic Fantasy hero is able to select between several different outcomes. Their journey is predictable, but only as a series of possibilities.

Similarly, the lives of the people in the Five Hundred Kingdoms are predictable, as they follow known Fairy-Tale stories; but, even so, their lives are predictable only as possibilities, not as determined fate. At every stage of their life, they are poised at a crossroads at event P, contemplating the possibilities of their actions. For instance, as described above, Elena is able to divert the traditional Sleeping Beauty tale from its well-known path, allowing the potential for different story endings to be carried out:

> [Elena states:] I knew [...] I could turn The Tradition, not just this one time, but open a new possibility for the future.

[... Bella responds:] The potential magic you used was just a fraction of what was available, and the rest of it went into cutting a new Traditional Path. (148–149)

As with Figures 2.1 and 2.2, Elena and Bella describe the process of following a path down a fated line until a fork in the road opens and "a new possibility for the future" is created, one which "cut[s] a new Traditional Path."

Elena soon discovers that she is able to create new paths by making minor choices that slowly shifts the well-tread trails: "la[ying] down a trace to follow at some other time, in some other place. She was, in effect, using The Tradition itself to build new paths" (242). When Elena is determined to travel a different path from the prescribed Tradition, The Tradition attempts to push her along more familiar paths. By choosing lesser-known alternatives, Elena is able to shift the prescribed storylines, setting the foundation or grooves for future characters to tread the same lines. With each repetition of the tale, these alternatives become re-affirmed and stronger.

Other Fantasy writers also utilise a conscious awareness of the concept of treading familiar stories like a Fairy-Tale path; a metaphor that is expressed in a variety of ways. For instance, in Terry Pratchett's *Discworld* series (1982–2015), the narration confirms that:

[T]heir very existence [the stories] overlays a faint but insistent pattern on the chaos that his history. Stories etch grooves deep enough for people to follow in the same way that water follows certain paths down a mountainside. And every time fresh actors tread down the path of the story, the groove runs deeper. (*Witches Abroad* 13)

As a satirist, Pratchett often demonstrates explicit depictions of well-known structures and motifs of Fantasy fiction. But Lackey and Pratchett are not the only authors (Fantasy authors or otherwise) that describes the narration of one's life as a path with potential forks on the road. It is a common metaphor to describe one's life and has become popular since Jorge Luis Borges's "The Garden of Forking Paths" (1941). Neil Gaiman directly evokes this idea in *Seasons of Mists* (1990–1991), volume 4 of *The Sandman* graphic novel series (1989–2015):

WALK ANY PATH IN DESTINY'S GARDEN, AND YOU WILL BE FORCED TO CHOOSE, NOT ONCE BUT MANY TIMES. THE PATHS FORK AND DIVIDE. WITH EACH STEP YOU TAKE THROUGHOUT DESTINY'S GARDEN, YOU MAKE A CHOICE; AND EVERY CHOICE DETERMINES FUTURE PATHS. ("Episode 0," original emphasis)

As in many Heroic Epic Fantasy fictions, the conception of destiny as multiple forking paths is an exposed structure in the way that the metaphor interacts with the plot and character development in an apparent way. For instance, in Lois McMaster Bujold's *The Curse of Chalion* (2001) the characters Cazaril and Umegat have a conversation about fate and destiny that includes the metaphor of destiny as a path that one is meant to follow. They determine that, though there may be many people that start on the same path, "only those arrive who choose to" (257). As the characters are able to directly interact and speak with the divine entities that set them on their path, they are able to determine that this perception of fate and the future is correct. For Bujold's *Chalion* series, this structuring is reaffirmed in the sequel, *Paladin of Souls* (2003), when the Bastard, one of the gods, informs Ista that: "The Son of Autumn dispatched many men in answer to your prayers, sweet Ista. They turned aside upon their roads, and did not arrive. For He could not bend their wills, nor their steps" (172). The Bastard here confirms that another god, the Son of Autumn, attempted to send many people on the path to resolve the events of *The Curse of Chalion*, but they all chose against selecting this path. As the model of branching-futurism suggests: "time's flow amounts to the dropping out of existence of the many real possibilities" (Bourne 12); in Heroic Epic Fantasy fiction, this is a direct result of the choices that characters make.

The model of branching-futurism is one method of fluid time that can be used to describe the events of the Heroic Epic Fantasy narrative. But although we can depict major and minor events throughout the hero's journey using this model, the final resolution of the major conflict of the narrative must be discussed in more nuanced ways. As chapter eight will expand on, rather than following pre-scribed potential paths, a substantial change – one that breaks the path – may be required in order to resolve the narrative. Consequently, while branching-futurism describes events in the narrative, the model of no-futurism may be more appropriate to describe the final conflict of the story. Here, "only the past and present exist" (Bourne 13), as the future is unreal or is still being forged.

For instance, in her attempt to create a new path, Elena believes that she has broken the Traditional path: "there isn't a scrap of Tradition to give them a hint of what to do" (465). However, the other Godmothers and Wizards inform her that, instead of breaking the Tradition completely, Elena has manipulated the Tradition into creating new paths:

> "[...T]hat's two Traditional paths you've combined there, the disguised female serving a boob of a man who hasn't figured out his servant is a she and the brave and cunning girl who follows her lover into battle, [...]." [says one Wizard]
>
> "You've opened up the Traditional warrior-woman paths a bit wider now, [....]." [adds another Fairy Godmother] (466–467)

Instead of breaking the Tradition, Elena has combined two Traditional paths into one. She is also able to create a new Tradition: an Order of Champions. The circumstances that led to her being able to do these things are built out of the potentials of older traditional paths. Rather than choosing between forks in the road, Elena is able to use the remnants of broken paths to forge a new one. Recall that: "[n]o-futurism conceives of reality growing, whereas branching-futurism conceives of reality shedding" (Bourne 13). As the model of no-futurism describes, instead of possible futures dropping out of existence, the hero is able to break the possible paths and re-forge them into a new possibility.

A Brief Note on Stock Characters

The Fairy Godmother is a good example of a text that combines stock character-types with free choices. As a 'Fairy Godmother' character, Elena attempts to manipulate the characters around her – the heroes of the Fairy-Tale stories – into choosing a path that *she's* determined. Accordingly, while Elena functions as the hero of the central narrative, she also performs the role of being the 'higher power' for the other stories in the novel; Elena is able to identify the narratives of the Tradition and act accordingly: "it all fell into a pattern" (60). Though she cannot guarantee the outcome of her actions, she can visualise possibilities of the future and act in a way that attempts to favour one specific path. In doing so, she not only sets other minor characters onto the path that she has chosen, but she also fulfils her purpose of functioning as the 'Fairy Godmother' type.

Does the choice to fulfil a purpose or to follow a pre-determined path indicate that these characters are 'flat'? E. M. Forster in *Aspects of the Novel* (1927) designates flat characters as those: "constructed round a single idea or quality" (73). They, the flat characters, "remain in [the reader's] mind as unalterable for the reason that they were not changed by circumstances" (74). This is similar to M. M. Bakhtin's assertion explored in the previous chapter that a hero in a story of fate emerges with an "identity absolutely unchanged" as fate simply reaffirms their character (*Dialogic Imagination* 105). Of course, whether the hero is flat or round does not matter when considering the structural necessity of the hero to the plot. While there is a defence to be made of character, that defence stands on a different ground to structure. But contemplating the depth of the character is an important element in the critical field of Fantasy fiction, as it is easy to condemn the Heroic Epic Fantasy as a narrative with flat characters and reductive formulas. Certainly, characters in Heroic Epic Fantasy fiction may be viewed as 'types' constructed around an idea, such as the 'hero type.' However, I argue that while the character fulfils a functional necessity, this function does not automatically indicate that the character is 'flat.' As the previous chapter determined, the Heroic Epic Fantasy protagonist *becomes* a hero, moving from a potential state to actualised state. This can be seen in the way that Heroic Epic Fantasy writers demonstrate the 'growth' of the characters as they are initially characterised by innocence and naivety and, through the process of the journey, develop self-awareness and knowledge of the world which profoundly changes them.

Character function or 'type' is different from character depth (or lack thereof), but it may be easy to interpret 'character type' as 'flat' because of the usages of the word. This is the manner in which Farah Mendlesohn interprets "portal-quest fantasies" (a categorisation that may be comparable to the Heroic Epic Fantasy) in *Rhetorics of Fantasy* (2008): "This may be one reason why the hero in the quest fantasy is more often an actant rather than an actor, provided with attributes rather than character precisely to compensate for the static nature of his role" (7). Mendlesohn here indicates that actants, characters with "attributes rather than character," are usually static. Though she does not refer directly to his name, Mendlesohn is referring to terminology of the actor and actant introduced by A. J. Greimas (1966). But Greimas' terminology is less weighted than the value judgment implied by flat and round characters or by 'static' characters. Brian Attebery summarises the difference in *Strategies of Fantasy* (1992) accordingly:

> A. J. Greimas has provided a less loaded terminology: as an element in the construction of a story, a character may be called an *actant* – the French participial ending conveying the sense of *doing* that is essential to such characters. A character who is more interesting for his individual qualities than for his place in a shaped narrative is an *acteur* (Scholes, *Structuralism* 103), or, substituting the English form, an *actor*. (73, original emphasis)

Attebery's discussion of Greimas' terminology indicates that the 'actant' character is not inferior to the 'acteur.' More importantly, Attebery concludes that the Fantasy hero is neither acteur nor actant, but something in between, *both* "character as imitated person and character as story function" (73). Likewise, as Northrop Frye asserts in *Anatomy of Criticism* (1957):

> [T]he sentimental notion of an antithesis between the lifelike character and the stock type is a vulgar error. [...] That stock type is not the character but it is as necessary to the character as a skeleton is to the actor who plays it. (172)

Similarly, in Heroic Epic Fantasy, the hero type may be considered a stock type, but this does not exclude them from being a round character as well. A character that demonstrates a lack of the contemplation process and follows the demands of fate unquestionably would result in a hero character that *is* flat. But that structural paradox – of choice and contemplation when confronted with their destiny – must come first.

The characters in *The Fairy Godmother* are portrayed as 'stock' Fairy-Tale characters, but ones that are conscious of their positioning. For instance, the character Prince Alexander begins as a Failed Quester type (or the ou-hero, a type that will be discussed in detail in chapter four). This role is a minor character in a Fairy-Tale story. But, as the story continues, Alexander "discover[s] that he was little more than a fancy pawn on some giant chessboard" (339). Note the conscious awareness of the motif of being a pawn. With this realisation, Alexander then actively chooses a different fork in the road and becomes a different character type. He moves from being a pawn (a failed quester) to becoming a champion knight. As a knight, he is still a player on the chessboard, but one that actively chooses the role. Elena similarly makes a conscious decision to become a different character type at her fork in the road, moving from a Cinderella character into a more active Fairy Godmother role for multiple Fairy-Tale storylines. Both characters realise their position as a stock character-type, one that is swayed by the story (The Tradition) around them. But, once they realise that they are characters in a story, the knowledge allows them the freedom to consciously choose a new path when faced with event P. As the previous chapter concluded, knowledge allows these characters to open up the text and exert their own choices onto pre-scribed potential paths.

In Heroic Epic Fantasy, "no outcome is *certain*, not even with The Tradition pushing it along" (*Fairy Godmother* 123, original emphasis). Instead, the act of fate or prophecy: "predicts a number of different possible outcomes and tells us how likely each of these is" (Hawking 64). Though authors may not be explicitly conscious of it, these theories of time and possibilities are embedded directly into the structure of Heroic Epic Fantasy. Although the act of prophecy or fate predicts a possible future, it is only *one* possible outcome in the narrative. The final few words of *The Fairy Godmother* ends on the message that: "It all comes down to what we make of ourselves, eh? Tradition or no" (478). The exchange demonstrates a conscious awareness of the dictates of fate and the character's free will in response to these commands. If a hero has knowledge of the potential narrative outcomes, then they make act and manipulate their path accordingly. *The Fairy Godmother* overtly exhibits the hero's awareness of their position in a narrative and their negotiation of this position. In the next chapter, I will discuss further how the choices a character makes leads to a development of character and an affirmation of the path they take through a more implicit awareness of the character's position in a narrative.

Note

1 Note that the structural device of reality shedding or growing is not a wholly new conception in literary criticism; there is precedence for the idea of branching paths that occurs in the genre of Alternate History. In Alternate History, a 'jonbar point' or 'point of divergence' indicates a nodal point where the world may change as a consequence of a change in an historical event. Parallel worlds can often form as a result.

Bibliography

Attebery, Brian. *Strategies of Fantasy*. Indiana University Press.1992.

Bakhtin, Mikhail Mikhaïlovich. *The Dialogic Imagination*. 1975. Ed. Michael Holquist. Trans. Caryl Emerson and Michael Holquist. University of Texas Press, 1981.

Borges, Jorge Luis. "The Garden of Forking Paths." 1941. *Collected Fictions*. Trans. Andrew Hurley. Penguin, 1998. pp. 119–128.

Bourne, Craig. *A Future for Presentism*. Clarendon Press, 2006.

Bujold, Lois McMaster. *The Curse of Chalion*. 2000. HarperCollins, 2011. Chalion 1.

———. *Paladin of Souls*. HarperTorch, 2003. Chalion 2.

Forster, Edward Morgan. *Aspects of the Novel*. 1927. Penguin Books, 1990.

Frye, Northrop. *Anatomy of Criticism*. 1957. Princeton University Press, 1973.

Gaiman, Neil. *Seasons of Mists*. 1990–1991. DC Comics, 2010. The Sandman 21–28.

Hawking, Stephen. *A Brief History of Time*. 1988. Bantam Books, 2011.

Haydon, Elizabeth. *Rhapsody: Child of Blood*. 1999. Gollancz, 2001. Rhapsody 1.

Jordan, Robert. *The Great Hunt*. 1990. Tor, 1991. The Wheel of Time 2.

Lackey, Mercedes. *The Fairy Godmother*. Luna Books, 2004. Five Hundred Kingdoms 1.

Mendlesohn, Farah. *Rhetorics of Fantasy*. Wesleyan University Press, 2008.

Pratchett, Terry. *Witches Abroad*. 1991. Corgi Books, 2013. Discworld 12.

3 Building Layers of Character

Analysing the Construction of the Hero in Robert Jordan's *The Great Hunt* (1990)

The previous chapter described how fate can be depicted as a path, with a hero following the road of a journey down possible forking branches. These paths can simultaneously form a pattern, such as a repetitive cycle or a tapestry of interwoven events. The conception of fate as being woven evokes the three Fates in Greek mythology, the Moirai. Note that the Moirai do not determine 'destiny' in terms of specific actions or deeds in one's life; instead, the three would limit the threads of life from birth to death, distributing only enough life to a mortal that was allotted to them. While the moment of death may be pre-determined, the deeds of one's life are free. Having considered the notion of the free will of the character and the fluidity of time, this chapter will explore how the hero mediates events around them. Through the process of deciphering their destiny for themselves, heroes can then determine how to act according to their own interpretation of events. Through this interplay, I argue that the hero is constructed by the text, and, reciprocally, the hero constructs the text.

In this chapter, I first consider the notion of a strange attractor in chaos theory as described by James Gleick in *Chaos* (1987). A strange attractor is an element that attracts and mediates turbulence. Although a strange attractor draws turbulence, it simultaneously "has the important property of stability" (Gleick 138). This description is also appropriate for the hero of the Heroic Epic Fantasy (and one we will return to again in Chapter 8). After outlining the premise of a hero as stranger attractor, I then examine metafictional structures of the hero's interpretation of prophecy, exposing how the intertextual awareness of their place in a narrative allows for the character to act as reader and construct both the narrative and their own identity. I argue that, rather than closing the meaning of the text, the character's interpretations of prophecy opens the text and allow for nuances of meaning to emerge. I conclude with an examination of the recursive structures that are built into the fabric of Heroic Epic Fantasy, structures which further allow for the characters to take an active position in constructing both identity and narrative by posing epistemological and ontological questions.

This chapter utilises *The Great Hunt* (1990), the second book of Robert Jordan's *The Wheel of Time* series (1990–2012), as a case study.

The Wheel of Time follows the journey of Rand al'Thor along with numerous companions. As with many Heroic Epic Fantasy texts, the motif of prophecy is a running thread throughout the series. While the hero's introspection and interrogation of fate is central to all narratives which contain prophecy, Jordan's[1] fifteen-book series offers a lengthy and comprehensive example of this interrogation as Rand comes to recognise himself as the hero of prophecy and determines the ways in which to interpret and confront this destiny of facing the Dark Lord in an apocalyptic "Last Battle." I have selected *The Great Hunt* in particular (with wider reference to the entire series) as the novel presents several recursive structures contained within the book. Using *The Great Hunt* as an example, I examine the character's processes of interpretation in detail, illustrating how layers of reading are built up in a Heroic Epic Fantasy text.

The Hero as Strange Attractor

Repetition and pattern are important and made overt in Jordan's *The Wheel of Time* series; the series, after all, *is* entitled *The Wheel of Time*. Events are repeated again and again, and people might be reincarnated and live their life over and over. For instance, as the Dragon Reborn, Rand al'Thor is also the reincarnation of another hero, Lews Therin. The narrative describes time as a tapestry with threads of individual lives weaved into it in a pattern. Three of the main protagonists of the novel are "ta'veren," which means that they are "centerpoints of the weaving" (*Great Hunt* 35). Rand's companion Loial describes this concept accordingly:

> For a time, the Wheel will bend the Pattern around you three, whatever you do. And whatever you do is more likely to be chosen by the Wheel than by you. *Ta'veren* pull history along behind them and shape the Pattern just by being, but the Wheel weaves *ta'veren* on a tighter line than other men. (35, original emphasis)

Loial's conception that the heroes must endure the game that fate or the Wheel plays is simultaneously counterbalanced by the idea that ta'veren also "*shape* the Pattern [of the Wheel of Time] just by being" (my emphasis). While fate may influence heroes, heroes simultaneously influence the world around them. These ta'veren characters are able to draw people to them and trigger events simply through their passage through a space. For instance, in *The Dragon Reborn* (1991), Rand's journey through a series of villages prompts a whole host of positive or negative events, such as everyone in one village getting married within a span of two days.

This conception of ta'veren weaving events around them is similar to an idea introduced by Chrysippus, a Stoic philosopher, as explained by Susanne Bobzien in *Determinism and Freedom in Stoic Philosophy* (1998):

> Chrysippus named the way the things are connected as "interweaving" or "interconnection" (ἐπιπλοκή). [...] The idea of interconnection is found also in his etymological exegesis of "fate" (εἱμαρμένη) as "connecting cause of the things" [...], which is reported also as a Stoic definition of fate. (70)

This Stoic definition of fate suggests that the movements of all things are connected or interwoven together. In *The Great Hunt*, characters that are ta'veren seem to be the centre-points of these connections. The first chapter of this monograph concluded that heroes have certain shapes to their souls. In Jordan's series, the shape of the hero is a ta'veren, centre-points of the wheel; they move according to their circular shape and are often pulled along by *The Wheel of Time*. But like spokes on the wheel, they also pull people and events around them as they move and interweave people and events together:

> "How many times have you said that *ta'veren* pull those around them like twigs in a whirlpool? Perhaps I was pulled, too." [...]
> "*Ta'veren*," Moiraine sighed. "[...]. Rather than guiding a chip floating down a stream, I am trying to guide a log through rapids. Every time I push at it, it pushes at me [...]." (*Great Hunt* 325, original emphasis)

Whereas in Mercedes Lackey's *The Fairy Godmother* (2004), the characters are 'pushed' by The Tradition, here, the characters acknowledge that the heroes themselves push them along in the narrative.

The idea that ta'veren are figures that push or pull people and events around them is remarkably similar to the description of strange attractors in chaos theory. Chaos theory offers a study of *patterned* behaviour that is *not predictable*. Similarly, while Heroic Epic Fantasy has patterns and is repetitive, that does not necessarily indicate that it is predictable. Turbulence is one example of a chaotic system: you have a flow in a stream, but something causes turbulence in this flow which creates eddies which are not predictable. Gleick describes turbulence as such:

> It is a mess of disorder at all scales, small eddies within large ones. It is unstable. It is highly dissipative, meaning that turbulence drains energy and creates drag. It is motion toward random. But how does flow change from smooth to turbulent? (122)

What is it that causes turbulence, that changes a calm flow to a chaotic one? The scientists who study turbulence answer this question with a "strange attractor" (Gleick 119–153), which is something that 'attracts' eddies towards its centre. Gleick describes this process with a simple example of a magnet: "This central fixed point 'attracts' the orbits" (134). Compare this definition of strange attractors to the description of ta'veren in *The Great Hunt*: "*ta'veren* pull those around them like twigs in a whirlpool" (273); the simile evokes the idea that ta'veren are strange attractors in a turbulent flow. As Gleick later describes, "Flow was shape plus change, motion plus form" (195). This is also the model of the hero, flowing through boundaries through the shape of the hero, causing change through form.

In *Order out of Chaos* (1984), Ilya Prigogine and Isabella Stengers express how:

> For a long time turbulence was identified with disorder or noise. Today we know that this is not the case. Indeed, while turbulent motion appears as irregular or chaotic on the macroscopic scale, it is, on the contrary, highly organized on the microscopic scale. (141)

Turbulent motion, while appearing chaotic, is highly organised. Compare this concept of turbulent motion to John Clute's second stage of Fantasy, that of "thinning," which he describes in "Fantastika in the World Storm" (2007):

> [T]he diminution of the old ways; amnesia of the hero and of the king; failure of the harvest; a literal drying up of the Land; and *cacophony*: the diversion of story into useless noise, dynastic quarrels, battle after battle, trilogies in twelve parts. (26, original emphasis)

While Clute uses "cacophony," it also suggests a "disorder or noise" (Prigogine and Stengers 141). Combining these ideas together, I argue that in Heroic Epic Fantasy, due to this increase of turbulence and cacophony in the land, the strange attractor as hero increases turbulent motion.

But the strange attractor simultaneously also add stability: "By definition, [strange] attractors had the important property of stability – in a real system, where moving parts are subjects to bumps and jiggles from real-world noise, motion tends to return to the attractor" (Gleick 138). This is the way in which the ta'veren in *The Great Hunt* operate, attracting turbulence and disorder while simultaneously weaving a pattern of order around them as motion returns to the attractor. While Chapter 8 will return to the full impact of the strange attractor, it is important to note here that Rand's role as hero, as ta'veren or strange attractor, is to draw motion and events to him, simultaneously creating both movement and chaos, along with stabilising that movement.

While in *The Great Hunt*, Jordan's ta'veren is an essential motif in the text, this does not exclude other Heroic Epic Fantasy texts from demonstrating a similar model of the strange attractor. For instance, in Terry Goodkind's *Stone of Tears* (1995), the hero is described as a "pebble in the pond" (852): "Everyone has an effect on others. [...] The ripples caused by you affect everyone else. Without you, all those ripples would not have happened" (852–853). Here, Goodkind's conception of a "pebble in a pond" is similar to Jordan's "ta'veren." Both metaphors describe a hero that disturbs the flow of events around them, similar to Stephen Hawking's analogy of ripples in a pond described in the previous chapter. The hero as a stone in the pond creates ripples which influence others around them. In other Heroic Epic Fantasy novels, the idea may be more implicit. The model of hero as strange attractor explains why the hero is constantly drawn to action and danger – or vice versa. For example, why *is* J. K. Rowling's Harry Potter the one who stumbles across a nefarious plot year after year? Of course, the obvious practical answer is that, as the hero of the story, the writer will create events around the hero instead of a background character. But there is a greater significance to examining the construction of a hero as a strange attractor. The strange attractor helps to model the idea that the hero *mediates, attracts, and induces events around themselves*. It is with this model that I will now discuss the idea of how the hero interprets and constructs the narrative and, in turn, is constructed by the narrative.

The Hero as Reader

In "Structuralism" (2012), Brian Attebery asserts that:

> One difference between fantasy and the genres of realism and naturalism is that fantasy typically displays and even celebrates its structure. If it were a shirt, the seams would be on the outside. This tendency is one reason that fantasies often take on a metafictional dimension. (83)

By overtly depicting its structures, Heroic Epic Fantasy fiction encourages metafictional readings. Patricia Waugh in *Metafiction* (1984) defines that: "*Metafiction* is a term given to fictional writing which self-consciously and systematically draws attention to its status as an artefact" (2, original emphasis); "Metafiction may concern itself, then, with particular conventions of the novel to display the process of their construction" (4). These qualities of 'metafiction' can be applied to any text that is in some way conscious of its structure. This is especially true for the Heroic Epic Fantasy form, for the reason that, as Attebery indicates in *Stories about Stories* (2014): "the fantasist [the author of fantasy fiction] appropriates from, engages with, travesties, and reconstitutes the myth" (3). Heroic Epic Fantasy – consciously or unconsciously – engages with the body of work that has come before it, taking part in an intertextual mode of creation by "reconstitut[ing] the myth" with each repetition.

In *Chaos Bound* (1990), a critical examination of the comparison between chaos theory and literary developments, N. Katherine Hayles describes that in chaos there is:

> a shift in focus from the individual unit to *recursive symmetries between scale levels*. For example, turbulent flow can be modeled as small swirls within larger swirls, nested in turn within still larger swirls. Rather than trying to follow an individual molecule, as one might for laminar flows, this approach models turbulence through symmetries that are replicated over many scale levels. (13, original emphasis)

Throughout the remainder of this chapter and at several points throughout this book, I will describe and identify "symmetries that are replicated over many scale levels." There are levels of symmetries between layers of readings which occur in metafictional reading. For the purposes of this chapter, these symmetries result in recursive structures with characters recognising themselves and functioning as both reader and character. Hayles connects recursive structures and repetitions to the idea of deconstructing a text in a metafictional or intertextual manner:

> Far from being ordered sets of words bounded by book covers, they [texts] are reservoirs of chaos. Derrida initiates us [...] through his concept of iteration. Any word, he argues, acquires a slightly different meaning each time it appears in a new context. Moreover, the boundary between text and context is not fixed. Infinite contexts invade and permeate the text, regardless of chronology or authorial intention. (180–181)

Each repetitive pattern is an iteration that "acquires a slightly different meaning" with each repetition. Attebery asserts something similar for Fantasy fiction in *Strategies of Fantasy* (1992): "Each parallel movement effectively rewrites those that went before. Each prepares the way for those yet to come" (59). This is the model in which this chapter examines recursive structures in *The Great Hunt*, as an iteration that builds on the layers of meaning that has come before it, creating a resonance by adding to the construction of identity and interpretation of the text.

This repetition is especially apparent with the presentation of prophecy and fate. Often in Heroic Epic Fantasy fiction, prophecy is retold several times with each repetition providing another level of analysis and interpretation. A critical stage in this repetitive process is the self-recognition of the hero *as* a hero figure and their subsequent response to their purpose in life. Recall Thomas Carlyle's assessment that the hero is one who "know[s] for certain, concerning [their] vital relations to this mysterious Universe and [their] duty and destiny there" (2–3). In Heroic Epic Fantasy, the protagonist's interpretation of their own future is when the hero-as-reader becomes essential to the resolution of the story. Other characters may also identify themselves as hero and interpret prophecy to place themselves in the narrative. As the next two chapters will explore further, what differentiates the hero from these characters is that the hero is able to comprehend the world and their place in it. For example, in Brandon Sanderson's *Mistborn* trilogy (2006–2008), three different people wrongly identify themselves as the hero of prophecy, before the fourth true hero deciphers the prophecy correctly and fulfils their role as actualised hero. In J. K. Rowling's *Harry Potter* series (1997–2007), the prophecy originally allows for two heroes, Harry Potter and Neville Longbottom, to be the possible hero, before Voldemort marks Potter as the chosen hero.[2] In *Stone of Tears*, Goodkind identifies a common problem with interpreting prophecy: the prophecy is written in a language that few people understand, and thus, translation problems occur with the text: "when they translate it, they give it only one version. They can't translate its ambiguity" (768). The hero Richard Cypher names himself the "bringer of death," and it is only later that he encounters a prophecy that is concerned with a man that also names himself the "bringer of death" (280). Note the last name of Goodkind's hero, Cypher, which embodies the idea of a code that needs to be decrypted. In all of these examples, the heroes of Heroic Epic Fantasy must not only interpret and engage with the prophecy themselves when confronted with it, but, as the first chapter determined, this confrontation comes not just once but many times. The characters' decisions and interpretation of prophecy are debated at each step; moments of choices which add to the repetition of the narrative structure.

While the process of self-recognition is an essential part of the hero's journey, Farah Mendlesohn repeatedly contends in *Rhetorics of Fantasy* (2008) that the interpretative processes of the hero in the portal-quest narrative (a type of narrative comparable to the Heroic Epic Fantasy) limits the reader's own interpretation:

> [R]everie and self-contemplation, far from creating depth, break the sense of immersion in a society, and are fundamentally antithetical to either character development or an immersive structure. It is a false mimesis that reminds us that we are in a narrated text and that *the protagonist's version must be true*. (10, original emphasis)

Mendlesohn maintains that the protagonist's introspection exerts authority over the narration as their view is privileged over others. However, I counter that the 'truth' is dissected from a multiplicity of storytelling. For instance, in Jordan's *The Wheel of Time* series (which Mendlesohn later uses as a model), the narration is developed from numerous viewpoints from other protagonists as well as antagonists. It is notable that these perspectives are often conflicting. As the series develops, information is often suppressed or missing, and the reader is repeatedly left guessing at which "*version must be true.*" This is especially the case as the central hero, Rand, develops into an imperialist tyrant and the other protagonists in the series start questioning the choices that Rand makes. Thus, the character's narration of events is not "antithetical to [...] character development" and, as I conclude below, while the Heroic Epic Fantasy hero may "remind [...] us that we are in a narrated text," this is done so deliberately.

Frequently, Heroic Epic Fantasy fictions are presented within frame-narratives. Although Mendlesohn contends that: "the presentation of these extracts [from a fictional historian] is rarely placed against other, disputatious sources" (14), as this chapter will demonstrate below, these extracts *are* placed against others, and, even if they are not, rather than closing the text, the presentation of these narratives open up the text as the reader may not be sure whether to trust the authority of these excerpts or a character's interpretation. For instance, James Clemens *Wit'ch Fire* (1998) begins with a frame story with the opening lines: "First of all, the author is a liar" (ix). These opening lines of Clemens' *The Banned and the Banished* series (1998–2002) are framed in a forward "by Jir'rob Sordun, D.F.S., M. of A., directory of University Studies – U.D.B." (ix). That this cautionary frame is presented as a foreword by an academic and scholar seems to give authenticity to this claim: that the Heroic Epic Fantasy story about to be told should not be trusted. But as the series develops, the reader is invited to question the authorial voice of both frame and narrative as themes of dishonesty paired with the assertion of a tyrannical authority abound.

Moreover, like with the ambiguity of the translated prophecies in Goodkind's *Stone of Tears*, the frame-narrative also identifies that the story about to be told is in translation from a lost text. This motif is common in Heroic Epic Fantasy fiction, as frame-narratives and especially texts containing prophecies are presented as texts in translation or from a lost history, and thus the reader must determine whether there are any biases in the interpretation. For instance, *The Great Hunt* begins with a prophecy that is presented as a preface with the following inscription:

> *The Prophecies of the Dragon*
>   as translated by Ellaine Marise'idin Alshinn,
>   Chief Librarian at the Court of Arafel. (xi, original emphasis)

Throughout the series, the characters discuss various interpretations and alternate versions of these prophecies. Each character that discusses the prophecy adds their own interpretation to the text. These interpretations are presented as repetitions with nuances, a chaotic pattern. In this way, the reader is invited to engage with the texts themselves and offer their own interpretation of prophecy and lost texts.

The appealing and fascinating part of *The Wheel of Time* is as the series continues it becomes harder to identify which character can be trusted: not only is there a fragmented narration resulting from focalisations from numerous multiple characters, but the central hero Rand becomes an unreliable narrator. Rand is a male Aes Sedai (magic user) and is cursed to become mad through the continued use of his power. As the series continues, Rand starts hearing a voice in his head. This voice is suspected to be an earlier incarnation of himself, Lews Therin, who is presented as a separate entity from Rand and Rand starts engaging the voice in conversation accordingly. These dialogues are often paired with Rand questioning whether the voice is real or whether Rand is mad: "*You are real, aren't you?* he wondered. There was no answer. *Lews Therin?* [...] He was not mad; the voice was real, not imagination. Not madness. A sudden desire to laugh did not help" (*A Crown of Swords* 365, original emphasis). At times this incarnation takes over and so subsumes Rand's personality that Rand is unsure whether it is Rand acting or Lews Therin. Thus, even though Rand is presented as the prophesised hero of the narrative, the reader is cautioned that the character may not be trustworthy.

Even if the reader is able or willing to accept Rand's interpretation of events, the character himself struggles with how best to interpret translations and nuances in the prophecy:

> Rand had studied the Karaethon Prophecy. Unfortunately, teasing out its meaning was like trying to unite a hundred yards of tangle rope. [...] Everyone knew the prophecy, but few asked the question that should have been inevitable. Why? *Why* did Rand have to take up the sword? Was it to be used in the Last Battle? (*The Gathering Storm*, 730–731, original emphasis)

Rand's questioning and examination of the prophecies demonstrate that the prophecies themselves are ambiguous and even when given 'instructions' on how to proceed, these instructions are never clear. He interprets the words of prophecy just as an external reader would. The prophecies are also retold in different versions throughout the ages and in different nations and cultures. These prophecies are all iterations of each other – slightly similar in structure, but with enough nuances that translation and interpretation are made difficult. Thus, the presentation of prophecy and other historical texts in Heroic Epic Fantasy fiction serves, not as a source of authority, but a means through which constant interpretation and re-telling add nuances to the reading.

While the heroes must decode and deconstruct prophecy, the external reader also engages in a similar process. In *S/Z* (1970, translated 1975), Roland Barthes presents five codes to reading, writing, and interpreting the text. The first code is the hermeneutic code: "by which an enigma can be distinguished, suggested, formulated, held in suspense, and finally disclosed" (19). While in Heroic Epic Fantasy, the hermeneutic code is most apparent via the structure of prophecy, in cases where prophecy is merely implied the hero must still come to interpret and understand the narrative and their place in the story. The external reader likewise takes part in a similar engagement with the text as the reader decodes and comes to understand the hero's purpose in the narrative. In *Strategies of Fantasy* (1992), Attebery asserts that: "the postmodern fantastic, by adopting a playful stance toward narrative conventions, forces the reader to take an active part in establishing any coherence and closure within the text" (53). The reader must take on an active role of engaging with the text as metafictional narrative conventions undermine surface readings: the interpretation of these prophecies or a character's understanding of a hero's purpose may be conflicting or open to manipulation.

For instance, in Sanderson's *Mistborn* trilogy: "*the words of the prophecies are changing. The alterations are slight. Clever, even. A word here, a slight twist there. But the words on the pages are different from the ones in my memory*" (*The Well of Ascension* 760, original emphasis to indicate lines from a journal). The characters are cautioned that they should not trust the printed word as the words may change with each reproduction. The same message is made to the external reader. In an account of an earlier (mis-)interpretation of the prophecies, the fictional author writes: "*It felt almost as if we constructed a hero to fit our prophecies, rather than allowing one to arise naturally*" (478, original emphasis). This caution, of an early interpreter of the prophecies (the writer of the journal) to its implied reader (the character in the novel), to beware *constructing* a hero to fit the prophecy, is also made to the external reader. Throughout the trilogy, Sanderson invites the reader to identify which of the protagonists is the correct hero of destiny. The careful, meticulous external reader may be able to catch the discrepancies in the text, identifying the correct hero before they are revealed and delight in the knowledge that they caught the author at their own game. In contrast to the careful external reader, the enthusiastic, heedless reader, while they may have been misled by the deliberate manipulations of the author, may still find an appeal in being caught out by the expected rules of the story.

As John Cawelti in *Adventure, Mystery, and Romance: Formula Stories as Art and Popular Culture* (1976) argues:

> Audience find satisfaction and a basic emotional security in a familiar form; in addition, the audience's past experience with a formula

gives it a sense of what to expect in new individual examples, thereby increasing its capacity for understanding and enjoying the details of a work. (9)

In Heroic Epic Fantasy, as in other formula genres, the expectations provided by the reader's familiarity with the formula and an author's manipulation of them not only provide satisfaction and enjoyment for the reader, but also adds to the development and understanding of the form, so that the conventions of the form resonates with a reader who is already familiar with the structure due to previous engagements with the form. Waugh identifies how this familiarity is also an essential process of metafiction: "There has be some level of familiarity. In metafiction it is precisely the *fulfilment* as well as the *non-fulfilment* of generic expectations that provides both familiarity and the starting point for innovation" (64, original emphasis). Barthes in *The Pleasure of the Text* (1975, translated 1976) and Attebery in *Stories about Stories* suggests something similar: "The pleasure of the text is not the pleasure of the corporeal striptease or of narrative suspense. [...] the entire excitation takes refuge in the *hope* of seeing" (Barthes 10, original emphasis). If the Heroic Epic Fantasy author delivers the story as if it were a game, then they must do so artfully: satisfying the demands of the audience's expectations of their hope of seeing the expected ending, while simultaneously playing with the structure enough to surprise the reader, "taking indirect paths to the inevitable outcome" (*Stories about Stories* 97). As the Heroic Epic Fantasy author often uses the expectations of formula to mislead both reader and character, both the enthusiastic reader and the careful reader engage with a metatextual awareness of how the structures of Heroic Epic Fantasy develop.

Heroic Epic Fantasy straddles that line between familiarity, articulated through patterns and motifs that one comes to expect with the genre, and distance, as a character or narrator must mediate and interpret the fantastical world to the external reader. In *History, Rhetorical Description and the Epic* (1982), Page Dubois argues that in the Epic tradition:

> The hero mediates the audience's relationship to these histories. The trajectory of his individual life brings these representations into existence. It is his presence before them – as legends recounted, as dreams or visions, as works of art – that bring them to his audience. His consciousness awakens these versions of history, and therefore his understanding of them tempers, qualifies, and enriches his audience's understanding of their own history. (3–4)

Dubois here emphasises the importance of the Epic hero mediating the story to the listener or reader. Accordingly, the mediation of the hero is a long-standing tradition arising from the Epic; the hero needs to function as reader in order to translate the world to its audience. This process is similar to the narrator-reader interaction in a metafictional reading. For instance, in the introduction to *Metafiction* (1995), Mark Currie uses the example of Joseph Conrad's *Heart of Darkness* (1902) as a marginal metafictional case, where "Marlow is a dramatised narrator, a kind of surrogate reader trying, as protagonist of the narrated journey to make sense of events and to interpret its significance in a manner analogous to that of external reader" (4). The hero does not necessarily *exert* their interpretation on the external reader, but the hero still functions as reader by trying to make sense of the events around them.

As this section has demonstrated, the hero's mediation of the text does not posit the naivety of the external reader. With Jordan's *The Wheel of Time*, the focalisation is split through various characters; the narration rarely follows the central hero; and when it does, his authority is questioned due to madness. Through repetition of these structural devices, when the meaning of the narrative is finally delivered, the uncovered meaning resonates to both reader and character. Within *The Wheel of Time*, each novel in the series also build layers of repetitions until the final climatic moment resonates. Within each individual novel, such as in *The Great Hunt*, these moments are presented through repetitive structures so that Rand's construction of his own identity is crystallised by the end of the novel – at least, until the next novel in the series, when the questioning of identity begins anew.

Recursive Structures Constructing the Hero

The hero's introspection of prophecy and identity allows the hero to form a narrative of their own journey. For Jordan's *The Wheel of Time*, Rand's interpretation and questioning of prophecies suggest that he recognises his place as a character or a figure in these prophetic texts: "'That's what I am,' Rand said. 'A Story. A legend. To be told to children years from now, spoken of in whispers'" (*The Gathering Storm* 519). By reading and interpreting texts where they themselves are the focus of the material, the hero almost shows a meta-fictional awareness of themselves as character. In essence, by interpreting the material written about themselves, the hero attempts to construct their own identity by forming a narrative about a predicted future.

This process of identity construction is extracted in multiple ways. Currie in *Postmodern Narrative Theory* (1998) contemplates that identity construction is drawn out through creating a narrative: "because it exists only as a narrative. [...] the only way to explain who we are is to tell our own story, to select key events which characterise us and organise them according to the formal principles of narrative" (25). This is the manner in which the heroes consciously form their own identity in Heroic Epic Fantasy narratives, through the process of repeated confrontations with divergent narratives.

Several types of recursive structures of time occur in *The Great Hunt* which allows the characters to confront their identity in the narrative; we will examine two of them here. One recursive structure occurs early in the novel, when Rand al'Thor along with two companions find themselves in an alternate world to their own. Loial, as a scholar and bibliophile, identifies the world as a "world that might be" (*Great Hunt* 217): "If a woman goes left, or right, does Time's flow divide? Does the Wheel then weave two Patterns? A thousand, for each of her turnings? As many as the stars? Is one real, the others merely shadows and reflections?" (217). Like the model of branching-futurism discussed in the previous chapter, the novel overtly depicts the idea of whether time branches based on the choices any one person makes in life.

The idea of "shadows" in the excerpt evokes Plato's 'Shadows on a Cave' or 'Theory of Forms' in *The Republic* (380 BCE), where men kept prisoners in a cave see only the shadows thrown on the cave wall by the light of a fire and assume these shadows to be real objects:

> Then if they were able to talk with one another, do you not think that they would suppose what they saw to be the real things? [...] What do you think he would say if he were told by someone that before he had been seeing mere foolish phantoms, [...]? (207–208)

Plato's conception of shadows on a cave indicates the impossibility of knowing what is real and what are shadows on the wall. The shadow worlds in Jordan's *The Great Hunt* are presented similarly, with the characters questioning the reality of the world in which they find themselves. They suggest that the worlds that might be are: "[w]orlds our world might have been if things had happened differently. Maybe that's why it is all so … washed-out looking. Because it's an 'if,' a 'maybe.' Just a shadow of the real world" (*Great Hunt* 249). These worlds are not actualised, as they are shadows of the real one, and thus places and objects lack corporeality.

The real world, then, is similar to Plato's Theory of Forms, in that the world the characters regularly inhabit hold the 'real' object, the essence of that object's being, and the objects in the alternate worlds are merely shadows cast by that object:

> Those worlds truly are mirrors in a way, [...]. Some of them reflect only great events in the true world, but some have a shadow of that reflection even before the event occurs. [...] Reflections of what will be are fainter than reflections of what is or what was. (*Great Hunt* 269)

These mirror worlds are not only created by events branching time, but also cast reflections based on possible events that are yet to occur (similar to the ripples in the pond or Stephen Hawking's light cones, as discussed in the previous chapter). These 'future' events are fainter than the 'past' ones, suggesting that these events are not as 'real' as past ones, as their possibilities have not yet manifested. Thus, as discussed in the previous chapter, Jordan presents time as tensed: mirrors or reflections of the 'real world' are branching paths in space-time, less 'real' variations of the real world or variations that are only possible.

In *Postmodernist Fiction* (1987), Brian McHale notes that: "Science fiction, by staging 'close encounters' between different worlds, placing them in confrontation, foregrounds their respective structures and the disparities between them" (60). Like in Science Fiction, the shadow or mirror worlds in Jordan's *The Great Hunt* can be seen as an example of this, of "foreground[ing] structures and the disparities" through "encounter[ing...] different worlds." Jordan presents this confrontation through the structure of alternate parallel worlds. McHale suggests that: "Among the oldest of the classic ontological themes in poetics is that of the *otherness* of the fictional world, its separation from the real world of experience" (27, original emphasis). *The Great Hunt* also poses this ontological theme, drawing attention to the artificiality of the worlds, by making it uncanny, making it both strange and familiar.

McHale postulates a difference between fictions that poses ontological questions and those that ask epistemological questions. Epistemological questions ask, "How can I interpret this world of which I am a part? And what am I in it?" (McHale 9). In contrast, ontological questions inquire: "What is a world?; What kind of worlds are there, how are they constituted, and how do they differ?; What happens when different kinds of world are placed in confrontation, or when boundaries between worlds are violated?" (10). In *The Great Hunt*, these are the questions that the characters are faced with when they enter the mirror worlds. The mirror worlds with their fractured timelines pose these ontological questions of "what kind of worlds are there [...] and how do they differ?" (McHale 10). But these ontological questions are paired with epistemological questions, as the ontological question of other worlds evokes epistemological questions of identity and meaning. Are the choices they make in the mirror world 'real'? That is, if the worlds are created by branching due to choices, do the worlds accurately represent an individual's identity? "How do they know it, and with what degree of certainty?" (McHale 9).

Although McHale declares that most critical approaches to the Fantastic have been epistemological (the most influential study, he notes, is Tzvetan Todorov's), this does not impede ontological critical approaches to Fantasy. Additionally, the literature itself may evoke a combination of ontological and epistemological questions, as Jordan's *The Great Hunt* does. This combination is notable in those Heroic Epic Fantasy series where the characters question their own sanity or in examples where characters actively question the reliability of information they are provided with, as described in the examples above. However, it should be noted that not all Heroic Epic Fantasy texts pose ontological questions. In others, an epistemological line of questioning may be more prevalent as protagonists and heroes attempt to interpret prophecies and navigate their place in the narrative. This is what occurs in the David and Leigh Eddings' *Belgariad* (1982–1984) and *Malloreon* (1987–1991) series, where the hero Garion constantly struggles with his 'destined' role. Garion realises that:

> He had finally found the answer to the plaintive "Why me?" which he had voiced so often in the past. He was inevitably chosen for those dreadful, frightening tasks because he was perfectly suited for them.
> "It's what I do," he muttered to himself. "Any time there's something so ridiculously dangerous that no rational human being would ever consider trying, they send for me." (*King of the Murgos* 45)

As the first part of this book concluded, the hero is constantly faced with the choice to fulfil their destiny. Expanding further on that argument, I assert that the hero is confronted with a choice or an alternate path which provokes epistemological questions where the hero comprehends and then accepts or rejects their own identity.

A second recursive structure in *The Great Hunt* demonstrates this questioning and confrontation further. When Rand attempts to travel to these shadow worlds again, he loses control of the spell and instead he and the group he is travelling with experience countless variations of their lives. They (re-)live their lives over and over again, but these lives are all different based on choices they have made. Yet the lives Rand experiences all share a common element: At the end of his life, Rand hears: "*I have won again, Lews Therin. Flicker*" (529, original emphasis). The "flicker" is a signal representing the move into the next world or life. McHale also uses the word "flicker" when discussing the oscillation between different ontological worlds:

> This is not a matter, in other words, of *choosing* between alternative states of affairs, but rather an ontological oscillation, a flickering effect, or, to use Ingarden's own metaphor, an effect of "iridescence" or "opalescence." And "opalescence" is not restricted to single objects; entire *worlds* may flicker. (McHale 32, original emphasis)

As in McHale, the flicker in Jordan's *Great Hunt* becomes almost an audible signal of movement between the oscillating worlds.

Like the mirror worlds, the ontological questioning of this second recursive structure is placed alongside epistemological questions of identity. Through these repetitive patterns, Rand re-lives different variations of his life. In each of these lives, the same pattern is repeated, with a voice – presumably that of the Dark Lord – whispering at the end of his life, "I have won again, Lews Therin," followed by a flicker. McHale identifies how these recursive structures function in ontological fiction:

> Here recursive structure serves as a tool for exploring issues of narrative authority, reliability and unreliability, the circulation of knowledge, and so forth. [...] One such strategy, the simplest of all, involves *frequency*: interrupting the primary diegesis not once or twice but *often* with secondary, hypodiegetic worlds, representations within the representation. (113, original emphasis)

Similarly, Heroic Epic Fantasy authors utilise frequent recursive structures throughout their novels and also from book to book within the series as events often repeat themselves; these structures explore issues of "narrative authority, reliability and unreliability, [...] and so forth." McHale maintains that these recursive structures: "have the effect of interrupting and complicating the ontological 'horizon' of the fiction, multiplying its worlds, and *laying bare the process of world construction*" (112, my emphasis). This narrative style, with the frequent, *infinite* repetitions, brings attention to the deliberate fractured structuring of the world.

This is the effect of the recursive structures in *The Great Hunt* as well. The repetitions of their lives resonate, allowing the hero to confront a part of their own identity. As Currie argues, identity "exists only as a narrative" (25). In Heroic Epic Fantasy, this identity formation is brought about through constant repetitive confrontation with other potential narrative selves. Witnessing these repetitions forces Rand and the other characters to question their identity by confronting alternate narratives: "Does it surprise you that your life might go differently if you made different choices, or different things happened to you?" (*Great Hunt* 533). The characters question how the choices they make result in a creation of a different world, a different life path.

For instance, Rand is forced to re-live his life over and over:

> He was a soldier. He was a shepherd. He was a beggar, and a king. He was farmer, gleeman, sailor, carpenter. [...] And at the end of every life, as he lay dying, as he drew his final breath, a voice whispered in his ear. *I have won again, Lews Therin. Flicker flicker flicker.* (531–532, original emphasis)

The constant repetition of the phrase "I have won again, Lews Therin" followed by the repetition of the word "flicker" which continues for twenty-six counts – an almost audible and visible signal of transmitting between worlds – operates to disrupt the text. The narration is broken as it switches to the next time stream and the reader might be disoriented, but this is done so deliberately. The hybridisation of ontological and epistemological questions posed by the text through the repetitive structures demands a constant interpretation on behalf of the protagonist. Each life is different in a number of ways due to the choices made. By stacking these lives next to each other so that differences and similarities between them become overt, the characters are able to affirm, alter, or reject their own identity. The presentation of their multiple lives become a process of textual comparison – a hermeneutics of identity.

Through repeated confrontation with different worlds, the characters must self-reflect on their identity, as they must, first, question whether the events that occur in these different lives are possible as a function of their own actions, and then next, construct and declare their identity out of these narratives. The self-reflection of the hero is always a moral dilemma, as the characters must struggle with the consequences of their actions. The element of fate offers a complexity to these ethical questions. Though Rand lives vastly different lives, in all of these realities they all end the same. Whenever he dies, he hears the voice of the antagonist, the Dark Lord, whispering in his ear: "I have won again, Lews Therin" (529). Consequently, the ways in which Rand's lives end can presumably be read bleakly. At the end of each life, the Dark Lord's words suggest that the character is destined to be defeated. But there is another interpretation of events which Rand comprehends at the end of the novel: All lives must end. All people must die. Hence, *what matters is the journey* and the *choices* made on this journey. In each life, whether a beggar or a king, Rand stays true to the "Light," to the Creator and the spirit of goodness. Rand tells the antagonist: "I will never serve you, Father of Lies. In a thousand lives, I never have" (666). At the end of the novel, Rand denies the Dark Lord's words "I have won again" and proclaims that they are a lie. He realises that in each repetition of his life he chooses to never surrender to the antagonist by *choosing death* instead. As Chapter 5 will explore, this act, of choosing death, is essential to the heroic function. Though the characters are free to interpret their destinies in any way they choose, the actualised hero is one who willingly embraces their heroic function of death and sacrifice.

Both the use of the mirror world and repeated lives results in a distortion that forces both character and reader to question the internal reality of the text. There are more recursive structural patterns of distortion in the text which operate similarly to the two described here. For instance, there is a *ter'angreal*, a magical device that tests the commitment of those seeking to train as Aes Sedai. By entering the device, characters are made to confront alternative versions of their lives and choose whether they wish to follow that path or their current one. Another structure is the dreamscape, where characters are faced with similar questions of commitment. Dreamscapes are one of the more popular ways in which

Fantasy fiction expresses recursive structures. As J. R. R. Tolkien indicates in "On Fairy-Stories" (1947): "it is true that Dream is not unconnected with Faërie. In dreams strange powers of the mind may be unlocked" (14). Thus, dreamscapes, through their connection to these ethereal (almost Jungian) potentials, allow several avenues in which a Fantasy author can develop recursive structures in which a character confronts their identity. The dreamscape is also important as it undermines the boundaries between the physical and metaphysical world. Recall how the first chapter explored that gods are removed from the physical world. Acting as a median space between the physical world and metaphysical world, dreamscapes and similar spiritual dimensions allow gods or comparable entities to interact with the heroes. These dreamscapes offer a distortion, as the consequent interpretation of events in the dreamscape is paired alongside a Todorovian hesitation as the characters then question the 'realness' of the events.

Recursive structures function to distort and redefine each character's sense of identity and purpose. Through repeated confrontations of recurring structural devices, devices that are the same but different from the one before it, the heroes' choices and reactions to these structures leads to a character development, one that builds or denies the character's stance as hero. While Rand's madness brings into question his position as authority, as a hero, his madness is that point where Clute's second stage of Fantasy, that of thinning, reaches its peak. Rand's degeneration results in cacophony and chaos, his authoritative role progressively questioned (both by the characters in the book and also by the external reader) until Rand reaches a point of unpredictability and instability. And yet, Rand as strange attractor also has the property of stability: "By definition, attractors had the important property of stability [...] motion tends to return to the attractor" (Gleick 138). If Rand attracts and spins out turmoil and chaos, he also mediates these events through himself, in order to create something new. It is at the point that meaning collapses that he is able to construct a new interpretation of events, mediating an elucidation of the narrative that was previously unclear or hidden.

In the next two chapters, I expand further on how the choices that characters make lead to the fulfilment of the heroic potential. Chapter 4 will discuss the temptation of the hero in choosing an alternative path, one that casts them as a failed hero or ou-hero. Chapter 5 then will examine how these choices are influenced by the hero's commitment to the community, especially in their willingness to sacrifice themselves on behalf of the community.

Notes

1 Following Jordan's death, Brandon Sanderson completed the last three books of the series using notes left by the late author.

2 Interestingly, in this case it is the antagonist and not the protagonist that marks the hero as the child of prophecy. Yet, Harry still must accept his role through a process of self-reflexivity. Furthermore, as the next chapter will discuss, the antagonist and protagonist are often shadows of each other and this dualism is especially true in Rowling's *Harry Potter* series.

Bibliography

Attebery, Brian. *Stories about Stories: Fantasy and the Remaking of Myth*. Oxford University Press, 2014.

———. *Strategies of Fantasy*. Indiana University Press.1992.

———. "Structuralism." *A Cambridge Companion to Fantasy Literature*. Eds. Edward James and Farah Mendlesohn. Cambridge University Press, 2012. pp. 81–90.

Barthes, Roland. *The Pleasure of the Text*. 1975. Trans. Richard Miller. Jonathan Cape, 1976.

———. *S/Z*. 1970. Trans. Richard Miller. Jonathan Cape, 1975.

Bobzien, Susanne. *Determinism and Freedom in Stoic Philosophy*. Clarendon Press, 1998.

Carlyle, Thomas. *On Heroes, Hero-Worship, & the Heroic in History*. 1841. Chapman and Hall Limited, 1904.

Clemens, James. *Wit'ch Fire*. 1998. Del Rey, 1999. The Banned and the Banished 1.

Clute, John. "Fantastika in the World Storm." 2007. *Pardon this Intrusion: Fantastika in the World Storm*. Beccon Publications, 2011. pp. 19–31.

Currie, Mark. *Metafiction*. Longman, 1995.

———. *Postmodern Narrative Theory*. 2nd ed. 1998. Palgrave, 2011.

Dubois, Page. *History, Rhetorical Description and the Epic*. D. S. Brewer, 1982.

Eddings, David and Leigh Eddings. *King of the Murgos*. Del Rey, 1988. Malloreon 2.

Gleick, James. *Chaos: The Amazing Science of the Unpredictable*. 1987. Vintage Books, 1998.

Goodkind, Terry. *Stone of Tears*. 1995. Tom Doherty, 1996. The Sword of Truth 2.

Hayles, N. Katherine. *Chaos Bound: Orderly Disorder in Contemporary Literature and Science*. 1990. Cornell University Press, 1994.

Jordan, Robert. *A Crown of Swords*. 1996. Orbit, 2007. The Wheel of Time 7.

———. *The Dragon Reborn*. 1991. Orbit, 2014. The Wheel of Time 3.

———. *The Great Hunt*. 1990. Tor, 1991. The Wheel of Time 2.

———. *The Wheel of Time*. Tor, 1990–2005. The Wheel of Time 1–11.

Jordan, Robert and Brandon Sanderson. *The Gathering Storm*. Orbit, 2009. The Wheel of Time 12.

———. *The Wheel of Time*. Tor, 2009–2012. The Wheel of Time 12–14.

Lackey, Mercedes. *The Fairy Godmother*. Luna Books, 2004. Five Hundred Kingdoms 1.

McHale, Brian. *Postmodernist Fiction*. 1987. Routledge, 1994.

Mendlesohn, Farah. *Rhetorics of Fantasy*. Wesleyan University Press, 2008.

Plato. "Book VII." *The Republic*. 380 BCE. Trans. A. D. Lindsay. 1906. J. M. Dent & Sons Ltd, 1961. pp. 207–237.

Prigogine, Ilya and Isabella Stengers. *Order out of Chaos: Man's New Dialogue with Nature*. 1984. Flamingo, 1985.
Rowling, Joanne K. *Harry Potter*. Bloomsbury, 1997–2007. Harry Potter 1–7.
Sanderson, Brandon. *Mistborn Trilogy*. Tor, 2006–2010. Mistborn 1–3.
——. *The Well of Ascension*. 2007. Tom Doherty, 2008. Mistborn Trilogy 2.
Todorov, Tzvetan. *The Fantastic: A Structural Approach to a Literary Genre*. 1970. Trans. Richard Howard. Cornell University, 1975.
Tolkien, John Ronald Reuel. "On Fairy-Stories." 1947. *Tree and Leaf*. 1964. HarperCollins, 2001.
Waugh, Patricia. *Metafiction: The Theory and Practice of Self-Conscious Fiction*. 1984. Routledge, 1993.

4 The Ou-Hero

Considering the Possibility for the Hero to Become Villain (and Vice Versa) in David Farland's *The Wyrmling Horde* (2008)

The first part of this book explored heroes in Heroic Epic Fantasy, indicating how repetitions function as iterations that build the structure of the story and lead the hero into fulfilling their role as actualised hero. This chapter examines how aspects of the heroic pattern can be found in another character, the 'ou-hero.' Although 'villain' is the traditional nomenclature used to refer to the hero's opposite, Heroic Epic Fantasy does not always contain a villain who embodies the quality of absolute evil; indeed, many antagonists demonstrate nuances of grey morality. The terminology 'antihero' is also inadequate as the antihero often indicates a protagonist with undesirable (unheroic) qualities. Consequently, I have established the terminology ou-hero – the οὐ-hero or not-hero – to indicate a protagonist *or* antagonistic that demonstrates the potential to be hero but fails to actualise the role.

Throughout this chapter, I assert that the similarities between hero and ou-hero indicate the potential and possibility of the one to become the other. I argue that, while the ou-hero exhibits the failed potential to be hero, the hero, in turn, reveals the possibility of turning into an ou-hero themselves. By examining the relationship between the two character-types, I also begin a discussion on the concepts of 'balance' and 'binaries' which are important themes in every Heroic Epic Fantasy text. While Heroic Epic Fantasy fiction traditionally expresses a battle between 'Good versus Evil,' this plot structure is overly simplified. The relationship between the hero and the ou-hero, or equally, the hero's battle with their own shadowy-self, is evident of the complicated layers of structure that develops these binaries.

In this chapter, I examine these layers of binaries using David Farland's *The Wyrmling Horde* (2008), the seventh book of the *Runelords* series (1998–present), as a case study. While the potential for the hero to become ou-hero and vice versa is notable in many Heroic Epic Fantasy narratives, Farland presents this concept in an explicit way. In his incomplete *Runelords* series (eight books produced so far in a two-part series[1]) Farland depicts an interesting relationship between antagonist and protagonist figures. The central protagonist of the first series, Gaborn Val Orden, is identified early in the first book, *The Sum of All Men* (1998),[2] as the man who will become the Earth King: a man crowned by the spirit of Earth itself to be its protector in a time of need. However, in the sequel series, the positioning of hero and villain is *reversed* as Gaborn's enemy Raj Ahten takes the place of a protagonist and Gaborn, in contrast, is possessed by a demonic figure. Consequently, as I expand on through my examination of *The Wyrmling Horde* (with reference to the rest of the series), identifying the protagonist and antagonist in their respective roles is convoluted. This complication, however, reinforces the conclusions of the first part of this book: that the choices characters make following a period of introspection redefines their identity as hero, or, indeed, as, ou-hero.

Maintaining the Balance of Good and Evil

Heroic Epic Fantasy fiction is often viewed in terms of binary relations with the plot motivated by the struggle between the forces of good and evil. In "Considering the Sense of 'Fantasy' or 'Fantastic Fiction': An Effusion" (2000), Darko Suvin identifies the basic premise of Fantasy is that: "in the doctrinal Master Plot the forces of Good and Evil, working through natural as well as supernatural existents, must battle it out between a Fall and the Happy Ending" (223). While this battle is certainly present in Heroic Epic Fantasy, defining the structure in terms of "the forces of Good and Evil" is more complicated than Suvin indicates. In "Structuralism" (2012), Brian Attebery asserts that these binaries function at different levels:

> Fantasy is often criticized for being too obvious in its oppositions. Light versus dark, good versus evil: such pairings seem glaringly evident, even simple-minded, [...] But Lévi-Strauss says, not so fast. There are different sorts of complexity. A myth is complex vertically, as it were, it lays out its pairings again and again, piling opposition upon opposition. (86–87)

Attebery here depicts the layers of binaries as a verticality, one that transcends the binaries and builds the complexity of it. This idea, of "piling opposition upon opposition" is similar to his argument in *Strategies of Fantasy* (1992) where he discusses repetitions: "Each parallel movement effectively rewrites those that went before. Each prepares the way for those yet to come" (59). Here, the repetitions are built horizontally, as parallel movements, where the repetition rewrites and changes the iteration that has come before. In both cases, repetition adds complexity to the original structure by building on or rewriting the previous layer. As with N. Katherine Hayles's model of *"recursive symmetries between scale levels"* discussed in the previous chapter (*Chaos Bound* 13, original emphasis), with each repetition the 'binary' of good and evil is constantly evolving.

As such, dualistic language such as that of 'good' and 'evil' may be inadequate to describe the qualities of the characters in Heroic Epic Fantasy. In her essay, "The Child and the Shadow" (1975), Ursula Le Guin argues that:

> In the fairy tale, though there is no "right" and "wrong," there is a different standard, which is perhaps best called "appropriateness." Under no conditions can we say that it is morally right and ethically virtuous to push an old lady into a baking oven. But, under the conditions of fairy tale, in the language of the archetypes, we can say with perfect conviction that it may be *appropriate* to do so. (56, original emphasis)

Just as Le Guin indicates that the Fairy-Tale hero does not choose between what is right and wrong but what is appropriate, similarly the Heroic Epic Fantasy hero chooses the best possible action to do at the time. Moreover, the characters often ponder this complicated relationship between 'right' and 'wrong,' as they reflect on whether their actions in the world hinder or harm. For instance, Gaborn in Farland's *Runelords* contemplates the meaning of virtue and vice in the third novel:

> When I was a lad I knew a woman so charitable that everyone praised her. She baked bread for the poor, gave coins to the poor, gave her cow – and finally her house. At last she found herself begging on the streets outside of Broward, where she died one winter. Thus her virtue grew into a vice that consumed her. (*Wizardborn* 40)

The passage demonstrates that instead of employing the language of 'right' and 'wrong,' a hero must deliberate on whether their actions when confronted with a fork in the road (Figure 2.2) are appropriate. In contrast, as will be explored, the ou-hero makes the *inappropriate* choice when confronted with the same decision.

Le Guin continues:

> Evil, then, appears in the fairy tale not as something diametrically opposed to good, but as inextricably involved with it, as in the yang-yin symbol. Neither is greater than the other, nor can human reason and virtue separate one from the other and choose between them. The hero or heroine is the one who sees what is appropriate to be done, because he or she sees the *whole*, which is greater than either evil or good. (56–57, original emphasis)

As Le Guin reveals, the binary between good and evil in the Fairy Tale is one which is not *opposite* to each other but is involved in a complicated relationship. The binary of good and evil in Heroic Epic Fantasy fiction operates similarly; it is not a relationship of good *versus* evil, but a relationship that sees the whole of good *and* evil and finds a *balance* between the two. Viewing the binary of good and evil as a whole is an important facet in describing the relationship between the antagonist and protagonist. As the next chapter will explore further, it is especially important for the hero to understand this view. For instance, in the fourth book of the *Runelords* series, the first Earth King Erden Geboren leaves a message to his successor: "*No tree or plant can grow in daylight alone. Given only light, a seed will not germinate, roots will not take hold. It takes a balance of sunlight and shadow. Men, too, grow their deepest roots in the darkness*" (*The Lair of Bones* 406, original emphasis indicating written text from a journal). Erden Geboren, a hero that is treated as a legendary or mythological figure within the text, cautions Gaborn that the hero must understand both light and darkness in order for growth to occur. In essence, the hero must maintain a balance of good and evil as both protagonist and antagonist journey towards a path that leads to greater good or greater evil, tipping the balance of the world accordingly. As Richard Mathews asserts in *Fantasy: The Liberation of Imagination* (1997): "Every minute of time represents a choice and thus a potential downfall or salvation that will affect not only the individual moral agent but also the delicate balance of good and evil in the world at large" (72). Thus, the choices that the characters make in their journey not only determine their own path, but also the world's path.

This concept of 'world balance' is articulated by many Heroic Epic Fantasy authors. For instance, in Jim Butcher's *Academ's Fury* (2005), the second book of the *Codex Alera* series (2004–2009), Gaius discusses how: "History is replete with them. Moments where the fate of thousands hangs at balance, easily tipped one way or the next by the hands and wills of those involved" (11). Here, Gaius argues that the fate of the world (the events of the first book), were tipped out of harm's way by the actions of "one obstinate apprentice shepherd and the courage of those holders" (11). Similarly, in L. E. Modesitt Jr.'s *The Magic of Recluce* (1991) one of the theological texts embedded in the book reads: "Order and chaos must balance, but as on a see-saw. The power of chaos is for great destruction in a confined area, for order by nature must be diffused over vaster realms" (378). In *The Magic of Recluce*, the hero Lerris comes to recognise that the power of order magic has become so focalised on the country of Recluce that it has created an unbalance in the rest of the world, increasing the powers of chaos magic throughout. Although there is no clearly defined antagonist or 'evil' in the novel, the hero must still bring a sense of balance into the world. Lerris does so by creating a mirror; a process that involves understanding the pattern of chaos and then reflecting this pattern in order to destroy it: "I struggled to reflect the odd twists, turning them into a deeper harmony, substituting order for chaos, in equal shape and force" (383–384). As in the previous chapter, the recursive pattern of mirroring is made explicit here. Note that Modesitt demonstrates a balance through a conception of order versus chaos. Other Fantasy authors may use conceptions of light and darkness, of life and death, or a whole variety of binaries that operate as if on a seesaw. As the latter half of this book will expand on, it is important to note that a sense of a balance *must* be present in the Heroic Epic Fantasy structure as the plot of the narrative is motivated by an *unbalance* in the system.

Because the plot of the narrative is motivated by an unbalance in the world, often the identity of antagonist (and occasionally the protagonist) is repeatedly deferred. This is especially the case in long-running Fantasy series; as an antagonist may be defeated at the end of each novel, another, greater, antagonist must take their place in the next novel. For instance, in Robert Jordan's *The Wheel of Time* series (1990–2012), the heroes defeat several antagonist characters throughout the series. In the first of these confrontations, they assume that the figure they had defeated is "the Dark One." They later understand that these figures are only minions of the Dark One. Though less of a threat than the Dark One, each minion they encounter demonstrates greater and greater abilities. As well, characters that they have already defeated may arise again in a more powerful form.

Such is the case with Farland's *Runelords* series, with the identity of the antagonist shifting into greater and greater entities as the fulcrum of balance in the world becomes increasingly unstable. In the first book, the conqueror Raj Ahten is presented as the antagonist but there is an underlying suggestion that a greater evil exists. After a conversation with the Earth (a personification that takes the place of a metaphysical entity or divinity), Gaborn, the hero of the first series, reconsiders the identity of the antagonist and mistakenly thinks that the Earth wishes him to destroy the reavers, an intelligent but carnivorous animal race. This misconception continues until the third book, when another hero, Averan, discovers that she is an Earth Wizard, one who is meant to be the protector of the reavers. Thus, the identity of the antagonist is deferred once again when Averan informs the other protagonists that the reaver army that marched on the people are mostly made up of peasants and "only did it because their master told them" to do so (*Wizardborn* 238). As Gaborn is a protector of the Earth, that protection extends to all life on it; the wizard Binnesman constantly reminds him that: "all life is precious. All must be revered" (*Wizardborn* 381): this includes the lives of both his enemy Raj Ahten as well as the monstrous reavers. Consequently, if all life is precious to Earth, then a 'greater' enemy than either Raj Ahten or the reavers must exist, one that is *abnormal* to Earth. While Chapter 6 will explore this idea of an enemy abnormal to the land in greater detail, it is important to note the continual deferment of identifying the antagonist indicating the constant teetering for balance.

As Chapter 6 will explore further, a disruption of the world balance leads to the dissolution of the world itself. In Farland's *Runelords*, prior to the events of the series, the worlds are fractured into numerous parts when the One True World divided. The creation saga embedded in the series tells of a time where:

> "[...] Once there was only one world, and one star, and beneath it grew the One True Tree. [says Binnesman. He continues:]
>
> "And One Rune bound them all together. But an enemy sought to change it, to take control. The enemy smashed the rune, and the pieces flew apart. [...]
>
> "Now there are a billion, billion worlds or more, each one spinning around its own sun. Each a broken piece of the One True World, each one more or less true in its own way." (*Wizardborn* 347)

This passage in the third novel indicates the need to heal the fractured worlds together into one whole totality in order to regain an Edenic utopia, a utopia before a Fall. The theme of a One World breaking into a million shadow worlds is also echoed in other Heroic Epic Fantasy texts such as in James Clemens' *The Godslayer Chronicles* and Jordan's *The Wheel of Time* series. In British author's Joe Abercrombie's *Shattered Seas* trilogy, a Localised young adult Fantasy, the gods themselves are divided: "Before the elves made their war upon Her, there was one God. But in their arrogance they used a magic so strong it ripped open the Last Door, destroyed them all and broke the One God into the many" (*Half a King* 108). The theme of one world, one god, one being, emphasises the importance of the unity of the world network. As the latter half of this book will discuss, the primary duty of the Heroic Epic Fantasy hero is to reunite the broken world and restore the balance. Those that fail do not actualise their role as hero and instead remain as ou-heroes.

The Shape of the Ou-Hero's Soul

While the first part of this chapter explored the idea of balance on a macroscale, the need for balance is also represented recursively in the depiction of individual characters. In fact, all the major characters may demonstrate this attempt to achieve balance, although many may fail. It is these characters that I label as an ou-hero, a protagonist or antagonist who has failed in their journey to become a hero. For instance, Brandon Sanderson's *Mistborn* (Lord Ruler), James Clemens' *Shadowfall* (Chrism), David and Leigh Eddings' *Belgariad* series (Torak), and Jordan's *The Wheel of Time* series (Logain and Mazrim Taim) all depict antagonists who attempt to fulfil the role of hero themselves. As such, they operate as a foil to the hero. In Lois McMaster Bujold's *The Curse of Chalion* (2001) Lord dy Lutez, attempts to fulfil the prophecy but fails and dies in the attempt. His failure allows Cazaril to gain the knowledge and conviction to realise his role as hero. Thus, a failed hero may come first, being a forerunner for the actualised hero; the failure of the ou-hero may aid the hero in gaining adequate knowledge which will allow them to fulfil their destiny.

It is also conceivable for a central protagonist – one who is *eventually* confirmed as hero – to demonstrate the *possibility* of failure. For instance, both Richard Cypher in Terry Goodkind's *Sword of Truth* series (1994–present) and Rand al'Thor in Jordan's *The Wheel of Time* series express this potential. As the latter half of this chapter will consider, at each fork in the road it is possible that the hero might fail and become ou-hero, or that, once failing, the choice may be presented again leading to a re-establishment of the identity of hero. Thus, the identification of a character as hero or ou-hero (or good and evil, or protagonist or antagonist) is often fluid.

The identification of hero and ou-hero is especially convoluted in Farland's *Runelords*. The fractured universe structure presented in the first series (books one to four) is expanded on and complicated in the second series (books five onward). While the One True World was broken into a million parts prior to the events of the first series, in the sequel series Gaborn's son Fallion heals the rift between two of these worlds and joins them together. Those people who are alive in both worlds have their spirits or souls joined, transforming into a hybrid being with memories of both of their lives. But a person who is dead on one world does not combine with their missing half and can only recollect the one life. Such is the case with the emir Tuul Ra, who was Raj Ahten, an antagonist, on Gaborn's world. In the shadow world, he is presented as a protagonist. But when the worlds combine the people realise what his shadow Raj Ahten had done in the world of the first series and decry his deeds:

> "That was not the emir," Daylan argued […]. "It was but a shadow, a creature that this emir could have become."
>
> "And yet," Thull-turock countered, "it seems that there is a pattern to things. In Indhopal, Raj Ahten was the most powerful lord of his time. In this world, the emir is much the same – a man with an unnatural talent for war."
>
> "And so you fear that he will become another Raj Ahten?"
>
> "I cannot help but see the potential," Thull-turock said. (*Wyrmling Horde* 147–148)

Note the emphasis on "pattern," on this idea of repetition, as well the notion of fulfilling a "potential." The characters themselves identify the resonance between the two characters. Similarly, Areth Sul Urstone, who was Gaborn in the first world, is also presented as a failed hero. In the sequel series, Gaborn does not realise his potential as Earth King as his body is possessed by a demonic figure, Lord Despair, who manipulates Gaborn's Earth powers for his own purposes. Furthermore, while he is main protagonist of the first series, he is barely mentioned in the sequel.

As both the hero and ou-hero mirror each other, they must at some point take different trajectories from each other in order to arrive at different and opposing paths, a narrative fork in the road. In essence, they both traverse what can be termed a bifurcation point in chaos theory as James Gleick describes in *Chaos* (1987): "By stressing the methods of nonlinear dynamics, [...] a small change in one parameter – perhaps a change in timing or electric conductivity – could push an otherwise healthy system across a bifurcation point into a qualitatively new behavior" (291). To translate that to narrative terms, stresses – choices and events in a character's journey – can push a character across a bifurcation point where they emerge as either the hero or ou-hero, depending on how that character responds to the stress: the branch they chose at the fork in the road at event P, as in Figure 4.1.

The possibility of a 'bifurcation' may be depicted explicitly in the way that a Heroic Epic Fantasy author negotiates the concept of fate and destiny as a possibility of the future. For example, in Terry Goodkind's *Stone of Tears* (1995), when the seer Nathan discusses the prophecies that he foresees, he says that: "There has been a fork in the prophecies" (51), overtly using the language of branching paths that was discussed in Chapter 2. The narration continues: "Some prophecies were 'if' and 'then' prophecies, bifurcating into several possibilities. There were prophecies that followed each branch, prophecies to foretell events of each fork, since not even the prophecies always knew which events would come to pass" (52). The narrative examines how the bifurcation of the prophecies are dependent on the choices that the 'hero of prophecy' make; based on these decisions, the possibility exists that the hero unleashes evil into the world, rather than saving it. Thus, the ou-hero has the potential to be a hero and vice versa; presented with the same choices as the hero, *they choose a different path*. The first part of this

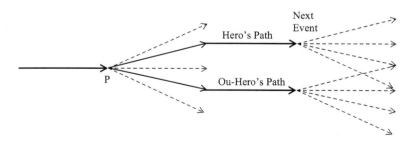

Figure 4.1 The Path of the Hero and Ou-Hero with Bifurcation Points.

monograph established that by making the correct choice, a character affirms their potential to be the hero. In Stoic philosophy, the free will aspect of choice-making "is the sole source of evil" (Marcia L. Colish, *The Stoic Tradition from Antiquity to the Early Middle Ages* 35). Evil, then, is a human construct fuelled by free choice, instead of an ethically ingrained human nature.

Recall that heroes have a shape that dictates some manner of destiny, but, to use the language of Stoic philosophy, it is up to their free will whether to move "in obedience to its given shape" (Colish 35). Like heroes, ou-heroes also have a pre-determined shape, "a pattern to things" (*Wyrmling Horde* 148), but as we can see with the characters of Tuul Ra and Raj Ahten, although the 'shape' of the character is the same, their choices have resulted in different paths, as hero or ou-hero. Tuul Ra's and Raj Ahten's initial sense of destiny comes about due to their abilities as flameweavers (wizards of fire): this is the shape of their soul. But they react to this innate skill in different ways:

> "Not all flameweavers are evil," Daylan said. "There are men who have mastered their passions to such a degree that Fire could not control them. In ancient times, some of these men were more than monsters. They became vessels of light, pure and radiant, filled with wisdom and intelligence and compassion. (*Wyrmling Horde* 150)

Daylan concludes the passage by identifying Fallion, the hero of the sequel series, as a powerful flameweaver. As the sequel series is incomplete at this time, it is not yet determined whether Fallion fails or succeeds in his role as hero. However, it is striking that the hero of the sequel series has the *same* powers and abilities as the antagonist of the first series; while the first *Runelords* series depicts flameweavers as evil, the hero of the sequel series *also* has the nature (the shape) of a flameweaver. This reinforces the idea that either protagonist or antagonist have capability to fulfil the role of hero or ou-hero, but with the possibility only realised through the choices made. Instead of embracing the path of destruction, a choice that may fulfil the 'shape' of the flameweaver, Fallion's adopts the other aspect of fire's nature, of warmth, becoming a "vessel[] of light," evoking the language discussed in the first chapter. This heroic shape of a cup will hopefully lead him down the path of fulfilling the role of hero and saving not only his world, but all the broken worlds of the *Runelords* universe.

Identifying the Ou-Hero through the Uncanny Other

While either protagonist or antagonist has the potential to become a hero, past this bifurcation point there still exists the possibility of reversal, of the hero to become a failed hero, or for the ou-hero to realise a role as hero. Note how in Figure 4.1, the hero and ou-hero have the potential to return to each other's path based on the decisions they make at the next fork in the road. Though the bifurcation leads them to different journeys, the choice to continue on this path is made repeatedly. As the characters must confront these bifurcation points many times in order to constantly affirm their potential as hero, the idea of temptation and failing as hero, is important.

To add further complication, as the balance between good and evil must be maintained, the hero is not wholly 'good'; they must *also* have aspects of the 'evil' side within themselves. Thus, a potential for failure is heightened as the hero learns to confront and balance this 'dark' side. In his analysis of Mythological heroes in *The Epic Hero* (2001), Dean Miller concludes that 'evil' is inextricably tied to the hero figure:

> [E]vil is, as it were, "in the family": it must be conceived as the shadowy realm of the antagonist, who is himself heroic. There is, of course, the definition of evil as absolutely something else: an utterly alien, malign, or antihuman force or personification, some "thing" purely opposite and Other to the human. But in fact the theme of most epics is heroic opposition not to forces outside the human frame but, ideally, to *other* superhuman images and forces, forces defined as heroic in their interior nature. The hero fights his own – even himself, in a sense. The hero's opponent may near or declare some *differentia* identified with the Other, or even of evil, but usually he is simply the hero's mirror image. (322–323, original emphasis)

While evil is presented to the hero as an Other in the form of the antagonist, the hero may recognise this Other as a resonant form of themselves, a part of the hero's shadow or mirror self.[3]

The previous chapter discussed the interaction of mirror worlds on the recursive structure of a Heroic Epic Fantasy novel. Mirror worlds, by the very nature of being *mirrors*, would also suggest the idea of doubling. As David Langford notes in *The Encyclopedia of Fantasy* (1997), mirrors are often seen as magical devices in Fantasy and Folklore:

> A mirrored face is uncannily lifelike and can easily be imagined as speaking autonomously; hence the talking magic mirror best known from the Snow White tale [...]. Mirrors can also work against magic. They may reflect spells, [... and] offer images *truer* than human perception, and do not show unrealities like vampires or ghosts. (651, my emphasis)

Mirrors blur the line between the real and unreal because, as Langford suggests, mirrors can, on one hand, reflect true events, and on the other, distort events as well.

The multiple usages of the word 'shadow' within Heroic Epic Fantasy also indicates this notion of distortion and reflection. In the *Runelords* series, as the world is fractured into a million pieces, fractured worlds (including the one where the narrative takes place) are referred to as "shadow worlds" because they are mere shadows of the "One True World." Like the shadow worlds in Jordan's *The Wheel of Time* discussed in the previous chapter, the imagery of shadows evokes the idea of Plato's shadows on the cave wall. There are people on these worlds that might be a reflection of themselves but they differ slightly:

> We are all distorted reflections of something greater, of what we once were. [...] We all yearn to return to the One True World. Some say that our spirits, our wights, are pieces of our true self, longing to return home. (*Wizardborn* 348)

There is a play on words, where shadows suggest 'spirits,' not only of the dead but also the shadow beings of a projected world. In *Runelords*, 'shade' can also refer to the ghosts of men and women, the word suggesting that the spirit left on earth is simply a portion or part of the original human being. Like the mirror motifs, 'shadow' expresses various qualities of distortion and fracturing.

A reflective and simultaneous distortion process occurs when the hero and ou-hero confront each other and reflect parts of themselves in each other. The mirroring demonstrates the potential for the hero to recognise the Self within the Other, an effect that creates an uncanny doubling as the hero is reluctant to acknowledge the similarities between their self and the ou-hero. The uncanny, as Freud describes ("The Uncanny" 1919, McLintock translation 2003), is "something familiar ['homely', 'homey'] that has been repressed and then reappears" (152, translator's annotations). This is the process that the hero undergoes when they come into contact with the ou-hero. The hero and ou-hero often embody doubles of each other as they have the potential to be the other: "a person may identify himself with another and so become unsure of his true self; or he may substitute the other's self for his own. The self may thus be duplicated, divided and interchanged" (Freud 142). Accordingly, the hero recognises the ou-hero as something familiar, but then this association is repressed.

A popular example occurs in J. K. Rowling's children's novel *Harry Potter and the Chamber of Secrets* (1998), where both Harry Potter and Voldemort have the ability to communicate with snakes. It is only later (*Harry Potter and the Deathly Hallows*, 2007) that the reader discovers that the reason the two characters share this ability is because Voldemort had inadvertently embedded fragments of his own soul within Potter. Similarly, in Orson Scott Card's *Ender's Game* (1977), a Heroic Epic Science Fiction novel, the hero comes to understand that: "In the moment when I truly understand my enemy, understand him well enough to defeat him, then in that very moment I also love him" (238). The hero must come to comprehend and embrace his enemy in order to gain the knowledge to defeat in. In the first *Runelords* novel, Gaborn is made to take an oath to the Earth who comes to him wearing the face of Raj Ahten. Earth tells him:

> "You say you love the land. But would you honour your vows to me, even if I wore the face of an enemy?"
> [...] "Someday you shall comprehend me, when your body mingles with mine. Do you fear that day?"
> Death. Earth wanted to know if he feared death. [...] Raj Ahten. The thing looked so much like Raj Ahten. Gaborn knew what Earth desired of him. Something more than embracing life. Something more than serving man. To embrace death and decay and the totality that was Earth. (*The Sum of All Men* 153–154)

The scene is significant, as the Earth wishes for Gaborn to submit to it while wearing the face of Gaborn's enemy, indicating the need for Gaborn to yield to his shadowy aspects in order to maintain the balance of Earth. This exchange also suggests first, a foreshadowing in which Gaborn will have to embrace his enemy, and second, a foreshadowing where the hero will have to welcome a literal or metaphorical death, an idea that will be explored in the next chapter. When Gaborn is unable to accept his enemies at the end of the second book, the Earth withdraws the power it had granted to Gaborn, leading to his identity as Earth King being questioned and setting him on a path to possibly becoming or remaining as an ou-hero.

In order for the protagonist to return to the path of the hero, they must fully comprehend and embrace their enemy, acknowledging the ou-hero as a shadow of themselves. For instance, in Ursula Le Guin's *A Wizard of Earthsea* (1968), a foundational Fantasy text, the hero Ged releases an unnamed shade from the underworld and spends the rest of the novel pursuing this shade. He ultimately defeats the shade by recognising the shadow as part of himself:

> And he began to see the truth, that Ged had neither lost nor won but, naming the shadow of his death with his own name, had made himself whole: a man: who, knowing his whole true self, cannot be used or possessed by any power other than himself, and whose life therefore is lived for life's sake and never in the service of ruin, or pain, or hatred, or the dark. (*Wizard of Earthsea* 199)

By naming the shadow as part of himself, Ged is able to embrace it, and thereby remove its presence as a separate entity.

Other instances of Heroic Epic Fantasy may demonstrate a more rigid binary of good and evil. Although many examples show nuances in this binary, this does not indicate that *all* antagonists in Heroic Epic Fantasy must demonstrate the potential to be hero. However, even in examples where a binary of 'good versus evil' is more rigid, a doppelganger figure may still exist but in the appearance of a *hero*. For instance, in Mercedes Lackey and James Mallory's *The Outstretched Shadow* (2003), the demon antagonist appears to the hero Kellen with the hero's own face and shape. This Other-Kellen tempts the hero with false promises, seducing him with ideas of glory. Here, refuting the doppelganger holds up the binary of good and evil rather than breaking it down. The scene is similar to the confrontation of Luke Skywalker with the "Dark Side" in *The Empire Strikes Back* (1980); in facing the symbolic presence of his enemy, Luke sees himself in the enemy he has destroyed. Both scenes indicate the temptation of the hero choosing the 'Dark Side,' the path of evil, and the possibility of becoming an ou-hero themselves.

Many of the post-1990 texts that are utilised as case studies in this book are explicit in challenging the binary of good and evil, but, as the examples above indicate, this is not to say that the binary is dissolved in all Fantasy texts – or that it was not complicated in earlier examples of Fantasy. J. R. R. Tolkien's foundational *The Lord of the Rings* trilogy (1954–1955) sets a precedent where the group of heroes break apart because of the selfishness of the individual characters and their desire for power motivated through the ring. Furthermore, the sole character charged with the destruction of the ring, Frodo Baggins, progressively begins to take on the characteristics of the ou-hero Gollum/Sméagol. The schism between Gollum and Sméagol also demonstrates the anxieties of labelling a character as wholly good or evil. Both characters – Frodo and Gollum – demonstrate the temptation of a character to embrace and lose themselves in darkness. The consequent confirmation of the character as hero or ou-hero is based on the choices they make when confronting their shadowy selves.

This motif of tempting towards the shadow side is an important feature of the hero's journey as the hero *must* have the potential to be tempted from their path. Le Guin expounds on the Jungian use of the word 'shadow' in "The Child and the Shadow":

> Jung saw the ego, what we usually call the self, as only a part of the Self, the part of it which we are consciously aware of. […] The ego, […] must turn inward, away from the crowd […]. These regions of the psyche Jung calls the "collective unconscious," and it is in them, where we all meet, that he sees the source of true community; […]. How do we get there? […] Jung says that the first step is to turn around and follow your own shadow. (52–53, original emphasis)

Thus, in Le Guin's *A Wizard of Earthsea*, the ego of the hero Ged must turn inward in order to reach the community. Like other Heroic Epic Fantasy heroes, Ged can only do so by facing himself, or "turn[ing] around and follow[ing] his own shadow." Likewise, in *The Writer's Journey* (1992), a guide to writing Fantasy fiction, Christopher Vogler describes the dramatic function of the Shadow as such:

> The function of the Shadow in drama is to challenge the hero and give her a worthy opponent in the struggle. [...] The challenging energy of the Shadow archetype can be expressed in a single character, but it may also be a mask worn at different times by any of the characters. Heroes themselves can manifest a Shadow side. When the protagonist is crippled by doubts or guilt, acts in self-destructive ways, [...] or becomes selfish rather than self-sacrificing, the Shadow has overtaken him. (84)

Through the repeated confrontation with the Shadowy set, the character redefines and reinforces their identity as hero or ou-hero. Thus, the character's evaluation of themselves as hero is an essential process to the journey of the hero. There are moments where the hero may falter, tempted by the 'Shadow side,' but, as the next chapter will explore, the assertion of the hero's selflessness, through the motif of sacrifice, redefines their positioning.

Accordingly, in *The Wyrmling Horde*, the way that two characters respond to the same punishment is what determines their status as hero or ou-hero. The story of the breaking in *Runelords* is told in multiple ways, labelling the destroyer, Yaleen, as a malicious force who intended to destroy the world, or, in other versions, in order to subvert the Great Seal of Creation to their will.[4] But in another retelling, Fallion recollects that: "*She [Yaleen] had only thought it a childish prank,* [...] *though she was a person of terrible avarice*" (*Wyrmling Horde* 17, original emphasis to indicate story within a story). This version recasts the story of the Fall as a naïve mistake, perhaps brought about by selfishness, but lacking the qualities of absolute evil that slowly grows to embody the persona of Lord Despair. Yaleen's transformation into Lord Despair comes about through her punishment: those Bright Ones (angel-like creatures) that were left alive after the destruction of the One True World trace a rune (a written spell) of compassion onto Yaleen, so that they "*shared their own grief and loss with Yaleen, heaping it upon her*" (18, original emphasis). This act, of sharing their mourning of the loss of their loved ones with Yaleen through a rune of *compassion*, brings about a profound change in character:

> *Where before there had been contrition and sadness in her face, Yaleen hardened and grew angry.* [...] *Thousands stood in line to heap their pain upon her, but something in her broke long before*

> her torment was ended. When the punishment was done, there was nothing but hatred left in Yaleen's eyes.
>
> "I harmed your world by accident," Yaleen said, "and now you have made me glad of it. You gave me torment, and I will torment you in return. [...]." (18, original emphasis)

Yaleen is broken by the overwhelming feeling of compassion that is thrusted on her. By explaining the reasons why Lord Despair turned to hatred and animosity, Farland explains the character's 'evilness' and therefore creates a measure of sympathy towards the antagonist, recasting a character of horror into one that is pitied.

And yet, within the same novel, the same act is done to the hero Fallion, who holds up to the torture, and demonstrates his potential as hero rather than a failed ou-hero. Lord Despair traces runes of compassion onto Fallion, thereby connecting other people (dedicates) to Fallion through the rune. Through this rune of compassion, feelings of pain are transferred from the dedicates to Fallion. Lord Despair then proceeds to torture the dedicates so that Fallion would feel the pain of the tortures without being physically harmed himself. However, rather than breaking him so that Fallion is hardened and turns to evil, Fallion thanks Lord Despair, for he feels "grateful that he could suffer instead of these innocents" (19). The repetitions within the novel, of the similarity of their punishments, create a resonance where a potential exists for Fallion to fail and become ou-hero. But whereas Yaleen responds to this same act by realising a role as the antagonist, the bifurcation point for Fallion affirms his role as potential hero instead.

As can be seen with the dual characters of Raj Ahten and Tuul Ra, the dual characters of Gaborn Val Orden and Areth Sul Urstone, and the repetition of punishments between Fallion and Yaleen/Lord Despair, all heroes are presented with the possibility of becoming ou-heroes. After all, as Joseph Campbell asserts in *The Hero with a Thousand Faces* (1949): "The hero of yesterday becomes the tyrant of tomorrow, unless he crucifies *himself* today" (303, original emphasis). This potential for the hero to become ou-hero is confirmed through the choices they make as they confront the branches in their journey. Throughout this chapter, I have asserted that the similarities between hero and ou-hero indicate the potential and possibility of the one to become the other. In the next chapter, I demonstrate that the success of the hero to fulfil this heroic function depends on their messianic status, which in turn is contingent on the choices they make for their community and their willingness to embrace death.

Notes

1 The books are produced in a two-part series from books one to four and books five onward. *The Wyrmling Horde* is the third book of the sequel series.

2 Note that the first book is printed under various titles including *The Runelords* and a combination of the two names – *The Runelords: The Sum of All Men*. In order to differentiate between the series title and the book title, I refer to the first book as *The Sum of All Men* and the series as *Runelords*.
3 A discussion on the many nuances of the Other would further break down the binary of the good and evil in the Heroic Epic Fantasy. As this discussion would need to include a wider consideration of politics and power, it is outside the scope of this book. Fredric Jameson's critical analysis of Northrop Frye's description of Romance in "Magical Narratives: On the Dialectical Use of Genre Criticism" (1981) in which he comments on the discourse on binaries by Derrida and Nietzsche is a good starting point.
4 Note that the gender for this character changes. Originally female, Yaleen later possesses the body of man and renames herself "Lord Despair." The issue of gender is important, especially when considering Yaleen's connection to an Edenic Fall; unfortunately, this discussion is outside of the scope of this book.

Bibliography

Abercrombie, Joe. *Half a King*. 2014. HarperVoyager, 2015. Shattered Seas 1.
Attebery, Brian. *Strategies of Fantasy*. Indiana University Press. 1992.
———. "Structuralism." *A Cambridge Companion to Fantasy Literature*. Eds. Edward James and Farah Mendlesohn. Cambridge University Press, 2012. pp. 81–90.
Bujold, Lois McMaster. *The Curse of Chalion*. 2000. HarperCollins, 2011. Chalion 1.
Butcher, Jim. *Academ's Fury*. 2005. Ace, 2010. Codex Alera 2.
Campbell, Joseph. *The Hero with a Thousand Faces*. 1949. New World Library, 2008.
Card, Orson Scott. *Ender's Game*. 1977. Tor, 1994. Enderverse 1.
Clemens, James. *Shadowfall*. 2005. Roc, 2006. Godslayer Trilogy 1.
Colish, Marcia L. *The Stoic Tradition from Antiquity to the Early Middle Ages*. E. J. Brill, 1990.
Eddings, David and Leigh. *Belgariad*. Del Rey, 1982–1984. Belgariad 1–5.
Farland, David. *The Lair of Bones*. 2003. Tom Doherty, 2005. The Runelords 4.
———. *Runelords*. Tom Doherty, 1998–2009. The Runelords 1–8.
———. *The Sum of All Men*. 1998. Tom Doherty, 1999. The Runelords 1.
———. *Wizardborn*. Tom Doherty, 2001. The Runelords 3.
———. *The Wyrmling Horde*. 2008. Orbit, 2011. The Runelords 7.
Freud, Sigmund. "The Uncanny." 1919. Trans David McLintock. Penguin Books, 2003. pp. 123–162.
Gleick, James. *Chaos: The Amazing Science of the Unpredictable*. 1987. Vintage Books, 1998.
Goodkind, Terry. *Stone of Tears*. 1995. Tom Doherty, 1996. The Sword of Truth 2.
Hayles, N. Katherine. *Chaos Bound: Orderly Disorder in Contemporary Literature and Science*. 1990. Cornell University Press, 1994.
Jameson, Fredric. "Magical Narratives: On the Dialectical Use of Genre Criticism." *The Political Unconscious: Narrative as a Socially Symbolic Act*. 1981. Methuen, 1983. pp. 103–150.

Jordan, Robert. *The Wheel of Time*. Tor, 1990–2005. The Wheel of Time 1–11.

Jordan, Robert and Brandon Sanderson. *The Wheel of Time*. Tor, 2009–2012. The Wheel of Time 12–14.

Lackey, Mercedes and James Mallory. *The Outstretched Shadow*. 2003. Tor, 2004. The Obsidian Trilogy 1.

Langford, David. "Mirror." *The Encyclopedia of Fantasy*. 1997. Eds. John Clute and John Grant. Orbit, 1999. p. 651.

Le Guin, Ursula K. "The Child and the Shadow." 1975. *The Language of the Night*. 1979. Berkley, 1982. pp. 49–61.

———. "A Wizard of Earthsea." 1968. *The Earthsea Quartet*. Penguin, 1992. pp. 9–168. Earthsea 1.

Mathews, Richard. *Fantasy: The Liberation of Imagination*. 1997. Routledge, 2002.

Miller, Dean A. *The Epic Hero*. 2000. John Hopkins University Press, 2002.

Modesitt, Leland E., Jr. *The Magic of Recluce*. 1991. Tor, 1992. The Saga of Recluce 1.

Plato. "Book VII." *The Republic*. 380 BCE. Trans. A. D. Lindsay. 1906. J. M. Dent & Sons Ltd, 1961. pp. 207–237.

Rowling, Joanne K. *Harry Potter and the Chamber of Secrets*. Raincoast Books, 1998. Harry Potter 2.

———. *Harry Potter and the Deathly Hallows*. Raincoast Books, 2007. Harry Potter 7.

Sanderson, Brandon. *Mistborn Trilogy*. Tor, 2006–2010. Mistborn 1–3.

Star Wars: The Empire Strikes Back. Dir. George Lucas. Lucasfilm Ltd. 1980. Star Wars 5.

Suvin, Darko. "Considering the Sense of 'Fantasy' or 'Fantastic Fiction': An Effusion." *Extrapolation*, vol. 41, no. 3, 2000, pp. 209–247.

Tolkien, John Ronald Reuel. *The Lords of the Rings*. Allen & Unwin, 1954–1955. The Lord of the Rings 1–3.

Vogler, Christopher. *The Writer's Journey: Mythic Structure for Storytellers and Screenwriters*. 1992. Boxtree Limited, 1996.

5 The Messianic Hero
Exploring the Hero's Willing Confrontation with Death in Gail Z. Martin's *The Summoner* (2007)

While the previous chapter discussed the possibility of the hero's failure, this chapter will further expand on the qualities that redefines the character. The identity of the character as actualised hero is confirmed through their function as a messianic figure. This position is first, conveyed through their relationship to their community, and second, is realised through the moment of sacrifice by a willing confrontation with death on behalf of that community. More importantly, the hero's fulfilment of their messianic role is dependent on the knowledge and understanding of the balance of the world (as described in the previous chapter) and the ways in which their interactions impact on this balance.

I explore these concepts further using Gail Z. Martin's *The Summoner* (2007), the first book of the *Chronicles of the Necromancer* series (2007–2009), as a case study. In *The Summoner*, Martin sets up a clear dichotomy between the protagonist, Matris Drayke (Tris), and one of the antagonists, his half-brother Jared Drayke. Early in the novel, Jared murders the royal family and usurps the throne. He is depicted as a stereotypical evil villain with all the melodramatic qualities the term conveys. Jared is quick to use and abuse those around him with Tris coming to the rescue of these victims. The contrasting depiction of both characters presents a distinct example of how the protagonist and antagonist interact with their respective communities. As brothers, both characters have access to the same possibilities, or branches on the road, but as the previous chapter considered, the characters react to these choices in drastically different ways (Figure 4.1).

I have selected *The Summoner* as a case study as *The Chronicles of the Necromancer* concerns, as the title indicates, necromancy, or the act of communicating with the dead. Accordingly, the lines between life and death are more deliberately and overtly blurred compared to a number of other Heroic Epic Fantasy texts where the relationship is subtler. For instance, in David and Leigh Eddings' *Enchanters' End Game* (1984), the final novel of the *Belgariad* series (1982–1984), the hero Garion is able to cross the veil of life and death and resurrect one of his companions. He is only able to do so, however, as he gained the knowledge in an earlier part of his journey: in *Magician's Gambit* (1983), he reaches across the veil of life and death to resurrect a stillborn colt. Though this knowledge is crucial to the resolution of the first series, the scene in comparison to the rest of the narrative is relatively minor. Consequently, the symbolic aspects of Garion's relationship to death – as opposed to the literal relationship where he must kill a god or be killed in turn – is minimised. In contrast, in *The Summoner*, the relationship of life and death is a major theme throughout the book. The act of necromancy is rare and is considered a special skill, one that the hero Tris demonstrates throughout the novel. Thus, the hero's association with death prior to any messianic sacrifice is made overt. As this chapter explores, the hero's comprehension of death is an essential aspect of the hero's journey as this knowledge allows the hero to fulfil a messianic sacrifice on behalf of their community.

The Horizontal versus the Vertical

In *Fantasy: The Liberation of Imagination* (1997), Richard Mathews identifies the Fantasy hero as either a horizontal or vertical hero using the hero's placement in the community – as evidenced through spiritual transcendence – to differentiate between the two:

> The vertical hero seeks resolution by departing the world for heaven or hell. The horizontal hero struggles to know himself and to share himself in love with another, to affirm his tribe's rights, land, and values against encroachments of an enemy, and to assume, and later responsibly discard, the mantle of the supernatural, instead taking on a godlike prerogative for moral continuity. [...] He rejects the contrived supernatural force that would preserve his life, for it would at the same time separate him from his tribe and from his very identity as a man. (90)

Mathews identifies the horizontal hero as one who has an identity as part of a community, and while the hero may take on a 'supernatural mantle,' they later "discard" it in order to remain with the community. The vertical hero, in contrast, is one "whose actions move upward or downward as he is propelled toward or away from absolute good or evil" (92); the vertical hero transcends and leaves the community behind. Similarly, in *The Epic Hero* (2000), Dean Miller also uses the language of horizontal and vertical heroes to discuss the Mythological hero. Miller indicates that the horizontal hero originates from the dominion of the king with a hero as vassal: "The ideal zone for the *hero* extends outward and horizontally from that 'civilized' royal control point" (133, original emphasis); while the vertical hero comes about as an *assault* to the upper and lower regions (134). Like Mathews' assessment of the horizontal and vertical Fantasy hero, the horizontal Mythological hero is linked to community while the vertical hero is associated with upper and lower metaphysical spaces (heaven and hell).

Mathews suggests that the horizontal hero and vertical hero are incompatible because the vertical hero departs the world while the horizontal hero rejects transcendence in order to stay with their community. However, instead of identifying the hero as *either* horizontal or vertical, I argue that throughout the journey, the Heroic Epic Fantasy hero *continuously* struggles with balancing their horizontal components with the vertical. While the Heroic Epic Fantasy hero is identified as a horizontal hero through their interaction with the community, the hero is simultaneously distinguished as a vertical hero through a movement between life and death. Just as the conception of good and evil discussed in the previous chapter indicates the need to see the two as a whole rather than opposite binaries, so too is it important to see the horizontal and vertical hero as part of a whole rather than incompatible opposites.

The hero is distinguished from the other characters by a messianic sacrifice – one that allows the hero to restore balance to the world. But the hero can only fulfil this messianic function by acknowledging a love and deep connection to their community. The departure then does not need to be a physical one – the hero does not need to literally die or death does not need to be permanent – so long as the hero shows a willingness to meet their death and, more importantly, the act allows the hero to restore balance. In doing so, the hero transcends in a spiritual or social advancement where the hero rises beyond the community. The hero may then return to the community after transcending or, equally, may depart society and remain in a transcendent state. But for the purposes of discussing structure, this final decision to return or remain is inconsequential; the pertinent moment is the act of transcendence itself where the hero fulfils their messianic function. As this chapter explores, the point at which the hero is differentiated from other characters is in the choices the character makes with regards to their interaction with their community (the horizontal) and with death (the vertical).

The Horizontal Hero

As the previous chapter considered, the Heroic Epic Fantasy hero does not choose between right and wrong, but instead makes an *appropriate* choice. This choice, which may lead to harm for the hero, places the needs of the community first. For instance, within the first few pages of *The Summoner*, a clear dichotomy is set up between Tris and Jared and their relationship with the servants in their castle:

> Tris could make out a grappling pair, the dark figure of a man looming over one of the chambermaids who struggled to escape.

"Release her!" Tris raised his sword in challenge. [...] "You dare to raise steel against me?" Jared roared. "I could have you hanged! No one threatens the future king of Margolan!" (15)

Both Tris and Jared are princes, but their conception of princehood are dramatically different. Tris sees that his role is to serve and protect his people, while Jared presumes that his people should serve his every whim. He does not consider the rape of a maid as an atrocious act, but instead views Tris's prevention of the rape as an act that denies him his rights. Tris puts himself in harm's way – risking being fatally stabbed by his older brother – in order to rescue the chambermaid. This act of protection while placing his own life in jeopardy is repeated throughout the novel. In this way, Tris demonstrates his willingness to serve the community by putting their well-being first.

While serving the community, the hero is also an inside/outside figure in the community: they both stand with a group of protagonists and are set apart from them. For example, at the end of Australian author Trudi Canavan's *Black Magician* trilogy (2001–2003), after a period of exile, the community of magicians determine that the hero is a threat to their society, and thus, while Sonea remains part of the Magicians Guild, she is also set apart from them. If the hero's status as inside/outside figure is made apparent before the climax of the novel, then the character must re-join the community before they can fulfil their role as hero. Often in these cases, the hero's interaction with the community suggests the possibility that the hero may fail and be affirmed as ou-hero. For instance, while Rand in Robert Jordan's *The Wheel of Time* series (1990–2012) is identifiable as the hero of destiny, he is often detached from his group of friends and there is a frequent suggestion made by his companions that his position as hero is a threatening one to society. Rand's eventual success as a hero is dependent on him finding a sense of peace and balance within himself; the act allows Rand's friends and peers to stop seeing him as a possible threat and to come to an accord with him long enough to join him in a final battle against the antagonist group.

While the heroes of Heroic Epic Fantasy often demonstrate some power or skill that would enable them to save their community, this ability simultaneously sets them apart from their peers. In Jordan's *The Wheel of Time*, Rand is an Aes Sedai and can channel magic. However, all male Aes Sedai are doomed to go mad. And yet, the world can only be salvaged if female and male Aes Sedai work together. Thus, by using the very abilities that will allow him to save the world, Rand sets himself on a path of corruption. Similarly, in *The Summoner*, Tris's ability as a powerful necromancer associates him with the world of death, a connection that his companions find disconcerting: "Tris could see warring emotions in the eyes of the two soldiers. [...] Soldiers were notoriously distrustful of mages" (83); "Something was different in their eyes, [...].

Perhaps not fear, but not quite comfort either" (436). Although his companions accept his magical abilities, their reaction is one of misgiving. In many cases, along with extraordinary super-human power the hero is identified as a unique individual, making them a solitary figure. For example, in Brandon Sanderson's *Mistborn* (2006–2008), Sazed the Terrisman is the last of his people. In David Farland's *Runelords* series (1998–present), Gaborn is the only Earth King after many thousands of years and it is unlikely that another will arise immediately after. In *The Summoner*, Tris is the lost "mage heir of Bava K'aa" (83), an extremely powerful necromancer. Necromancy itself is described as a rare skill. Accordingly, Tris is not only separated from his companions, but the strength of his ability sets him apart from other magic-users as well. Note, however, that while the hero might have skills and abilities that are unique from the rest of humanity, this does not necessitate that they are the strongest or most skilled, it only indicates that they are distinguished from the rest of the community.

Although isolated due to the skill and ability that will allow them to save the world, the hero is also part of a community. In Heroic Epic Fantasy, the protagonists – the heroes and companions – function as a communal group. While the hero sacrifices themselves in order to save the world, the protagonist group may simultaneously sacrifice themselves in order to aid the hero. These individual helper figures are macrocosmically representative (a synecdoche) of their race or different social groups.[1] They embody the body of their people just as a king would. Even though discrimination might occur between separate groups, the individuals of the group as representatives of their race or class set aside their prejudices and unite to defeat the antagonistic force. This is the case with J. R. R. Tolkien's *The Fellowship of the Ring* (1954) or in James Clemens' *The Banned and the Banished* series (1998–2002), which both consider race.

The Epic hero is often a traveller figure who may encounter new species, races, or classes that is different from their own. As the Epic structure contains a journey, this is a formal necessity. The hero's acceptance into the (new) group – usually demonstrated by the other characters' love or admiration for the hero – marks the hero's belongingness in the community. This is what happens in Jordan's *The Wheel of Time*, with Rand being orphaned at a young age and raised by a different culture than his own. He is acknowledged as a child of both the East and the West, bridging the two worlds. Or, for instance, in Sanderson's *Mistborn* trilogy, though Vin is from the slave class, her father has noble bloodlines. And thus she is able to straddle both social spheres. Another hero, Sazed, is a nomad who integrates with the community, similar to Paul Atreides in Frank Herbert's *Dune* (1965).[2]

It is absolutely crucial to the Heroic Epic Fantasy structure that the hero is not an individual but stands with a community. In an Adventure

Fantasy, where the locale shifts from series to series, the heroes travel from place to place often because of their *inability* to fit with the community, as occurs in Scott Lynch's *Gentleman Bastard* series (2006–present). The hero of Localised Heroic Fantasy, in contrast to the Epic, is often a solitary figure or with a sole companion; as the resolution is a much smaller one than the world scale, a large protagonist group is not required to save the world. The size of the community group may be represented in different ways, depending on where the text falls in the range (Figure 0.1). J. K. Rowling's *Harry Potter* series (1997–2007), for example, moves slowly from Localised to Epic. As such, the community group becomes bigger by the final book, moving beyond the adventures of the hero and his two friends until it includes the larger wizarding community, but, it should be noted, still does not encompass the entirety of the world, opening a potential for a sequel series if the balance should shift again.

In comparison to the Heroic Epic which focuses on the hero's journey, the Fragmented Hero follows the narrative of several ou-heroes; these ou-heroes are characterised by qualities of selfishness or isolation. For instance, in George R. R. Martin's *A Song of Ice and Fire* (1996–present), the narrative perspective follows the path of numerous characters. Any of them have the potential to become hero, and yet, many of them may lack the essential characteristics which distinguish them as a hero, demonstrating instead self-centredness and/or an inability to fit in with or re-join the community prior to the final conflict of the narrative. Ultimately, the hero must properly recognise how the fulfilment of their messianic function impacts the delicate balance of the world and be willing to sacrifice themselves for the good of the community accordingly. Any character that fails to fully comprehend this role remains as an ou-hero.

In another text, *The Warded Man* (2008; also published as *The Painted Man*), the first book of Peter V. Brett's *Demon Cycle* series (2009–2017), although Jardir does not function as a point of view character, he emerges in the final pages as a possible "Deliverer," the hero of destiny. However, this idea is counterbalanced with the knowledge that Jardir is only able to declare himself as "Deliverer" by betraying his friend (another potential hero) and leaving him to die. In the second book, *The Desert Spear* (2010), the first half of the novel is narrated from Jardir's perspective. By explaining some of his more questionable choices from Jardir's point of view, the author further allows the character to emerge as a potential hero. Even so, the atrocity of his acts may still be uncomfortable to the reader: Jardir is often a cruel man, quick to physically attack those that are weaker than him. Although these actions are explained as a custom of his culture,[3] the reader may hesitate to identify the character as hero due to the violence of these actions and the continued betrayal of his family and friends. And yet, the other potential heroes in the series are *also* set apart as distinct and separate from the rest of the community, as they are alienated and isolated from those around them. In order to take a position as hero, the characters must re-join their community.

One of the biggest differences between the hero and antagonist is their connection with other characters and humanity in general; this later allows them to make a sacrifice on behalf of humanity. Like the hero, the antagonist also has these markers which isolate them from the larger group but their association with the group is one of animosity rather than of compassion. For instance, the antagonist may set themselves apart from the group deliberately as they attempt to reign over them by force. In *The Summoner*, When Jared's soldiers fail to locate his brother Tris, Jared tortures one of the scouts and has him beheaded:

> [T]he scout whimpered. Hog-bound with chains and forced to kneel before his king, the man was barely coherent, and a row of fresh, seeping burns along his face and arm attested to Jared's frustrations.
> [...] Jared nodded once more to the torturer, who set aside his poker and lifted an axe. "You know the consequence for failure." (*Summoner* 143–144)

Throughout the novel, Jared's actions suggest that he has no care for his community, not even for the men who choose to follow him. A reversal is evident, where the antagonist sacrifices the community, rather than the hero sacrificing themselves on behalf of the community.

As noted in the previous chapter, the identification of the hero and villain is constantly deferred. In *The Summoner*, although Jared is identified as a clear antagonist, the novel also identifies that: "There is a threat to Margolan and the Winter Kingdoms that is greater than Jared, [...]. An old evil has arisen. The Obsidian King is stirring once more" (108). The Obsidian King was once a Light mage, one who began to experiment with dark magic:

> There has been no mage so great as the Obsidian King [...] and even he could not control the darkness. It consumed him, and made him its slave. [...] Some say he was possessed by the spirit of an evil one stronger than himself. [...]. Others believe he thought that the dark power could be harnessed for good, [....] That is how a good man became the greatest evil our world has seen. (304)

The Obsidian King sought more power, an act of hubris that led him to become "the greatest evil." The previous chapter concluded that all heroes have the potential to become ou-heroes if they make the wrong choice. Here, the Obsidian King's descent into darkness demonstrates that all 'good men' have that potential.

And yet, Bava K'aa, Tris's grandmother, makes a *similar* decision in her fight against the Obsidian King: "Believing she was wounded mortally, Bava K'aa loosed her last, most potent spell – a gray magic which would bind both of their souls. [...] Bava K'aa thought to seal the Obsidian King, even if she must forever stand guard" (550). Here, both protagonist and antagonist make the same choice in their fork on the road (Figure 4.1), and yet they emerge on different paths. Accordingly, while the free choices that the characters make are important, the justification behind each decision made is a more crucial factor in determining the path of the character. A character that makes the 'right' choice for the wrong reason may find themselves on the path of becoming an ou-hero. For instance, in the *Star Wars* film series (1977–present), Anakin Skywalker is initially identified as the hero of destiny as he was to bring balance to the force. However, his *selfish* love for Padmé is what triggers a Faustian downfall to the "Dark Side," setting him apart from the rest of the Jedi and leading him to being cast in the role of the antagonist throughout the majority of the films. It is only at the end of Episode VI (*Return of the Jedi*, 1983) that Anakin Skywalker redefines his position as a hero – and indeed, this reaffirmation is brought about due to his sacrifice made through an act of selfless love for his son.

Equally, a character can make the 'wrong' choice for the right reason and be confirmed as a hero. In *The Summoner,* while Bava K'aa unleashes a spell that is "gray," she does so that she can stand guard against the Obsidian King even in death. While she makes a choice that is nearly identical to that of the Obsidian King, the motivation behind that choice is fuelled by a choice for the greater good rather than a choice of hubris. Additionally, unlike the Obsidian King, Bava K'aa choice leads her to sacrifice herself for the community. This sacrifice not only results in death but also denies her peace in the afterlife. Thus, Bava K'aa willingly surrenders *eternal* rest in order to save the world from this ultimate evil. Unlike the ou-hero, the hero's choice is made on behalf of the community. More importantly, the choice results in a sacrifice that will aid or save the community in some way. As the remainder of this chapter explores, the choice to fulfil a role as a messianic figure is the crucial factor that distinguishes the hero from other characters.

The Vertical Hero

The Heroic Epic Fantasy hero is distinguished by their function as a messianic hero. As Miller explains for the Mythological hero:

> The heroic "good death" is supposed to be violent, a sword death – and it is voluntary [...]. Mary Douglas believes, and I think quite correctly, that part of the mysterious and lasting potency of the heroic individual comes from his voluntary submission to death: the hero wills himself to accept and even to welcome the danger of death. (121)

92 The Messianic Hero

Like the Mythological hero, the Heroic Epic Fantasy hero is identified through their "voluntary submission to death" (Miller 121). But, more importantly, the hero's choice to fulfil their destiny is inextricably tied with sacrifice through *service*. In *The Summoner*, Tris prays to the Goddess: "*[L]et me be the instrument of your judgment. Take my life, my soul, whatever you require, but let me put right what has been done this night*" (77, original emphasis to indicate inner monologue). Repeatedly, the Heroic Epic Fantasy hero makes a sacrifice of themselves for the good of the community. George R. R. Martin makes this notion explicit with the repeated phrase "Valar Morghulis," which translates to "all men must die" (*A Storm of Swords* 748). The phrase is later answered with "'*Valar Dohaeris.*' *All men must serve*" (*A Dance with Dragons* 836, original emphasis). It is notable that when Epic Heroes occasionally emerge from the Fragmented Hero narrative, they are identified through this messianic function. Any character that abandons the community is recast as ou-hero.

At the end of *The Summoner*, Tris descends; a literal journey downwards. The descendent also operates as a metaphorical descent, a journey to the underworld which results in a tipping of the fulcrum of the world back into balance (Figure 5.1). This is an idea that will be expanded on in in the latter half of this book. Here, it is important to note that messianic sacrifice is tied to this act of descent. By 'descending,' the hero 'pushes' on the lever and is able to tip the unbalanced world back into a balanced state. Expanding on the conclusions from the previous chapter – that the Heroic Epic Fantasy hero realises that good does not *triumph* over evil, but that good must be *balanced* with evil – the hero utilises this comprehension to restore balance to the world, thereby saving it. Consequently, before the hero reaches this final confrontation, they need to be able to realise all aspects of the balance of the world, of good and evil and of life and death, in order to restore this balance to a 'normal' state.

In *The Summoner*, before Tris can defeat the Obsidian King in the second book (*The Blood King*, 2009), he must first be able to comprehend

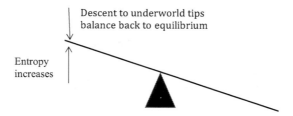

Figure 5.1 The Fulcrum Tipping Back into Balance.

all aspects of the one goddess, or the underlying balance of this Heroic Epic Fantasy universe: "[o]ne goddess, eight aspects – four Light and four Dark" (*Summoner* 61). It is imperative that the goddess of this Fantasyland is not simply a goddess of Light, but also has aspects that are equally Dark. Tris is likewise described as "the mediator between the living and the dead" (528). As a necromancer, Tris is able to communicate with the spirits of the dead and convey their wishes or grievances to the world of the living. In doing so, he is able to gain knowledge of the physical and metaphysical world which will help him in meeting the final confrontation.

The act of understanding and comprehending this balance is a moment of Recognition for the hero. In *Poetics* (335 BCE, Heath translation 1996), Aristotle defines Recognition as such: "*Recognition,* as in fact the term indicates, is a change from ignorance to knowledge, disclosing either a close relationship or enmity, on the part of people marked out for good or bad fortune. Recognition is best when it occurs simultaneously with a Reversal" (18–19, original emphasis). Note how Recognition is best combined with Reversal; in Heroic Epic Fantasy, Reversal indicates the (re-)establishment of a previously unbalanced world. In Heroic Epic Fantasy, Recognition is important in the manner in which the hero understands their own messianic destiny, thereby comprehending their purpose in life and how their actions will affect this balance. As the second half of this book will explore in greater detail, it is at the world's 'darkest' moments, when the balance is tipped dramatically, that the hero achieves enlightenment, a Recognition, and instigates a Reversal in the balance of good and evil.

The hero gains knowledge of the world through confrontations with death or by descending. As Frye in *Anatomy of Criticism* argues: "To gain information about the future, or what is 'ahead' in terms of the lower cycle of life, it is normally necessary to descend to a lower world of the dead" (321). While Frye uses the Epic examples of Homer's *Odyssey*, Virgil's *Aeneid*, and Dante's *Divine Comedy*, this idea is also pertinent in Heroic Epic Fantasy. There may be a literal journey to the underworld, as occurs in Farland's *Runelords* or in Philip Pullman's *His Dark Materials* (1995–2000). Martin's *The Chronicles of the Necromancer* presents an explicit meeting with death as necromancy allows spirits of the dead to communicate and pass knowledge on to the world of living. In Nnedi Okorafor's *Who Fears Death?* (2010), the hero Onyesonwu confronts death in a variety of ways: bringing people back to the living; crossing over into the spirit world; and by being reborn herself: "I'd died, been remade, and then brought back" (324). After her rebirth, she chases death again, pursuing a path she had foreseen earlier: "the death [she] was voluntarily heading toward" (325). The hero not only demonstrates several interactions with death, but bravely pursues it, an idea embedded in her name itself as Onyesonwu means "Who fears death?" (6). Thus, the hero can be associated with death or a descent in a variety of literal or metaphorical ways. As Chapter 7 will describe further, if a literal death or journey to underworld does not occur, then a hero may descend through a spiritual fall and/or a physical decline of the body.

As well, often embedded historical texts – newly discovered journals or prophecies, or the only surviving words of a dead generation, culture, or person – allow knowledge to be imparted. To access this knowledge, a hero must 'descend.' In Brett's *Demon Cycle*, for example, the hero searches lost ruins in order to find knowledge of ancient runes to inscribe on weapons. Here, knowledge takes the form of language itself. Farland's *Runelords* contains an interesting depiction of the connection to death and language. In the first series, runes allow dedicates to pass endowments (traits and abilities such as 'strength' and 'stamina') to Runelords. It is notable that these runes were created by mimicking the way reavers (monstrous creatures) eat the dead. The reavers only eat their dead in order to gain their memories; in this way, entire generations of knowledge can be passed on, creating stronger and wiser creatures. Something similar occurs in Robin Hobb's *Dragon Keeper* (2010). The dragons likewise feed on the dead: "This was the way of their kind, not to waste the bodies of the dead but to take from them both nourishment and knowledge" (9). By eating their dead, these creatures are able to absorb the knowledge of their lineage. Death here reflects the idea of continuity, with these intelligent creatures consuming death in order to pass knowledge on. This aspect of death is indicative of the connection between community and death, of the messianic sacrifice of an individual that results in good for the community.

In *The Summoner*, Tris gains knowledge of death and life through his experiences as a necromancer. When a vengeful ghost possesses the body of one of his companions, Tris follows the ghost into a metaphysical spirit world in order to drive her out:

> [Tris] closed his eyes and plunged into the darkness. [...] Once before, he'd borrowed from the glow of his own thread to hold Vahanian to life. Now, Tris threw himself on the blue-white thread, overlaying it with his own life's strand, and with all of his will, drove back the ghost in the brightness of its glow. (459–460)

Note the motif of threads to describe life, similar to Jordan's *The Wheel of Time* series described in Chapter 3. Building off the knowledge that he had learned in a previous incident, here, Tris is able to strengthen his companion's life thread, using his own soul's brightness to ward off the vengeful ghost. He then refines the skill further in order to overcome the final adversary in this first novel. At the end of the book, Tris must defeat the ghost of the mage Argus in order to win a sword that will help him in his battle against the Obsidian King. Tris is able to overpower Argus using his knowledge of life and death:

> This time the pathway was familiar, and Tris hurtled along it, [...]. Heedless of consequence, Tris envisioned his own glimmering soul strand and began to weave it around Argus's in a complex, shining knot. [...] "If I cannot leave without Mageslayer, then I will not stay as your servant," Tris shouted. "We will spend eternity together, bound at the soul, closer than brothers. [...]" (590)

Using his experiences with life threads that he encountered in the first half of the book, Tris builds on and develops this knowledge in order to defeat Argus. Notably, Tris uses this knowledge to attempt to sacrifice himself, telling the mage Argus that they will be combined for all eternity.

The messianic function is not only tied to sacrifice, but also to knowledge and comprehension of *what that sacrifice will entail*. For instance, in Lois McMaster Bujold's *The Curse of Chalion* (2001), comprehension of the prophecy – that a hero must die three times for Chalion – also includes comprehension of life and death. As Cazaril later reveals, the reason that the hero is required to die three times is "for the practice" (468). Cazaril must experience dying multiple times in order to properly fulfil his function as messianic hero so that in the third death Cazaril's body is able to allow the divine spirit to enter his body as a channel into the physical world. This act is only possible due to his experiences and 'practice' with accepting the first two deaths. Like Cazaril, the heroes of Heroic Epic Fantasy use their experience with death to gain knowledge that will allow them to perform their final messianic duty.

Accordingly, it is not only the hero's willingness to serve the community to sacrifice that serves as the vital distinction between hero and ou-hero, but also their understanding of the balance of the world and a comprehension of how their sacrifice will restore the balance of the world. In Sanderson's *Mistborn* trilogy, for example, several protagonists attempt to sacrifice themselves in order to save their world. While they all succeed in sacrificing themselves, they had failed to understand the balance of the world and the meaning of the prophecy, and thus, the means in which a sacrifice would aid the salvation of the world. In some sense, they are still 'heroes' as they have *willingly* fulfilled a messianic function and served their community. *But* their sacrifice is not the crucial sacrifice that is necessary to save the world. Thus, they have failed in their quest and are redefined as ou-heroes.

Because of this potential for characters to become ou-heroes, the distinction between the 'central hero' (the messianic hero that transcends and is able to save the world) and the collective group of 'protagonists' that accompanies the hero can be opaque, especially as the identification of a character as hero or ou-hero is often in flux throughout a series.

As the previous chapter concluded, while the choices they make in one novel reaffirms or redefines their identity, an alternative choice or the revelation of further comprehension of their world in a later novel may cast them in a different role. For instance, as noted above, Anakin Skywalker moves back and forth from an identification as hero and ouhero. Likewise, the most recent trilogy in this franchise demonstrates that the characters understanding of the "Balance of the Force," may have been faulty, as the Dark Side has still not been defeated. In Martin's *Chronicles of the Necromancer*, Tris's confrontation with both Jarden and the Obsidian King is resolved within the first two novels. However, the series continues past this confrontation and Tris's role as central hero lessens in the remainder of the series. As Chapter 9 will discuss, as Fantasy series often leave the possibility open for sequels or continuation of the series, the role of hero may be transferred to another. Often, a sequel series may reveal that the hero's initial comprehension of the balance was incomplete, or, indeed, that the balance, once established, has shifted again. Accordingly, while a protagonist character may initially realise a function as hero, this identity may be deferred at a later branch in the road, or in the sequel.

As well, in Heroic Epic Fantasy, death is not necessarily a final state. For example, in Farland's *Runelords* at the end of the first book, the ghosts or shades of the recently deceased kings and queens rise up to join the legendary figure Erden Geboren. A character later recollects this moment in the third book:

> "I was at Longmot when the wight of Erden Geboren came," Myrrima said. "He blew his warhorn, and men who had died that day rose up and joined him on the hunt. They were happy, Averan. Death isn't an ending. It's a new beginning." (*Wizardborn* 80)

Likewise, in Martin's *The Chronicles of the Necromancer*, death clearly does not need to be an end, as a person's soul can still remain on the human-plane as ghosts or spirits. In many of the battles throughout the series, the spirits of the dead join Tris in his fight against the antagonists. Strikingly, many of these ghosts are soldiers who rise again to continue the battle. Though these characters have died, they are still able to act in the living world, and thus, death is not a finished state. This conception of death suggests a continuation after one's physical life has passed.

As well, all things occur again and again. There is a pattern of eternal recurrence that is an overt motif in Heroic Epic Fantasy which is demonstrated metafictionally as well as implicitly in the structures of the text. As Earth tells Gaborn in Farland's *Runelords*: "Once there were toth upon the land. Once there were duskins [...] At the end of this dark time, mankind, too, may become only a memory" (*The Sum of All Men* 156). The cycle of death is inevitable, but the cycle also indicates that a new form will rise again. In *The Chronicles of the Necromancer* series, while the major conflict of the narrative may be resolved in the first two novels, through the deferment of 'evil,' other antagonists rise up in the next two novels, making way for different heroes to come to the forefront and offer themselves in sacrifice to defeat them. While balance in the world is restored at the end of book two, the third book reveals that this balance was a false restoration: "The Winter Kingdoms are at a tipping point. What Jared put in motion has not yet run its course. Before all is ended, old ways will be swept away, and old certainties will be broken" (*Dark Haven* 390). Note the use of the phrase "tipping point" as the characters demonstrate a conscious awareness of balance themselves.[4]

Despite the hero's messianic function, the death of the hero may not be a final state. While it is that element of sacrifice, of removing themselves from the physical world, which pushes the hero from horizontal hero to vertical hero, it is not strictly necessary that the Heroic Epic Fantasy hero *remain* in this state. They may be reborn or return to the living after having died, as Cazaril does in Bujold's *The Curse of Chalion*. Alternatively, it may be possible that a hero may arise again. For example, in Jordan's *The Wheel of Time*, the hero Rand al'Thor is identified as the *reincarnation* of Lews Therin, the Dragon Reborn. Similarly, in Farland's *Runelords*, the first legendary Earth King is Erden Geboren. He is, in a way, reborn in the persona of Gaborn val Orden, the *new* Earth King, suggesting a cyclic time, but one that also suggests a reverse cycle through the reversal of names.

The cyclical nature of death and balance/unbalance that is explicit in many Heroic Epic Fantasy fictions is part of the narrative structure, as it indicates the return of the hero when the Heroic form is required. In *Chaos* (1987), James Gleick presents how the chaos scientist Theodor Schwenk "believed in universal principles, and, more than universality, he believed in a certain spirit in nature that made his prose uncomfortably anthropomorphic. His 'archetypal principle' was this: that flow 'wants to repeat itself, regardless of the surrounding material'" (197–198). As discussed in previous chapters, the hero functions as sites of fluidity, and accordingly, this flow "wants to repeat itself"; the hero's death is almost reassured in a cycle of rebirth as the hero figure will be called upon again in time of need. Death, then, implies a plurality in the depiction of time: of progressing forward and being elevated, of being frozen in stasis (as spirits or ghosts), and of being reborn in a cycle. Thus, while their voluntarily submission to death as a messianic figure is the distinguishing facet of the hero, it is notable that death is not necessarily the end. The hero, or a form of a hero, will be reborn when a hero is required.

Notes

1 With either nobility or sorcery, there is an emphasis on bloodlines or on powers inherited from ancestry. While the hero may emerge from the 'normal' population – for example, Canavan's Sonea in the *Black Magician* trilogy comes from the slums and J. K. Rowling's Harry Potter is not

'pure-blooded' – there is often an underlying discussion of parentage and ancestry, with the hero inheriting power through lineage. Thus, while Heroic Epic Fantasy may contest a fear of miscegenation or crossing class systems, it still favours an inherited class system from at least one parentage. Tris's own powers are inherited from her maternal grandmother.

2 It should be noted that there are obvious implications of a 'white saviour narrative' with the premise of an outsider who enters the community and saves it. However, this reading may be complicated in post-1990s' Fantasy and especially in post-2010s' Fantasy with the movement towards inclusion of an antagonist, protagonist, or central hero character who is visibly Othered (like Sazed) or, with a coding that is more finely nuanced in order to contain a deliberate political message (such as in Nnedi Okorafor's *Who Fears Death?*).

3 Jardir is introduced as an Orientalised Other; ruler of a desert race in opposition to the people of the "Greenlands." While this positioning further complicates his identity as hero or ou-hero, further investigation is required with regards to race and Other in Heroic Epic Fantasy.

4 Note also the idea that the resolution can only be brought about by the path shattering completely, similar to the conclusions made in Chapter 2. This idea will be expanded on further in Chapter 8.

Bibliography

Aristotle. *Poetics*. 335BCE. Trans. Malcolm Heath. Penguin, 1996. Print.
Brett, Peter V. *The Desert Spear*. 2010. Ballantine Books, 2011. Demon Cycle 2.
———. *The Warded Man*. Demon Cycle 1. 2009. Ballantine Books, 2010. Demon Cycle 1.
Bujold, Lois McMaster. *The Curse of Chalion*. 2000. HarperCollins, 2011. Chalion 1.
Canavan, Trudi. *The High Lord*. 2003. Orbit, 2010. Black Magician Trilogy 3.
Clemens, James. *The Banned and the Banished*. Del Rey, 1998–2002. The Banned and the Banished 1–5.
Eddings, David and Leigh Eddings. *Enchanters' End Game*. Dey Ray, 1984. Belgariad 5.
———. *Magician's Gambit*. Del Rey, 1983. Belgariad 3.
Farland, David. *Runelords*. Tor, 1998–2009. Runelords 1–8.
———. *The Sum of All Men*. 1998. Tom Doherty, 1999. Runelords 1.
———. *Wizardborn*. Tom Doherty, 2001. Runelords 3.
Frye, Northrop. *Anatomy of Criticism*. 1957. Princeton University Press, 1973.
Gleick, James. *Chaos: The Amazing Science of the Unpredictable*. 1987. Vintage Books, 1998.
Herbert, Frank. *Dune*. 1965. Gollancz, 2010. Dune Saga 1.
Hobb, Robin. *Dragon Keeper*. 2010. Harper Voyager, 2012. Rain Wilds Chronicle 1.
Jordan, Robert. *The Wheel of Time*. Tor, 1990–2005. The Wheel of Time 1–11.
Jordan, Robert and Brandon Sanderson. *The Wheel of Time*. Tor, 2009–2012. The Wheel of Time 12–14.
Lynch, Scott. *Gentleman Bastard*. Bantam, 2006–2013. Gentleman Bastard 1–3.

Martin, Gail Z. *The Blood King*. 2009. Solaris, 2012. Chronicles of the Necromancer 2.

———. *Dark Haven*. 2009. Solaris, 2012. Chronicles of the Necromancer 3.

———. *The Summoner*. 2007. Solaris, 2012. Chronicles of the Necromancer 1.

Martin, George R. R. *A Dance with Dragons*. Bantam Books, 2011. A Song of Ice and Fire 5.

———. *A Song of Ice and Fire*. Bantam Books, 1996–2011. A Song of Ice and Fire 1–5.

———. *A Storm of Swords*. Bantam Books, 2000. A Song of Ice and Fire 3.

Mathews, Richard. *Fantasy: The Liberation of Imagination*. 1997. Routledge, 2002.

Miller, Dean A. *The Epic Hero*. 2000. John Hopkins University Press, 2002.

Okorafor, Nnedi. *Who Fears Death?* 2010. Daw Books, 2011.

Pullman, Philip. *His Dark Materials*. Scholastic, 1995–2000. His Dark Materials 1–3.

Rowling, Joanne K. *Harry Potter*. Bloomsbury, 1997–2007. Harry Potter 1–7.

Sanderson, Brandon. *Mistborn Trilogy*. Tor, 2006–2010. Mistborn 1–3.

Star Wars. Lucasfilm, 1977–2017. Star Wars 1–8.

Star Wars: The Return of the Jedi. Dir. George Lucas. Lucasfilm Ltd. 1983. Film. Star Wars 6.

Star Wars: The Revenge of the Sith. Dir. George Lucas. Lucasfilm Ltd. 2005. Film. Star Wars 3.

Tolkien, John Ronald Reuel. *The Fellowship of the Ring*. 1954. HarperCollins, 1999. The Lord of the Rings 1.

6 Breaking into Fantasyland

Investigating How Fracturing and Entropy Motivates the Plot in Terry Goodkind's *Stone of Tears* (1995)

Having considered the role of character in the first part of this book, the second part will continue the discussion of the relationship between character, plot, and setting in Heroic Epic Fantasy. The diminishment and consequent healing of Fantasyland is central to the Fantasy narrative. The plot of all four aspects of Fantasy fiction (Epic, Local, Heroic, Fragmented) in some way focuses on healing a diminished Fantasyland. In "Fantastika in the World Storm" (2007), John Clute outlines four phases for each of the major genres of Fantastika (Fantasy, Science Fiction, and Horror) which are all seen as iterations of each other. His stages for Fantasy are:

> Wrongness: some small desiccating hint that the world has lost its wholeness: the Nazgûl enter the Shire.
> Thinning: the diminution of the old ways; amnesia of the hero and of the king; failure of the harvest; a literal drying up of the Land; and *cacophony*: [...].
> Recognition: the key in the gate; [...] the hero remembering his true name; the Fisher King walking again; the Land greening. [...].
> Return: the folk come back to their old lives and try to live them again. (26, original emphasis)

While Clute presents these stages as a movement or progression, my own discussion on structures of Heroic Epic Fantasy focus on these stages as fluid back and forth movements.

The hero's understanding and comprehension of the world as discussed in the previous chapter can be seen as an exploration of Clute's "Recognition." This chapter will explore a combination of "Wrongness" and "Thinning" through the conception of entropy fracturing or thinning world boundaries. I will first clarify these theoretical assertions with a brief discussion of wholeness or holistic connections in Fantasyland, before applying this framework to Terry Goodkind's *Stone of Tears* (1995), the second book of Terry Goodkind's *Sword of Truth* series (1994–present). While the idea of fracturing is a part of all Epic Fantasy fiction, *Stone of Tears* can be read as a contained book and for practical reasons, it is easier to discuss the fracturing of the worlds within one novel rather than focusing on a text where the fracturing is spread out over several. This second book begins immediately after the events of the first, *Wizard's First Rule* (1994), in which the hero, Richard, defeats the enemy, Darken Rahl. In the beginning of this second novel, it is revealed that in the act of overcoming Darken Rahl, Richard accidentally tore the veil between worlds. Thus, the events of the first novel directly trigger the events of the second novel by *fracturing* Fantasyland. Throughout the second novel, the boundary between worlds is further torn, allowing greater and greater entropy to escape into Fantasyland.

Entropy directly operates to unbalance good and evil as discussed in the previous chapter (Figure 5.1). As I argue throughout this chapter, the penetration of the metaphysical into Fantasyland increases entropy, thereby stimulating and escalating the plot of the Heroic Epic Fantasy novel. Although Heroic Epic Fantasy is often seen as a struggle between good and evil, rather than the defeat of an antagonist, the overall obstacle that the hero must overcome is an increase of entropy which *results* in an unbalance of good and evil in the world. While an antagonist character is often emblematic of the increase in entropy, it is not necessary that an antagonist character must be present in a Heroic Epic Fantasy series, or even that the antagonist character is the focus of the plot. Instead, I assert that the plot is directly motivated by an increase in entropy. The chapter will conclude with a survey of a number of other Fantasy texts in order to establish this claim.

Entropy in Fantasyland

As Chapters 4 and 5 explored, Heroic Epic Fantasy narratives demonstrate a constant increase of the unbalance of the world as it shifts further and further out of alignment with equilibrium (Figure 5.1). This unbalance is motivated by the 'Thinning' of the world boundaries of Fantasyland, a Thinning that is caused by entropy. Thus, 'Thinning' can be taken literally, as the boundaries between worlds weaken. As 'Wrongness' or entropy increases in Fantasyland, the boundaries of the world weaken further, allowing more entropy to enter. The increase in entropy leads to a greater and greater unbalance of the world. Ultimately, it is the hero's role to tip the balance back into equilibrium, thereby resolving the major conflict of the narrative.

Entropy means disorder, a disorder at a molecular level within a macroscopic system. It is, as James Gleick explains in *Chaos* (1987), "the inexorable tendency of the universe, and any isolated system in it, to slide toward a state of increasing disorder" (257). The second law of thermodynamics indicates that in a *closed* system, entropy always increases. But, if a system were to open and combine with a second parallel system, this does not necessarily indicate that entropy would decrease.

As Stephen Hawking explains in *A Brief History of Time* (1988): "the entropy of an isolated system always increases, and [...] when two systems are joined together, the entropy of the combined system is greater than the sum of the entropies of the individual systems" (116). The combination of two closed systems results in an increase in overall entropy.

Similarly, in the fictional world of the Heroic Epic Fantasy, when the metaphysical world breaks into the Fantasyland, net entropy increases in both worlds. This entropy is depicted through a language of degradation, chaos, and disorder:

> After that Maerad began to notice signs of neglect or poverty: tiles missing in a barnhouse roof or rotting carts and wagons abandoned by the side of the road [...] and not infrequently they saw farmhouses which have been abandoned altogether, their windows broken, their roofs beginning to collapse [...]. It was not always so, and she still saw many houses with well-tended gardens and orchards [...]; but beneath the pleasant surface of Ettinor she sensed a pervasive sense of slow decay, of hopeless struggle against entropy. (*The Gift* 244)

In Australian author Alison Croggon's *The Gift* (2004), where the hero describes the diminishment of the land as she travels on her journey, alongside the idea of general degradation and decay the text itself uses the term "entropy." This idea of entropy is also expressed overtly in early Fantasy:

> Elric shook his head. "[....] my power is gone."
> "How? Why?"
> "I know not – unless the forces of Entropy rule more strongly here." ("While the Gods Laugh" 65)

In British author Michael Moorcock's *Elric* series (1961–2007), "Entropy" is not only depicted as a destructive force but is also connected to a divinity. Later in the series, the impact of both Entropy and Chaos causes "a sizable breach in the Law-constructed barrier which once kept the creatures of Chaos from wholly ruling the planet" ("Black Sword's Brother" 295). Here, entropy is seen as a divine disruptive force that causes ruptures and breaches. These ruptures allow entropy to increase further, a feedback cycle that climbs exponentially.

Fantasyland, as this chapter will demonstrate below, is a *fractured* world-system. If it is initially a closed system (Figure 6.1), as entropy increases, the boundaries of Fantasyland grow thinner and allow cracks or holes to form, allowing two parallel isolated systems to combine. Instead of reversing entropy, the open system works to increase entropy dramatically, as the diffusion of entropy spreads across the open membrane (Figure 6.2). The penetration of the abnormal – a metaphysical entity

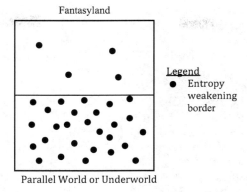

Figure 6.1 The State of Entropy in Parallel Worlds.

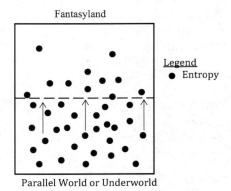

Figure 6.2 The Movement of Entropy When Two Parallel Words Are Bridged.

that does not belong in Fantasyland – tips the balance further, radically increasing disorder and entropy. Thus, entropy is the underlying stimulus that motivates the Heroic Epic Fantasy plot. It does so by causing Wrongness and Thinning by fracturing Fantasyland.

While it may be preposterous to question whether a fictional landscape operates similarly to a real-world closed system, as I reveal throughout this book, Fantasy is a logical system even if it is irrational in the real world. More importantly, this question of whether Fantasy is open or closed is the focus of much of the criticism surrounding Fantasy fiction. However, instead of investigating the relationship between the physical and metaphysical worlds *within* the narrative, Fantasy criticism draws a comparison between the fictional world and the real world (our reality). For instance, Tzvetan Todorov's categorisation of the Fantastic (*The Fantastic: A Structural Approach to a Literary Genre*, 1970), upon which much of current Fantasy criticism is predicated, is dependent on how the reader through the hero *enters* the Fantastical. In *Rhetorics of Fantasy* (2008), Farah Mendlesohn expands on this approach to further differentiate subgenres of the Fantastic, categorising Fantasy through the relation between the primary world (the real world) and the secondary world (the Fantastic world). For example: "A portal fantasy is simply a fantastic world entered through a portal. The classic portal Fantasy is of course *The Lion, the Witch and the Wardrobe* (1950). Crucially, the fantastic is *on the other side* and does not 'leak'" (xix, original emphasis). Mendlesohn's taxonomy of the portal-quest is comparable to the Heroic Epic, as many of the texts she uses as examples also fits the perimeters of the Heroic Epic. However, Mendlesohn contends that these narratives do not "leak," and the hero moves through one world to another through a contained passage.

As this chapter will demonstrate, Heroic Epic Fantasyland is fractured, and thus exhibits a back and forth movement between both worlds. As Adam Roberts makes note of in "Faulty Cartography" (2008), a review of *Rhetorics of Fantasy*:

> [O]ne of the striking things about it is that the border between the Shire and the rest of Middle Earth *leaks all the time*: [...]. Indeed, it occurred to me that the borderline between mundane and fantastical is porous in most of the examples of portal fantasies with which Mendlesohn deals. (511, original emphasis)

As Roberts correctly identifies, Fantasyland is porous, and not simply a movement from the real or "mundane" to the "fantastical." There is a constant flow of movement from all areas of the world. For instance, J. R. R. Tolkien's shire (*The Lord of the Rings*, 1954–1955), like all parts of Fantasyland, is holistically connected to all of Middle Earth. It is not isolated. Recall Clute's first phase of Fantasy: "Wrongness: some small desiccating hint that the world has lost its wholeness: the Nazgûl enter the Shire" (26). Clute's example of the Nazgûl entering the Shire demonstrates the fluidity of the boundary; while the hobbits depart the Shire on a portal quest, abnormal entities have reached into the Shire first. As well, the idea that "the world has lost its wholeness" would suggest that the world would function together holistically, and that any aspect of wrongness would be reflected in all areas of the land through this breakage. For example, when the hobbits return to the Shire after their journey, they discover that the war in Middle Earth has affected the Shire as well. Thus, Tolkien's shire is not an isolated landscape, or a contained space from which the heroes enters and departs.

Likewise, in Goodkind's *Stone of Tears*, all areas of the world are affected by the "Wrongness" and "Thinning" of the land, even if the communities at first glance appear to be isolated. The characters spend a great part of the novel with first the Mud People, a tribe that has limited contact with the outside world, and second, the Sisters of the Light, a community that are living in a time pocket isolated from the rest of the world. However, despite this isolation, the tearing of the veil comes to impact them as well. The veil between worlds is a boundary between the physical world and the underworld. Before the tearing, the Mud People would communicate with their ancestors by reaching across the veil. As described in the previous chapter, in this way, the characters are able to receive advice and knowledge from the world of the dead. But, following the tearing of the veil, false spirits are able to penetrate into Fantasyland. By pretending to be their ancestors, these spirits convince one tribe to go to war with another. Thus, even though these tribes are isolated from the rest of the world, the tearing of the veil still affects their community as well. As for the Sisters of the Light, the Sisters of the Dark (agents of the Keeper, or the Devil-like antagonist) had penetrated into their circle. Consequently, entropy increases within their society as well. Moreover, despite their isolation in a bubble that is outside of normal time, throughout the book the reader learns that the Sisters routinely emerge from their isolation in order to impact on events in the world. Their claim of isolation is thus false, as they continue to operate within the network of Fantasyland. Hence, an 'isolated' community is never truly isolated; they are part of an ecological whole. And when 'Wrongness' occurs in the land, it spreads, even to its most isolated sections. Accordingly, instead of viewing Heroic Epic Fantasy as a journey of the hero from the mundane world to the fantastic world, this chapter considers that the plot of the Heroic Epic is triggered by the movement of a metaphysical entity that is abnormal to the Fantasyland.

Breaking Boundaries

The very first page of *Stone of Tears* begins with a screeling – a creature of the underworld – loose in the world. Zed the Wizard reveals that the creature was released due to the events of the first novel, which resulted in the veil between worlds to be torn. Further: "If the veil is not closed, Commander, and the Keeper is loosed on the world, [...] It won't be just D'Hara, but the whole world that is consumed" (17). As indicated above, in Epic Fantasy, the world as a whole is affected. The 'hero of prophecy,' Richard, is identified as the only person who is capable of re-closing the border and resolving the conflict of the narrative. This concept, of the hero re-closing the border between worlds, is one that will be explored in the next chapter. The important thing here is that the Keeper of the Underworld, a figure with obvious connotations to the Devil, is able to enter the physical world if the "veil," the border between worlds, is not closed: "The veil holds [the Keeper] and his minions back. Holds the underworld back. It keeps the dead from the living" (170). Unleashing this figure in the world would have the effect of exponentially increasing entropy in the world.

The circumstances in which the veil comes to be torn are peculiar. In the first novel, Richard must defeat the evil lord, his own father, Darken Rahl. But the seeress Shota cautions Richard that he must *not* defeat Darken Rahl or a greater evil will be unleashed. Richard misinterprets this prophecy, and, though he does not physically kill Darken Rahl, he allows a magic to be released that pulls Darken Rahl into the underworld. This action is what causes the veil between worlds to be torn, as the magic rips a hole in the world. Thus, in the first book, Richard unwittingly begins to choose the path of the ou-hero by misinterpreting prophecy. This identity is not solidified, however, as the opportunity to choose the path of the hero returns multiple times throughout the second book. Unfortunately, Richard continues to make choices that place him on the path of becoming ou-hero. Each choice operates to tear the veil further, unbalancing the world even more.

Only a few pages after Richard is reprimanded for his actions, he decides to hold a spiritual ceremony to speak to his ancestor's spirits. Richard is told that in order to speak to his ancestors, their spirits temporarily cross over the veil. Despite an explicit explanation of how the ceremony works, Richard fails to understand that this crossing allows the veil to be torn further. As the previous chapter concluded, knowledge of life and death is important in how the protagonist fulfils their role as hero. Here, Richard fails to properly comprehend the metaphysical boundaries of death and its interaction with the world of the living. Mere moments after this conversation, another warning is delivered to Richard, in the form of an owl attacking him:

> [Birds] live in two levels – land and air. They can travel between their level and ours. Birds are closely connected to the spirit world. [...] *This bird gave its life to warn you.* [...] *This warning means the gathering will be dangerous, dangerous enough for the spirits to send this message.* (179, original emphasis to indicate speech in a different language)

Note the idea of balance presented in the form of the messenger, one who mediates and comprehends different aspects of the world. Despite these repetitive warnings from knowledgeable individuals, Richard insists on holding a gathering ceremony which would invite his ancestors' spirits to the world.

Similar to the tradition of Odysseus and Aeneas described in Chapter 5, Richard hopes to gain knowledge by speaking to the spirits of the dead. At the start of the ceremony, the spirits also offer their own caution. Instead of heeding these multiple warnings, Richard insists on speaking to his ancestors' spirits. The spirits then command the other tribesmen to leave the spirit house as it is dangerous for any who remain. The spirits *themselves* flee the spirit house in fear. The danger of his actions is asserted again and again to Richard, and yet he ignores all omens. And so, in inviting his ancestor's spirits to cross the veil to give him advice, he calls forth Darken Rahl, his own defeated father: "I am your ancestor. Only you could have brought me back, through the veil. Only you. [...] Not simply called me back, Richard, but torn the veil further to do so" (237). Richard's incomprehension of how the veil operates allows the border between worlds to tear even further. This enables further entropy to enter the world, as the Keeper's agents – including the formerly defeated Darken Rahl – cross over and attempt to destroy the veil completely.

Despite his original choices as an ou-hero, Richard is still presented with multiple opportunities to become a hero, and, as such, he still has the *potential* of restoring the veil to its proper place. As the first half of this book considered, the hero must be able to interpret the prophecy appropriately; they can only do so by first understanding all aspects of life and death. This process of interpretation is made explicit in Goodkind's *Stone of Tears*:

> The images [on the page] were drawing him in. It was almost as if they were murmuring to him. He had never seen such words before, but somehow they resonated with something deep within him.
>
> His hand slowly reached out, drawn to one of the words. [...]
>
> "This one," Richard whispered, as if from a trance. (769)

The manner in which Goodkind describes the hero's connection with his own prophecy is almost mystical. Despite not being able to read the language that the prophecy is written in, Richard is "drawn to one of the words," the word that is at the source of the contention between translators of the text. The word "resonate[s] with something deep within him," adding to the idea that language of the prophecy has the power to speak to the essence of the hero.

Significantly, the word that draws Richard is 'death': "That's the word that that is the center of the controversy. *Fuer grissa ost drauka* – the bringer of death" (769, original emphasis to indicate speech in a different language). Richard instantly understands that 'death' is a convoluted term: "Death. It has different meanings" (769), while his companion Sister Pasha has difficulty comprehending the layers of meanings it can coveys: "Death is plain as pie" (769). Richard explains that there are at least three meanings to the concept of death. It could signify 'death' as in 'to kill'; it could signify the metaphysical idea of 'death' as in 'souls'; and it could signify the space of 'death' as in 'the underworld.' Richard immediately grasps the different possible meanings of the word, and, moreover, comprehends that instead of choosing between different meanings as a translator, that the nuances of the word operate together. As the prophecy states that the hero will be the "bringer of death," Richard, as the hero, has been involved in bringing all three conceptions into being. He has killed, he has brought forth and communicated with spirits of the dead, and he has brought the underworld into the world as well:

> "But how could it mean 'the bringer of the underworld'? How can you bring the underworld?"
> Richard stared blankly ahead. "You tear the veil." (770)

It is notable that the hero in Goodkind's *Stone of Tears* plays an essential role in breaking the boundaries between the worlds. While this is not true of all Heroic Epic Fantasy heroes, it is pertinent that the hero is, in some way, intrinsically connected to the idea of borders and boundaries between worlds. This idea will be explored further in the next chapter. Here, it is important to note that it is Richard who correctly interprets the prophecy. In understanding the language of the prophecy, Richard is finally able to understand and comprehend his part in the balance between life and death.

It is with this comprehension that Richard is able to undo his actions from the first novel. The scholar Warren later explains to Richard that the "magic of Orden," the box that Richard helped Darken Rahl open at the end of *Wizard's First Rule*, is in fact a "gateway," "a passage between the world of the living and the world of the dead" (800). This gateway creates a hole in the veil, allowing the Keeper of the Underworld to touch or influence the world. But Warren cautions that one cannot simply close the gateway by closing the box. This act "ruptures the balance" (801), as it takes both Additive and Subtractive Magic to open and close the box. However, as Chapter 5 explored, the Heroic Epic Fantasy hero must be a character of balance. And thus, as can be expected, Richard is later identified as "a child of balance" (855). Unlike other wizards, he has the gift of *both* Additive and Subtractive Magic, and accordingly, he is the only one capable of opening and closing the Boxes of Orden properly and restoring the veil between worlds.

This act, of closing the Boxes of Orden and restoring the veil, is combined with a messianic duty, one that the hero must decide to make through an act of selflessness: "the Stone has the power to banish any soul to the infinite depths of the underworld. But if it were used in that way, through hate, through selfishness, it would feed power to that side, and destroy the veil" (859). Expelling Darken Rahl back through the gateway would create further fractures in Fantasyland. Accordingly, at the end of the novel, instead of banishing Darken Rahl back into the underworld, Richard decides to sacrifice himself instead: "I must suffer the consequences of my own actions. I cannot make others pay for what I have caused, intentionally or not" (951). Darken Rahl tries to incite Richard into punishing him for vengeance, but Richard here refuses. If Richard were to take revenge on Darken Rahl and seek to destroy his soul, Richard would break the veil completely, breaking the boundary of the Underworld so that the Keeper can enter the world. This act would confirm Richard's status as ou-hero. But Richard decides to make amends for his own actions and moves to sacrifice himself instead. In doing so he restores the torn veil, replacing the lock – the Stone of Tears – onto the underworld so that the Keeper's powers cannot escape. In restoring the broken veil between worlds, Richard finally moves away from the path of the ou-hero and fulfils his function as hero – at least, for this novel, as the series continues and the possibility of the equilibrium unbalancing again comes many times. As entropy always increases with time, it is up to the hero to continue choosing the path of the hero again and again and re-establish this broken balance repeatedly.

Fractured Fantasyland

As can be seen with the example of Goodkind's *Stone of Tears*, the fracturing of Fantasyland is the impetus that causes the plot of the novel as fracturing leads to an overall increase of net entropy, which causes the world to unbalance. As Mircea Eliade argues in *Myth and Reality* (1963 translation): "myths describe the various and sometimes dramatic breakthroughs of the sacred (or the 'supernatural') into the World. It is this sudden breakthrough of the sacred that really *establishes* the World and makes it what it is today" (6, original emphasis). Similarly, the breakthrough of the supernatural (metaphysical entities) into Fantasyland establishes the Fantasyland itself.

In many cases of Heroic Epic Fantasy, acts of fracturing and unbalancing also prompt magic to occur. These events are connected, as the special powers which are unlocked in the hero allow the hero, in turn, to re-establish the balance in the world. For instance, when the Sorceress Sister Verna encounters Richard, she tells him that Richard's actions have triggered his magical abilities to unlock:

> First, you used the gift the save the life of one who was being pulled back into the underworld. Not physically, but by her mind. [...] Second, you used the gift to save your own life. [...] You partitioned your mind. [...] Third, you used the gift to kill a wizard. (132)

Note that for Richard, all three specific events that trigger the development of magic are linked to the concept of balance: of splitting, dividing, and of life and death. It is the act of *unbalance* that allows "the gift" to develop in Richard.

As in *Stone of Tears*, the sense of Wrongness, "some small desiccating hint that the world has lost its wholeness" (Clute 26) often occurs in Fantasyland early in or prior to the events of a Heroic Epic Fantasy novel. Wrongness leads to Thinning: "the diminution of the old ways, [...] a literal drying up of the Land." Many Heroic Epic Fantasy novels demonstrate this conception of a broken Fantasyland. For example, in James Clemens' *Shadowfall* (2006), following a War of the Gods, the gods, and the worlds are Sundered: "the kingdom of the gods had been shattered and they appeared among the lands of Myrillia" (30–31). The story of the Sundering indicates that the gods existed on a plane separate from the world of humans but, due to the shattering of this world, the gods are cast into Myrillia, the physical world where the novel takes place. The story echoes an idea of a fall from heaven but is combined simultaneously with a story of a breaking of the worlds. Through this Sundering, the gods themselves are broken into parts, their bodies and souls split into three dimensions: into Myrillia, the naether, and the aether. This splitting acts to increase entropy, and, as the next chapter will explore further, the seepages between the three dimensions kindles the conflicts of the narrative as the gods from the naether and aether attempt to move into Myrillia and gain power. Thus, as in *The Stone of Tears*, the plot is directly triggered by metaphysical entities, abnormal to Fantasyland, who attempt to break into the physical world in order to gain power.

Additionally, like many Heroic Epic Fantasy fictions, the interaction between the metaphysical and Fantasyland is what creates the magical system of power within *Shadowfall*. Here the metaphysical is expressed through the broken divine body. Magic in *Shadowfall* comes about from humours – the bodily fluids of a god – which are said to be imbued with "Graces" or magic. The properties of Graces in their bodily fluids are the only real differentiation between godhood and humanity:

> It is said that the gods, before the great Sundering of their own kingdom, bore no special Grace. [...] It is supposed that a god's Grace manifests from some ethereal connection that persists between the gods of Myrillia and their torn counterparts, a bleeding of power that still flows through all three. (420)

It is the *fractured* world that results not only in the splitting of the divine bodies, but a holistic ethereal *connection* flowing between these three broken parts in each dimension that results in the special magical properties of the body's humours.

The humans in *Shadowfall* are then able to cast spells using these humours: "Blood [...] is indeed the key to all. It is tied to the will of the god" (134). The physicality of the bodily fluid that results in magic is connected to the *will* of the *god*. Recall how the first chapter presented the idea that the word 'fate' itself indicates the spoken word of the gods, and thus, accepting fate means embracing the will of the gods. Here, *magic itself is an expression of the will of god*. This idea is also seen in other works of Heroic Epic Fantasy, especially when a divine or metaphysical being is explicitly present. In David and Leigh Eddings' *Belgariad* series (1982–1984), for example, wizards act as disciples of one of the gods. As disciples, they have access to a divine magic, which is encapsulated through the idea of "The Will and the Word":

> "The Will and the Word, [...] You simply will something to happen," the old man said, "and then speak the word. If your will's strong enough, it happens. [...] Any word will do the job. It's the Will that's important, not the word. The Word's just a channel for the Will." (*Pawn of Prophecy* 255)

Note the idea that language is a *channel* for the expression of will. This motif of flow is one that is depicted in a variety of ways, not only through the language of magic, but also when discussing fractures in Fantasyland and the hero as vessel.

In some examples of Heroic Epic Fantasy, the breakthrough of the supernatural occurs on the physical or bodily plane. Take Brandon Sanderson's *Mistborn* trilogy (2006–2008), for instance. The heroes gain powers by ingesting or piercing their body with metals that grant them superpowers. However, they later learn that the metals are a physical manifestation of the *body* of a god, Perseverance, and, more importantly, that Perseverance sacrificed its body in this way in order to bring about the end of another metaphysical entity, Ruin. Accordingly, the conflict of the narrative is triggered by the clash between Ruin and Perseverance, as each seek to rid the world of each other. Through the physical penetration of the divine's body into each character, these entities are able to utilise people as their avatars.

This physical penetration has an impact on the complicated relationship between fate and free will, as the physical penetration acts to subvert the character's will and consciousness. Similarly in N. K. Jemisin's *The Broken Earth* trilogy, the characters discover that metal piercing a person body allows a connection to form between a conscious Earth and themselves; this connection allows the godlike entity to manipulate and subsume them so that they become "puppets of a greater will" (*The Stone Sky* 32). The characters later learn that the conflict of the narrative is triggered by the actions of early humans in trying to harvest the magical powers of the earth. Interestingly, humankind here is presented as the abnormal entity that seeks to conquer Earth, with the Earth, depicted as "Evil" for taking revenge against their actions. Whereas the first chapter concluded that heroes make a free choice to serve a metaphysical entity, in *Mistborn* and in *The Broken Earth* trilogy, a physical penetration of abnormal entities allows for a contamination of its host subject, one that completely subverts the will – but only if the will is weak to begin with. Characters in *The Broken Earth* are able to fight this contamination, "somehow manag[ing] to retain some measure of free will" (*The Stone Sky* 37). Here, the heroes resist submission to the metaphysical entity, exerting their strong will against the divine in attempt to restore the world.

There are differences between abnormal and normal metaphysical entities, as abnormal breakthroughs cause disruption and entropy, while elements normal to Fantasyland encourages prosperity and creation. For instance, in British author Philip Pullman's *His Dark Materials* (1995–2000), Lyra's movement between parallel universes, through the method of cutting or ripping holes between worlds, allows spectres to be released into these worlds. These spectres are abnormal to the worlds and their presence increases the death and decay of worlds. In contrast, the conception of "Dust" is initially seen as an abnormal substance, and thus the governing body in the world seeks to rid it from Fantasyland, perceiving it as the cause of disorder. The central conflict of the narrative is triggered by this perception. However, the hero Lyra speculates and later confirms that "Dust" is an essential makeup of the universe, a substance that leads to life and creation, and accordingly she confirms it to be *normal* to the universe. The breakthrough of "Dust" which permeates the universe allows consciousness to form, and thus is an integral part of Fantasyland.

Other examples of the penetration of the metaphysical into Fantasyland might be less overt, as divine or metaphysical entities may not be explicit in the text. However, in these cases, magic itself may operate as a metaphysical force, and, again, the breakthrough of this force leads to diminished Fantasyland, thereby creating the impetus of the plot. For instance, consider Sanderson's *Elantris* (2005), a halfway text between the Local and the Epic. Like the gods of *Shadowfall* who are rooted to one location, in *Elantris*, there is a relationship to the individual to the city of Elantris: "The farther one traveled from Elantris, the weaker the Aon-Dor powers became" (277). In the novel, Elantris is struck by a curse, the Reod, and the once transformative powers of The Shaod converts these near-divine Elantrians into wretched creatures. This diminishment of the Fantasyland occurs in the prologue of the novel before the narrative even begins, and it is up to the hero to restore and heal the diminished land. Here, it is the magic itself that operates as the metaphysical entity, transforming humans into semi-divine or wretched creatures.

The magic in Elantris is dependent on a non-semiotic language, so that, if one is able to access the power of AonDor, then that person, by writing Aons (the characters of the Aonic language) can alter the laws of the world. The hero Raoden later comes to realise that, through the interaction of language on the landscape, the "curse" of the Reod is in fact a misspelling of an Aonic character that resulted in the land to break:

> He studied Aon after Aon, noticing other features of the landscape in their forms. Aon Eno, the character for water, included a wiggling line that matched the meanderings of the Aredel River. The character for wood – Aon Dii – included several circles that represented the southern forests. The Aons were maps of the land, each one a slightly different rendering of the same picture. (504)

There is a direct connection between language and landscape as these magical characters describe the physical geography around Elantris. While initially an earthquake is viewed as a result of the loss of magic in Elantris, Raoden discovers that "the earthquake came just *before* the Reod" (507, original emphasis). With the formation of a large chasm caused by the earthquake, as the physical geography has changed, the characters of Aon are also unable to function as they no longer represent the landscape. When Raoden adds another line to the three basic lines, completing the previously fractured characters, he is able to release the trapped power of The Dor: "The Dor attacked with a roaring surge of power, and this time it hit no wall. It exploded through Raoden like a river" (507). The fracturing of the land here resulted in the blocking of the metaphysical power, acting as a dam that stops the 'normal' flow of power. Correcting the runic language allows this power to release.

Fracturing between lands or dimensions creates holes or spaces for metaphysical power to flow. For instance, recall that in Lois McMaster Bujold's *Chalion* universe (2001–2017), the five gods exist on a different plane of existence from humankind:

> Lord dy Cazaril claimed that the world of the spirit and the world of matter existed side by side, like two sides of a coin, or a wall; the gods were not far away in some other space, but in this very one, continuously, just around some strange corner of perception. (*Paladin of Souls* 85–86)

While the gods cannot enter the physical world, the gods' spiritual selves can interact with the characters through dream sequences (a metaphysical boundary space) or by inhabiting the body of a willing subject. The trigger for the events in Bujold's *The Curse of Chalion* (2001) is when a drop of blood from a god enters into the physical world; "a drop of the Father's blood" (477), which was somehow "spilled, soiled" (466) into the world. A drop of blood from one of the gods causes a generational curse across the land of Chalion. That only a single drop of blood flowing into the physical world results in such an immense curse – one that impacts on an either nation for generations – suggests to the reader the impact of transgressing these boundaries. As in other examples of Heroic Epic Fantasy, the flow of the metaphysical entity into the physical world causes disruption and disorder.

Fractured landscapes may also motivate the plot even in instances of Localised Fantasy. For example, in China, Miéville's *Perdido Street Station* (2002), Isaac, in his research of flying creatures, acquires a caterpillar which evolves into a dangerous slakemoth. While little is known about the creature, strikingly, the characters hypothesise that: "the current favourite theory is they come from the Fractured Land" (Miéville 325). It is noteworthy that the creature's illegal entrance into this contained space – the city of New Crobuzon – is connected to the notion of a fractured world. But, more importantly, the creature the power to disrupt dreamworlds and alternate realities, fracturing the planes of existence. In Naomi Novik's *Uprooted* (2015), another Localised Fantasy, the plot of the novel is triggered by the wizard Sarkan taking a young girl, Agnieszka, from her home. An outsider, Sarkan uses people born in the valley in order to form a link to the Wood that surrounds it: "You're bound to the valley, all of you; born and bred here [...] It has a hold on you. But that's a channel of its own in turn, and I could use it to siphon away some of the Wood's strength" (355). A metaphysical connection exists between the land and the people. The wizard Sarkan, as an outsider to this valley, uses the people's connection to access the power of the Wood. However, the Wood itself is a corrupted entity. Thousands of years before, the Wood-queen had married a human king, and, following his death, their people turned on her, entombing the queen while alive in the king's crypt. The events of the novel focus on the interactions with the corrupted Wood, and Agnieszka and Sarkan's attempts to defeat it. Thus, different levels of 'normal' and 'abnormal' function here, all of which operate to motivate the plot. Sarkan can be read as an abnormal metaphysical entity who motivates the plot by selecting Agnieszka as a conduit. Agnieszka has magical powers of her own, and, more importantly, is directly connected to the land, and can be read as a normal metaphysical entity accordingly. And yet, Sarkan's arrival into the valley is motivated by the Wood-queen, a being that was originally normal to the valley but has become abnormal.

Similar to the other descriptions of magic in Fantasy fiction, magic in Novik's *Uprooted* flows and has an energy: "On an impulse I tried to align our workings: I envisioned his like the water-wheel of a mill, and mine the rushing stream driving it around" (95). Note the language and the use of the channel in the excerpt above. As magic is conceptualised as an energy that flows, the person who has their roots in the Valley are envisioned as a channel through which that energy can move. Gail Z. Martin's *Chronicles of the Necromancer* (2007–2010) demonstrates a similar device of flow: "They say that power flows like the underground rivers, deep beneath us. All magic draws on that power" (*Dark Haven* 451); "It seemed like the magic was splintering ... as if the Flow itself was coming apart" (389). Note the language of splintering, indicating a fracturing. Likewise, in Robert Jordan's *The Wheel of Time* series (1990–2012), magic is described in motifs of flow or channelling. Here magic is identified as "The One Power," indicating a sense of wholeness and holiness: "'The One Power,' Moiraine was saying, 'comes from the True Source, the driving force of Creation, the force the Creator made to turn the Wheel of Time'" (*The Eye of the World* 168). Like many of the examples of magic above, this One Power is not abnormal to the Fantasyland, as it has a hand in the creation of the Fantasyland itself. The magic users, Aes Sedai, are able to touch this power by channelling the power through their bodies: "the True Source cannot be used up, any more than the river can be used up by the wheel of a mill. The Source is the river; the Aes Sedai, the waterwheel" (169). Just as characters are able to channel metaphysical entities through themselves to function as avatars, so to can they channel magic through their bodies. In these cases, magic itself is a metaphysical entity, as the hero (or anyone who is capable of connecting with this magic) uses their body as a channel for the power.

In *The Wheel of Time*, prior to the beginning of the first book, the ou-hero Lews Therin attempts to seal the Dark One (a Devil figure) into a metaphysical prison in order to remove his presence and influence from the world. Through this attempt, the male half of the magic becomes "corrupt" due to the touch of the Dark One on the flow of power:

> *Saidin*, the male half of the True Source, and *saidar*, the female half, work against each other and at the same time together to provide that force. *Saidin* [...] is fouled by the touch of the Dark One, like water with a thin slick of rancid oil floating on top. The water is still pure, but it cannot be touched without touching the foulness. (168, original emphasis)

Thus, as in Novik's *Uprooted*, a normal metaphysical entity becomes corrupted, and made abnormal. There seem to be different layers of power, and to access Saidin one must penetrate the fouled layer of abnormality on top of it. The power of "The One Power" is corrupted by an abnormal entity, the touch of the Dark One, resulting in distortion to the metaphysical underpinning of Fantasyland. Because of this corruption, slowly over generations entropy increases and the Dark One's prison begins to erode and break as the Dark One seeps back into Fantasyland, triggering the main conflict of the narrative. Fantasyland begins to disintegrate, which is expressed through the repetitive motif throughout the series that the Wheel of Time is unravelling. Properties of time and space begin to break down (locations and temporal periods shift) as the pattern of time weakens. The task of the hero is to re-seal the Dark One back into his prison, thereby removing his taint from the physical world.

All of these examples of Heroic Epic Fantasy demonstrate *the flow or movement of an abnormal entity* into or within Fantasyland *as the instigator* of Wrongness, "some small desiccating hint that the world has lost its wholeness" (Clute 26), thereby triggering the plot. These examples also depict magical powers as an expression of a relationship with a *normal* metaphysical entity; one that flows through Fantasyland and may become disrupted or corrupted by the presence of the abnormal entity that has broken into the land. The motif of crossing boundaries through fluidity is directly linked with the idea of fractures: these metaphysical entities are only able to cross the boundaries of the closed systems through cracks between these spaces. Thus, as this chapter has demonstrated, Fantasyland itself is a closed system that is prone to fractures which leads to a melding with parallel systems, one that results in an increase in imbalance and entropy. The narrative of the Heroic Epic Fantasy focuses on the hero's journey in expelling entropy and re-establishing this balance. In the next chapter, I will continue the discussion on the hero's movement in Fantasyland, integrating the idea of how the body of the hero acts as a medium between fractured worlds in order to reverse the flow of entropy and rebuild broken boundaries.

Bibliography

Bujold, Lois McMaster. *The Curse of Chalion*. 2000. HarperCollins, 2011. Chalion 1.
———. *Paladin of Souls*. HarperTorch, 2003. Chalion 2.
Clemens, James. *Shadowfall*. 2005. Roc, 2006. Godslayer Trilogy 1.
Clute, John. "Fantastika in the World Storm." 2007. *Pardon this Intrusion: Fantastika in the World Storm*. Beccon Publications, 2011. pp. 19–31.
Clute, John and John Grant, eds. "Fantasyland." *The Encyclopedia of Fantasy*. 1997. Orbit, 1999. p. 341.
Croggon, Alison. *The Gift*. 2004. Walker Books, 2012. Pellinor 1.
Eddings, David and Leigh Eddings. *Pawn of Prophecy*. Del Rey, 1982. Belgariad 1.
Eliade, Mircea. *Myth and Reality*. Trans. Willard R. Trask. Harper Colophon Books, 1963.
Gleick, James. *Chaos: The Amazing Science of the Unpredictable*. 1987. Vintage Books, 1998.
Goodkind, Terry. *Stone of Tears*. 1995. Tom Doherty, 1996. The Sword of Truth 2.
———. *Wizard's First Rule*. 1994. Tom Doherty, 1995. The Sword of Truth 1.
Hawking, Stephen. *A Brief History of Time*, 1988. Bantam Books, 2011.
Jemisin, Nora K. *The Stone Sky*. Orbit, 2017. The Broken Earth 3.
Jones, Diana Wynne. *The Tough Guide to Fantasy Land*. 1996. Gollancz, 2004.
Jordan, Robert. *The Eye of the World*. Tor, 1990. The Wheel of Time 1.

Lewis, Clive Staples. *The Lion, The Witch and the Wardrobe*. 1950. Harper-Trophy, 1978. The Chronicles of Narnia 2.

Martin, Gail Z. *Dark Haven*. 2009. Solaris, 2012. Chronicles of the Necromancer 3.

Mendlesohn, Farah. *Rhetorics of Fantasy*. Wesleyan University Press, 2008.

Miéville, China. *Perdido Street Station*. 2000. Del Rey, 2003. Bas-Lag 1.

Moorcock, Michael. "Black Sword's Brother." 1963. *The Stealer of Souls: Chronicles of the Last Emperor of Melniboné Volume 1*. Ballantine Books, 2008. pp. 274–325. Stormbringer 2.

———. "While the Gods Laugh." 1961. *The Stealer of Souls and Other Stories*. Granada Publishing, 1968. pp. 40–72. Elric.

Novik, Naomi. *Uprooted*. 2015. Del Rey, 2016.

Pullman, Philip. *His Dark Materials*. Scholastic, 1995–2000. His Dark Materials 1–3.

Roberts, Adam. "Faulty Cartography: Review of Farah Mendlesohn's *Rhetorics of Fantasy*." *Extrapolation*, vol. 49, no. 3, 2008, pp. 506–512.

Sanderson, Brandon. *Elantris*. 2005. Gollancz, 2011.

———. *Mistborn Trilogy*. Tor, 2006–2010. Mistborn 1–3.

Todorov, Tzvetan. *The Fantastic: A Structural Approach to a Literary Genre*. 1970. Trans. Richard Howard. Cornell University, 1975.

Tolkien, John Ronald Reuel. *The Lords of the Rings*. Allen & Unwin, 1954–1955. The Lord of the Rings 1–3.

7 The Hero as Portal
Examining the Hero's Role as Reversal of Entropy in James Clemens' *Shadowfall* (2006)

Having considered how the plot of Heroic Epic Fantasy is motivated by an increase in entropy resulting in the deterioration of the boundaries of the land itself, the next two chapters will explore how the major conflict of the narrative is resolved through the actions of the hero in reversing the decay of entropy, restoring the balance, and re-establishing a closed system. This particular chapter explores how the Heroic Epic hero achieves this resolution by functioning as a portal or threshold, much like James Clerk Maxwell's demon, separating out entities that are abnormal to Fantasyland back into its proper positioning. The hero is often viewed as inextricably part of the land. For instance, the prophecies of the Dragon in Robert Jordan's *The Wheel of Time* series (1990–2012) states that: "for the land is one with the Dragon Reborn, and he one with the land" (*A Crown of Swords* i). Similar to the Fisher King motif or the Osiris myth, the hero's connection with Fantasyland allows a messianic act to heal the land. The hero does so by functioning as a portal, a mediator between two world systems. In doing so, the hero is a liminal figure who stands at the threshold of Fantasyland.

As a portal between fractured Fantasyland and the metaphysical world, the hero's body is particularly significant, as it allows a metaphysical entity to pass through them into the physical world. As the hero is also physically or spiritually damaged, the healing of the hero and the healing of the land are often combined into one. In this chapter, I first examine the hero as a liminal figure who bridges the fractured Fantasyland, before exploring the body of the hero and the amalgamation of healing the land with the healing of the hero. In healing the broken Fantasyland, the narrative moves firmly into the Epic Fantasy spectrum. Accordingly, I briefly conclude with an examination of the movement of the narrative from the Localised Fantasy to the Epic Fantasy, or, using the language of Northrop Frye's *Anatomy of Criticism* (1957), the movement from Romance to Myth.

I discuss these concepts with an examination of James Clemens' *Shadowfall* (2006), the first book of the incomplete *Godslayer Chronicles* (2006–present), as a case study. Like many Heroic Epic Fantasy authors, Clemens expresses an idea of an intimate connection between Fantasyland

and the metaphysical body. This depiction is overt, and moreover, the physical effect on the body is also made significant. In Clemens' *Shadowfall*, the divine entities are not removed from Fantasyland (made 'invisible'), although they are fixed to a place and consequently must still function through other characters as pawns. However, like other Epic Fantasy novels, the divine body is still presented as abnormal to Fantasyland. As Chapter 6 considered, the breakthrough of the abnormal metaphysical entity directly results in the increase of entropy in Fantasyland, stimulating the plot of the narrative. As I demonstrate throughout this chapter, the Heroic Epic Fantasy hero resolves the major conflict of the narrative by expelling this entity out of Fantasyland by operating as a portal between the physical and metaphysical world.

The Hero as Liminal Figure

As the previous chapter described, in Clemens' *The Godslayer Chronicles*, following a war of the gods, the gods and the worlds are Sundered; through this Sundering, the gods themselves are broken into shattered parts into three different dimensions: Myrillia, the naether, and the aether. After the fall of the gods into the physical world of Myrillia, through this split in their personas the gods suffer a loss of identity (not knowing their 'true' name) and become "maddened and raving" (*Shadowfall* 104). This motif, of recovering the lost knowledge – especially that of a true name – is a common one to Fantasy fiction, one that is connected to the decaying Fantasyland. The gods are only able to regain their sanity and recover their names by tying themselves to the land. While many countless gods remain mad and roaming through the wild, a hundred gods settled the land of Myrillia: "It lasted three centuries until the god Chrism chose the first god-realm and imbued his Graces into the region, sharing his powers to bring order out of chaos. Other gods followed" (43). Though the kingdom of the gods is shattered, the gods are able to somewhat reverse the process of chaos by linking themselves to the land. This idea, of "bring[ing] order out of chaos," is integral to Heroic Epic Fantasy and will be explored further in the next chapter. Here, it is important to note that the gods are explicitly depicted as connected to the land, rooted so firmly that they are unable to leave physically. They become a part of the world so intimately that their personality reflects the land. For instance, "Gods of loam were as patient as a budding seed, as solid as rock and hard-packed soil, while gods of the air were aloof and farseeing, ethereal in mind and grace" (246). Following the tradition of many Epics, Clemens here depicts how intrinsically the divine is connected with the land, so that the health and temperament of the divine being is embodied in the landscape.

The process of the gods tying themselves to Myrillia is fuelled by the flow of blood into the landscape – an act that is similar to that of crucifixion[1]: "Chrism had bled himself into the land, fully and completely, drained empty, attempting to end his life. But death did not come. Instead, as his living blood bonded to the region, he discovered peace from the ravenings" (442). Through crucifixion, a physical penetration of a divine's body that allows them to bleed into the landscape, the divine is connected to the land in a bodily way: *"as the humours of a body course through a god, so they do its lands"* (97, original emphasis to indicate excerpt from dictionary for the word "god-realm"). The flow of bodily fluids into the landscape, an act that takes place via a sacrificial rite, binds the broken body of the divine entity to Fantasyland.

The interaction between the metaphysical and Fantasyland is what creates the magical system of power within *Shadowfall*, here specifically expressed through the broken divine body. The previous chapter explored how the flow of a metaphysical entity – one that is an abnormal substance that does not belong in Fantasyland – into Fantasyland *as the instigator* of Wrongness: "some small desiccating hint that the world has lost its wholeness" (John Clute, "Fantastika in the World Storm" 26). In Clemens' *Shadowfall*, although the broken bodies of the gods have fused themselves to the Fantasyland, much like a virus that has become part of a host body, they do not belong there. As they are abnormal to the Fantasyland, and especially because these broken bodies are still connected to the other parts of their selves in the naether and the aether, their presence in Fantasyland causes the cracks and fractures of the world to widen further. In the first page of *Shadowfall*, a naethryn (the shattered spirit of the divine that resides in the naether) enters the world of Myrillia (the physical world): "It has no form, no shape, no substance. [...] It glides up to one of those rare places where its existence overlaps into the world of substance. Few know of these moiety points. But they exist" (*Shadowfall* 1). The naethryn is a metaphysical entity that does not belong in the physical world. Its action, that of killing the goddess Meeryn, results in the stimulus that launches the hero Tylar dy Noche on his journey as he is blamed for Meeryn's death. Near the end of the novel, the reader discovers that the provocation of the events in the book is motivated by other naethryn entities entering the physical world two centuries prior to the start of the novel: "there were those among your people who used dark Grace to thin our world from yours. We broke through in tiny seepages" (486). These naethryn spirits do not belong in Myrillia, but they are able to cross through and widen the cracks between the worlds because of the presence of their counterparts in Myrillia. The motif of crossing boundaries through fluidity is directly linked with the idea of fractures that was explored in the previous chapter; these metaphysical entities are only able to cross the boundaries of the closed systems through cracks between these spaces.

In discussing the idea of a fractured Fantasyland, Chapter 6 also briefly considered Farah Mendlesohn's conception of a portal world

(*Rhetorics of Fantasy*, 2008), one in which the hero *enters* a Heroic Epic Fantasy world, thus suggesting that the hero is abnormal to Fantasyland themselves. This is rarely the case. Often the Heroic Epic Fantasy hero is frequently *removed* from their home prior to the events of the novel. In *Shadowfall*, the godchild Dart is brought out from the Hinterland and hidden at a children's school. In Jordan's *The Wheel of Time*, Rand al'Thor is similarly orphaned as a baby and adopted by a family who moves him to an isolated village. This motif occurs in earlier works of Heroic Epic Fantasy as well. For instance, in Poul Anderson's *Three Hearts and Three Lions* (1961), it is revealed within the frame story that Holger Carlsen was adopted by the Carlsen family. His movement into a Fantastical world is a seamless transition as his entrance indicates a type of homecoming: "she had spoken in a language he did not know – and he had answered her in the same tongue" (11). Even when they are not relocated from their homes as a child, the hero may be a traveller figure who is made to leave their home, as is the case with Tylar in *Shadowfall* or Paul Atreides in Frank Herbert's *Dune* (1965). The Epic form necessitates a journey in order for a hero to undergo spiritual transcendence. But the journey also indicates that the hero's movement across Fantasyland as *a return to the world they belong to*. The hero is thus not leaving a primary world and entering a secondary world, the *hero is part of both worlds*.

Fantasyland, as the previous chapter established, is a fractured system that allows entities to enter from other parallel systems. When this happens, the entropy of both systems is higher than the entropy of each individual system. In a real-world system, entropy is irreversible, as N. Katherine Hayles notes in *Chaos Bound* (1990):

> The reversal of this tendency requires a "restoration." But any attempt of reform only creates more dissipation. A *net* restoration is beyond the power of "organized matter;" the adjective implicitly acknowledges that matter may be unorganized, itself subject to entropic decay. (39, original emphasis)

If entropy is irreversible, how then is the hero able to reverse entropy in fractured Fantasyland and restore the boundaries?

Hayles summarises a famous argument by James Clerk Maxwell who, in *Theory of Heat* (1871), describes an entropic system where a microscopic being is able to separate out molecules and in doing so is able to decrease the system's entropy:

> If we conceive a being whose faculties are so sharpened that he can follow every molecule in its course, such a being, whose attributes are still as essentially finite as our own, would be able to do what is impossible to us. […] He will thus, without expenditure of work,

raise the temperature of *B* and lower that of *A*, in contradiction to the second law of thermodynamics. (Maxwell quoted in Hayles 42, original emphasis)

Maxwell describes a being that is able to lower the entropy of a combined system by separating molecules back into their original systems. This intelligent being that is able to reverse entropy becomes known as Maxwell's Demon, although, as Hayles notes, Maxwell himself never uses the term 'demon' to discuss his 'being.' But Hayles continues:

> Like guardians of portals to other realms in ancient myths, the demon is a liminal figure who stands at a threshold that separates not just slow molecules from fast but an ordered world of will from the disordered world of chaos. On one side is a universe fashioned by divine intervention, created for man and responsive to his will; on the other is the inhuman force of increasing entropy, indifferent to man and uncontrollable by human will. (43)

Note Hayles' idea that Maxwell's Demon "is a liminal figure who stands at a threshold" to separate entities of disorder back into their proper place of divine and human order. Hayles draws a connection to "guardians of portals to other realms in *ancient myths*" (my emphasis). Extrapolating these ideas to Heroic Epic Fantasy fiction, Maxwell's Demon can be seen in the figure of the Heroic Epic Fantasy hero: the hero likewise is a liminal figure who stands at the threshold of Fantasyland separating out entities that are abnormal to Fantasyland back into its proper positioning (Figure 7.1).

This idea, of the hero as a liminal figure who stand as the threshold of two different lands, is explicitly depicted in Clemens' *Shadowfall*.

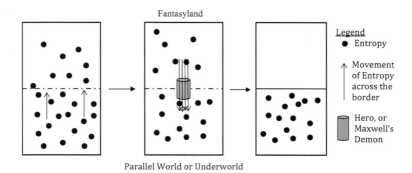

Figure 7.1 The Hero as Maxwell's Demon between Parallel Systems.

Throughout the novel, the spirit of the dying god Meeryn enters into the world of Myrillia using Tylar dy Noche's body as portal site in which to enter: "As the scintillating wave finished with the beast, it fed along the only channel left open to it: the snaking umbilicus that led to Tylar" (*Shadowfall* 82). The goddess Meeryn uses her dying graces (magical powers) to heal and remake Tylar's broken body so that his body can function as a portal site between the land of Myrillia and the naethryn. Thus, Tylar is very explicitly depicted as a liminal figure standing on the threshold between two worlds, his body allowing spirits to pass from one world into the other.

The idea of the Epic hero as a liminal figure has its roots in the Mythological hero, imitating the concept of a King's body as mediator between the land and the people. As Ernst H. Kantorowicz discusses in *The King's Two Bodies* (1957), the: "Christ-imitating king was pictured and expounded also as the 'mediator' between heaven and earth, a concept of some importance here because every mediatorship implies, one way or another, the existence of a twin-natured being" (88). As previous chapters considered, the hero is a character of balance, one that understands all aspects of good and evil, life and death. It is because of this very nature, of being a 'twin-natured being,' that the hero is able to function as a mediator between two metaphysical realms. While Kantorowicz's medieval study focuses on the concept of the 'Hero King' as imitator of Christ, the hero as mediator between heaven and earth has its roots in earlier Epics as well. In *The Epic Hero* (2000), Dean Miller identifies that the Greco-Roman Mythological hero is always connected to liminality, a transitional borderland space:

> The border is very often a transitional or liminal topos between the human, profane world and a supernatural zone or Otherworld; and one obsession of the hero [is] to find and penetrate into threatening or unknown places and terrains, [...]. The place of the hero on the border is thus almost a cliché: liminality is all but a given. (147–148)

Similar to the Mythological Epic hero, the Heroic Epic Fantasy hero is a liminal figure who mediates transitional space between the metaphysical world and the physical world.

The liminal space is defined as a religious transitional space: "Of or relating to a transitional or intermediate state between culturally defined stages of a person's life, esp. as marked by a ritual or rite of passage; characterized by liminality (liminality *n.*)" (*OED*). The liminal space is an intermediary between two states, and, especially in the Epic, this liminality is characterised by ritual and rites of passage. In *The Golden Bough* (1922), James Frazer indicates that, similar to the Heroic Epic Fantasy hero, the function of the King was also a messianic religious function. The King is ceremonially offered up for sacrifice for the good of his people:

> Kings were revered, in many cases not merely as priests, that is, as intercessors between man and god, but as themselves gods, able to bestow upon their subjects and worshippers those blessings which are commonly supposed to be beyond the reach of mortals. (n.p.)

In Heroic Epic Fantasy, heroes take the place of this King, voluntarily sacrificing themselves in order to function as "intercessors between man and god." The hero as liminal figure intercedes between two metaphysical planes, expressed through an act of sacrifice, combining the liminal figure with a messianic role. Accordingly, the conception of the hero as a liminal figure who separates out entropic entities like Maxwell's Demon, *also* has an overt connection to a religious function, and particularly that of their messianic role. By fulfilling their messianic duty, heroes are able to separate out entropic entities back into their proper positioning. Consider, for instance, Cazaril in Lois McMaster Bujold's *The Curse of Chalion* (2001). By dying three times, Cazaril is able to allow the divine to reach into his body and draw out a drop of blood: a substance that is abnormal to the Fantasyland and had directly created the "curse" that affected the entire land. By fulfilling his messianic duty, Cazaril is able to function as Maxwell's Demon as well.

In Heroic Epic Fantasy, as the fractures in the world create spaces for flow, this allows enough movement for divinity to manifest enough to set pawns (their chosen heroes) in motion or to act themselves through a hero as avatar. In *Shadowfall*, Tylar dy Noche is treated as both pawn and avatar in order to negotiate the divine's metaphysical entity into Fantasyland. His movement in Fantasyland as an emerging hero suggests that "even a broken pawn can arise again and shake the board" (*Shadowfall* 106). When Tylar comes across the dying goddess Meeryn, she heals his physically broken body and the other characters infer that Meeryn "must have championed [him] for some purpose" (45). Tylar discovers that Meeryn had hidden a part of herself – the part that connects to the naethryn half – in his own body, re-building his broken body in order to make "a cage out of [his] healthy bones, requiring only one crack, one broken bone, to set [the naethryn spirit] free" (94). Accordingly, while Meeryn dies on Myrillia, the connection between her other entities still persist through Tylar's own body as "[a] conduit for the naether-spawn, the naethryn undergod" (250). Tylar functions as Meeryn's avatar, taking on her connection to her other ethereal parts: "Had she marked Tylar as her avatar and set him loose with a piece of herself?" (452). Tylar comes to the conclusion that Meeryn marked him as her personal avatar in the physical world as she can no longer fulfil the duty herself. Thus, by acting as an avatar or pawn of a god, instead of simply *entering* Fantasyland through a doorway, the Heroic

Epic Fantasy hero often *functions as a doorway themselves*: they may anchor the divine spirit long enough for them to heal the world through the hero, or in order to fulfil the role themselves by taking on the powers of divinity, or by gaining knowledge from the metaphysical world in order to complete this role.

Many Heroic Epic Fantasy novels depict a hero who crosses over into a metaphysical dimension – either to interact with the spirits of another world (a symbolic death), or, by literally dying. This messianic function is not limited to the central hero as the larger protagonist group may also aid in working against entropy. Recall, as Chapter 5 considered, that the difference between the hero and larger protagonist group is that the hero's messianic sacrifice is able to bring balance to the world, but that the protagonist group may also sacrifice themselves in order to facilitate this act. For instance, in Brandon Sanderson's *Hero of Ages* (2008), several heroes die in their attempt to save the world. While they are not the central hero that are able to restore the balance in the world, their messianic death still allows them to aid the hero in an attempt to re-establish this balance. Indeed, in Sanderson's *Arcanum Unbounded* collection of short stories (2016), it is revealed that the first hero to die has influenced events throughout the remainder of the trilogy even after his physical death. Similarly, in the unfinished Fractured Fantasy of George R. R. Martin's *A Song of Ice and Fire* series (1996–present), several heroes may sacrifice themselves in order to aid their perceived hero. In the episode "The Door" (2016) in *A Game of Thrones* (2011–2019), the television adaptation of the series, the relatively minor character Hodor is asked to "hold the door," an act that results in sacrifice. The hero as mediator of a threshold space is also made overt in the form of the hero Bran's splitting of consciousness between different times and different bodies. Ista in Bujold's *Paladin of Souls* (2003) also functions as a porter for god, using her body as a doorway between the physical and metaphysical world, and carrying spirits through it to their proper place: "*We are all, every living one of us, doorways between the two realms, that of matter that gives us birth, and that of spirit into which we are born in death*" (397, original emphasis). Thus, the Heroic Epic Fantasy hero does not simply move between worlds, but also functions as a doorway themselves, anchoring the threshold long enough for entities to move between. As previous chapters confirmed, the Heroic Epic Fantasy hero must be a messianic hero, but one that must first contemplate and comprehend the different metaphysical boundaries of life and death. This comprehension allows the hero to manipulate these boundaries.

The Body of the Hero

Because of the hero's positioning as a threshold figure between metaphysical boundaries, the conception of the hero's body is particularly significant. Heroic Epic Fantasy heroes may be humble, and the physical description may emphasise their ordinariness, as is the case with the hero Garion in David and Leigh Eddings' *Belgariad* series (1982–1984): "He was so *ordinary*. He was a peasant, a scullion, a nobody. He was a nice enough boy, certainly, with rather plain, sandy hair [...]. He had a nice enough face – in a plain sort of way" (*Magician's Gambit* 12, original emphasis). Other Heroic Epic Fantasy heroes might be small in stature (such as Frodo Baggins in J. R. R. Tolkien's *The Lord of the Rings*, 1954–1955) or are often children on the cusps of adolescence (such as the Pevensies in C. S. Lewis's *The Lion, the Witch and the Wardrobe*, 1950).

The central protagonist of *Shadowfall* is notable for having a physically broken body. Clemens makes a point to describe Tylar as a figure physically opposite to a knight:

> [T]he empty vessel left behind had been broken by a half decade spent in the slave rings of Trik. His sword arm was a callused club, numb from the elbow down. [...]
> He was no knight.
> Not any longer. (*Shadowfall* 6)

Note the motif of the 'empty vessel' that is paired alongside the broken body of the knight. Bujold describes Cazaril similarly as a disabled knight: "His fingers didn't really straighten right, and he found himself waving a claw" (*The Curse of Chalion* 3). Both authors emphasise that their heroes are unable to carry a sword, like a proper knight of the Adventure mode. Like Tylar, Cazaril is also a former captain who was sold to the slave trade, indicating their fall from grace. The physical descriptions accentuate this fall: "His back, the ropy red mess of scars piled one across another so thickly as to leave no untouched skin between, legacy of the last flogging in the Roknari galley-masters had given him" (*The Curse of Chalion* 12). In post-1990 fiction, there seems to be an emerging trend of depicting protagonists that are damaged, physically or spiritually. While the 'fallen hero' has often been a part of the Adventure mode, more recently, along with a spiritual fall, authors have started depicting this fall in a more overt, physical way.

Why do these Heroic Epic Fantasy authors depict heroes that are damaged? The broken hero, I argue, is a structural necessity of the Heroic Epic Fantasy plot. To begin with, the damaged hero's body seems to be an externalisation of their spirit. The first hero of *Shadowfall*, Tylar, is often depicted as morally grey, a fallen and disgraced knight who has dabbled on the edges of the underworld society. Dart, the second hero of the novel, a girl of age thirteen, is brutally raped and spends much of the novel contemplating how she is physically and spiritually unclean: "It was shameful to offer such soiled palms, but then again, it was somehow fitting, considering the corruption of her body and spirit" (*Shadowfall* 71–72). Like

Dart's expression of shame, the physical deformities of Tylar and Cazaril seem to be an externalisation of their 'spirit.' They feel that they are broken in some way.

But along with being an externalisation of their fallen spirit, the broken hero comes about because it is their very brokenness that allows their body to function as a portal site for the metaphysical into the physical world. Recall from Chapter 5, that the hero must 'descend' or confront 'death' in order to fulfil their messianic function. The broken hero is emblematic of this fall. As well, recall that Chapter 1 established that the hero has a shape to their soul and that the hero can choose whether or not to fulfil the function of this design; while the soul is not physical, the body is the container, the mediator between the physical and spiritual world. In *Shadowfall*, at the moment when Meeryn's naethryn spirit enters Tylar's body, Tylar finds himself poised between two boundaries: "Where a moment ago he had stood at the edge of a bottomless abyss, now he hung over the same. But as he spun, he recognizes his mistake. There was not one abyss, but *two* – one above and one below" (18, original emphasis). Tylar's body functions as a site of merger between two abysses. Accordingly, the body of the hero is pertinent, as its shape may determine how the hero fulfils the function of their design. When Meeryn heals Tylar's broken body so that he can function as her hero after she has departed the world, the narration in *Shadowfall* echoes that of *The Curse of Chalion*: "Then the water finally emptied from the broken vessel that was his body. Tylar collapsed in on himself, spent and drained" (*Shadowfall* 19). Repeatedly the language in these texts evokes the idea of a vessel – the spirit of the divine passes through Tylar's "vessel," just as Cazaril's body functions as a cup in *The Curse of Chalion*.

In both examples, the vessel, the body that contains the spirit of the divine, is described as broken. Prior to the divine spirit entering his body, Tylar describes his body as an "empty vessel" (6). The broken body of Tylar is reformed and healed only when the goddess Meeryn ties her naethryn spirit to his body, allowing her spirit to flow into Tylar's body, using it as a container.[2] Tylar can only release the naethryn spirit into the physical world of Myrillia by breaking his body again, his broken body acting as a fracture that would allow the spirit to leak out: "It was as if she had made a cage out of your healthy bones, requiring only one crack, one broken bone, to set it free" (94). Accordingly, Tylar's physical body is a site of fracture between the physical world and the metaphysical world. Similarly, in *The Curse of Chalion*, Cazaril is required to die three times "for the practice" in order to be capable enough to accept a metaphysical spirit to enter the physical world through his body (*The Curse of Chalion* 468). The hero is broken because it is the *break* in their body that allows the metaphysical entity to pass through him into the physical world. In those texts where the hero is not physically broken, a spiritual fall may take its place, indicating that the fracturing of the hero's spirit allows the metaphysical entity to leak through.

The broken hero comes about because they are representative of the entropy of Fantasyland. As Brian Attebery argues in "Fantasy as an Anti-Utopian Mode" (1986): "Fantasy explores inward, examining the fears and ideals of the individual, projecting interior forces onto a symbolic landscape" (6). This expression of the landscape is also represented in the body of the characters. And thus, we have a broken hero who must fall before they can ascend and heal Fantasyland. Attebery further declares that two themes of Fantasy fiction are often combined:

> One is the movement from immaturity to maturity: the coming of age or the acquiring of wisdom. [...] The other is the healing of an ailing land or society, what might be called the Fisher King motif. [...] Many stories combine the two themes: Frodo's growth is tied to his role as savior. (7–8)

The two paths – the healing of the hero and the healing of the land – are often combined into one. The arc of the hero is restoration, recuperation, redemption; the healing of the damaged hero is part of the broader trajectory of the hero's journey to fulfill their purpose.

Transcendence of the Heroic Epic Fantasy Narrative

The hero is a transgressor figure in that they have the ability to cross boundaries and different dimensional spaces. Miller identifies this ability as a central aspect of the Mythological hero:

> [A] more central aspect of the hero [is] his mediation between one zone and another, between this world and an Otherworld. What I call Otherworld may have a nominal connection with divine persons and spiritual potencies (gods or goddesses), or it may be merely indicated as the place of death; either, or both, is possible. (6)

Miller asserts that the hero's mediation of the upper and lower worlds (divine heaven or demonic hell) is a central aspect of the hero. Likewise, in *Anatomy of Criticism* (1957), Northrop Frye associates the conflict of good and evil functions in the Quest structure of Romance or Myth with the movement of the upper and lower worlds:

> A quest involving conflict assumes two main characters, a protagonist or hero, and an antagonist or enemy. [...] The enemy may be an ordinary human being, but the nearer the romance is to myth, the more attributes of divinity will cling to the hero and the more the enemy will take on demonic mythical qualities. The central form of

> romance is dialectical: everything is focussed on a conflict between the hero and his enemy, and all the reader's values are bound up with the hero. Hence the hero of romance is analogous to the mythical Messiah or deliverer who comes from an upper world, and his enemy is analogous to the demonic powers of a lower world. (187)

Frye distinguishes Romance from a Myth as if on a spectrum; "the nearer the romance is to myth, the more attributes of divinity will cling to the hero and the more the enemy will take on demonic mythical qualities." Extrapolating this idea onto Figure 0.1, the Romance can be paralleled to Localised Fantasy, with the Myth taking the place of Epic Fantasy. As the narrative continues, the Epic Fantasy hero transcends, growing closer to the divine.

The hero's messianic function incorporates a movement across metaphysical spaces, a literal or symbolic descent to the underworld followed by a period of transcendence where the hero is temporarily able to ascend to the heavens. Initially, the divine is embedded in Fantasyland itself before they are made to depart. Once this entity becomes abnormal to Fantasyland, as the hero comes to replace the divinity, the divine's relationship with the land is replaced with the hero, who then, in turn, becomes representative of the broken land. Like the Fisher King motif, healing the hero also results in healing the land.

Through the act of healing, both hero and Fantasyland undergo a transcendence where they become something 'more.' The flow of the naethryn spirit into Tylar's body further unravels Tylar's essence: "*I am undone*, he thought, knowing it to be true" (18, original emphasis). But by being "undone," Tylar's body is crafted into something new, a body that is able to contain a divine essence and become immortal itself. These heroes must break – be undone – in order to be reformed into something new – *not* in the normative body – but something *more*: the hero's body; one that is capable of restoring and healing a broken Fantasyland. Recall C. D. Broad's conception of "becoming": "the sum total of the existent is continually augmented by becoming" (*Scientific Thought* 69). The first half of this book established that, through the repeated acceptance of the heroic function, the hero moves from being a *potential* hero to becoming ac *actualised* hero. As Chapters 4 and 5 confirmed, this heroic function is a messianic function, one which the hero must accept willingly. In doing so, the hero not only embraces their potential death, the hero also prepares for the possibility of being "undone" and then remade, transformed into something more than once was. In the moment where the hero's sacrifice allows them to fulfil the necessary role of dispelling the abnormal out of Fantasyland, the hero achieves transcendence, a process where the hero embodies or replaces the divine or metaphysical spirit.

Through this transcendence, the Heroic Epic Fantasy hero moves from the hero of Romance – a potential state – to the hero of Myth – an actualised state. In *Anatomy of Criticism*, Frye differentiates modes of fiction by the hero's power of relation to the environment and with other humans:

1. If superior in kind both to other men and to the environment of other men, the hero is a divine being, and the story about him will be a myth in the common sense of a story about a god. [...]
2. If superior in degree to other men and to his environment, the hero is the typical hero of romance. (33)

Frye indicates that there is also a movement between the five modes of fiction that he identifies: "Our five modes evidently go around in a circle" (42). While Frye discusses the movement of the modes from one text to another, it is not unfeasible that a single work of text can move from one mode to the other. Frye himself states that Science Fiction is "a mode of romance with a strong inherent tendency to myth" (49). The same holds true for Heroic Epic Fantasy fiction.

Through the hero's journey, the hero transcends. As Miller describes for the Mythic hero: "the mythological epic and its archetypical thematic elevates the hero, who is made the shadowy partner or the earthly avatar of divinity, to an awesome height" (31). Similarly, the Heroic Epic Fantasy hero is "elevate[d]" through their status as the "shadowy partner or the earthly avatar of divinity." There is a movement upward as the hero comes closer to the divine entity that they are in service to. Extrapolating on both Miller's and Frye's work, I assert that the trajectory of a work of Heroic Epic Fantasy fiction is one that moves from Romance to Myth. This movement is similar to the movement of the Local to the Epic in Figure 0.1. As the hero's powers become greater in an ever-expanding cosmos, the Heroic Epic Fantasy hero moves from the hero of Romance – the Localised hero – to the hero of Myth – the Epic hero. *Both* Local and Epic hero begins as Romantic hero, reflected in the broken landscape, but the Epic hero, as they achieve transcendence, arises from a fully healed lands as a Mythic hero. Whether or not the hero then returns and re-joins the community (as discussed in Chapter 5), is dependent on the level of transcendent and how near the hero has come to becoming one with divinity.

This transcendence comes about due to the hero's role as a messianic figure. This moment of death is what allows the Heroic Epic Fantasy hero to gain transcendence and cross into another world. In *The Hero with a Thousand Faces* (1949), Joseph Campbell describes this moment of transcendence accordingly:

> The idea that the passage of the magical threshold is a transit into a sphere of rebirth is symbolized in the worldwide womb image of the belly of the whale. The hero, instead of conquering or conciliating the power of the threshold, is swallowed into the unknown, and would appear to have died. (74)

Transcendence comes through a passage through a threshold, one that links the hero to death. In *Shadowfall*, as in many Heroic Epics, the hero experiences the actual moment of death. They have died or are "undone" (*Shadowfall* 18). But, the Heroic Epic Fantasy hero, like the Mythological hero, *is reborn*: "passage of the threshold is a form of self-annihilation. [...] But here, instead of passing outward, beyond the confines of the visible world, the hero goes inward, to be born again" (Campbell 77). In Heroic Epic Fantasy, the hero's messianic function, the voluntary sacrifice that the hero makes for their community, would indicate that through this act of dying, the hero reaches transcendence where the hero becomes one with god. Recall M. M. Bakhtin's argument in *The Dialogic Imagination* (1975, translated 1981) that: "The series of adventures that the hero undergoes does not result in a simple affirmation of his identity, but rather in the construction of a new image of the hero, a man who is now purified and reborn" (117). The hero may become a saint (like in Bujold) or a god (Clemens), or perhaps something in between, but, nonetheless, something that is clearly beyond even the most distinguished human, as the character fulfils their potential of hero and is "purified and reborn."

Through this moment of transcendence, the hero is able to reverse the entropy of Fantasyland as the hero removes the damaging influences of the abnormal entropic entity. Sometimes, this act necessitates that the hero slays a divine or immense metaphysical entity. There is an element of sacrifice in this as well, with a lineage back to a harvest or corn god that must be sacrificed in order for there to be a renewal of the land. For example, in *The Golden Bough*, Frazer relates the myth of Osiris: "a personification of the great yearly vicissitudes of nature, especially of the corn" (n.p.). When the Egyptian god Osiris is murdered, his body is cut into pieces and scattered across the land. His wife Isis finds his broken body and restores it in order to bear an heir. The fertility and healing of the land (represented by spring) is the other side of the coin that represents brokenness (impotence). This connection is seen in the cyclical movement of nature and the seasons, represented by nature-myths, as Frye asserts:

> The fundamental form of process is cyclical movement, the alternation of success and decline, effort and repose, life and death which is the rhythm of process. [...] Thus: 1. In the divine world the central process or movement is that of the death and rebirth, or the disappearance and return, or the incarnation and withdrawal, of a god. (158)

In comparison to the abnormal divine entities represented in Clemens' *Shadowfall*, other Fantasy texts may depict entities that have already removed themselves from the world; but for those gods that are active and manifest in the physical world, they need to *be* removed, as they no longer belong in that world. This is what occurs at the end of Eddings'

Belgariad series: while the other gods have already removed their presence from the physical world, the god Torak persists in Fantasyland and must be slayed at the end of the first series.

The removal of this divine force necessitates that a hero or another protagonist takes their place. At the end of Eddings' sequel series (*Malloreon*, 1987–1991) another hero must rise up to take the place of the lost god. This time, though, the divine is *normal* to Fantasyland, and is treated accordingly. The other gods in the pantheon depart for other worlds, leaving Eriond in charge of the current world:

> "[…] You'll probably live long enough to see the day when Eriond is the God of the whole world. That's what was intended from the beginning." [says the voice of the Prophecy of Light…]
>
> "[…] What happens to the other Gods then? Aldur and the rest of them?" [asks Garion]
>
> "They'll move on. They've finished with what they came here to do, and there are many, many other worlds in the universe." [replies the voice]
>
> "What about UL? Will he leave, too?"
>
> "UL doesn't leave any place, Garion. He's everywhere." (*The Seeress of Kell* 303–304)

Note that UL, the father of all the gods (along with the universe, who is their mother) does not depart the world, because the 'ultimate' creator is infused in all parts of this holistic world, but that the other gods are forced to leave, to become 'invisible' and move on to another world that requires their presence. The same resolution occurs in Sanderson's *Mistborn* trilogy. The first book ends with the death and destruction of the ou-hero 'god,' who is not replaced until the conclusion of the third novel of the trilogy. With the removal of the metaphysical entities Perseverance and Ruin, one of the heroes must step forward and take their place as a new god, leaving behind his human existence, as Eriond does in *The Malloreon*, in order to fill the vacuum left by the removal of these gods. Likewise, in the final pages of *Shadowfall*, Tylar dy Noche realises that he "had no choice. At the end, the godslayer had become a god" (498). At the climactic moment of the novel, the hero Tylar kills the ou-hero god and takes his place, his heroic potential fulfilled as he becomes a god himself. Note that the hero's transcendence following the removal and subsequent replacement of the divine or abnormal entity usually occurs in the climactic moment of the *series*, rather than in the first novel, as happens in *Shadowfall*. It is likely that the resolution of this unfinished trilogy (with a sequel trilogy already planned) will result in an even larger usurping of the divine order, as the hundred settled gods and the numerous hinterland gods will probably be removed entirely from the Fantasyland, rather than a single one ou-hero god, as in the first novel.

The act of killing a god (or to a lesser extent, a king) is the ultimate transgression of boundary; by the act of deicide or regicide, the hero replaces the god or king, usually with themselves. If the hero kills a king, then another form of hierarchy must take his place. If the hero kills the god, then again, a new god must arise. The hero's transcendence comes about because the hero has plummeted to the depths and slayed an awesome figure. When the madman in Friedrich Nietzsche's *The Gay Science* (1887, translated 1997) famously proclaims that "god is dead," he continues:

> Is the magnitude of this deed [of killing god] not too great for us? *Do we not ourselves have to become gods merely to appear worthy of it?* There was never a greater deed – and whoever is born after us will on account of this deed belong to a higher history than all history up to now! (181, my emphasis)

The act of killing a god is a great deed, and the one who does so must be equal to the slayed god in turn.

The replacement of the god with a new one would indicate a pattern of cyclicality. As Nietzsche's madman notes, a new history, a greater history, is born after the death of god: a new pattern is established. Clute's fourth phase of Fantasy, "Return," also suggests cyclicality to the progression of the Fantasy narrative. These ideas of the cyclicality of Fantasy are expressed consciously in Heroic Epic Fantasy texts. For example, in Australian author Alison Croggon's *The Gift* (2004), when the elemental (a fairy queen) Ardina fears the end for her people, the hero Maerad responds:

> "Say not an end. [...] Say rather another beginning."
> "Perhaps," said Ardina. "But an ending, nevertheless." (305)

As Campbell asserts, "The basic principle of all mythology is this of *the beginning in the end*" (231, my emphasis) – and vice versa of course. The death of a king or a god indicates the end of one type of social order and the beginning of something new. The citizens of this new Fantasyland (if they have survived the revolution) have a chance to re-build their society in a wholly new way. Consequently, the healing of Fantasyland does not always indicate a simple *reversal* of the forces of entropy; instead a new cycle is created, similar to the one before, and yet still different. The last two chapters in this book will examine these reversals and cycles of repetition in greater detail, suggesting an element of chaos in the cycle.

Notes

1 The first god to undergo crucifixion, Chrism, with a name that alludes to Christ, is later revealed to be an ou-hero. Clemens may be offering an

alternate reading of the Christ mythology, especially as the characters discover that Chrism's crucifixion was not voluntarily but was performed as punishment by the community.

2 An important facet is indicated by the use of the words 'cup' and 'vessel' – these words may indicate a female body. But here there is an inversion of the gender type, with the male body functioning as a vessel to hold the spirit of a female divinity. As often land is gendered as well – the notion of Mother Earth indicating a fertile female landscape – the healing of the land via the male body may indicate a renewal of fertility, evoking the Osiris myth of the scattering of the broken male body inseminating the female landscape. The language of the 'cup' and 'vessel' may also suggest a wider theological connection with Christianity, but whereas Bujold's Christian background can be read in the *Chalion* series, Clemens' *Shadowfall* depicts subversive Christian motifs. Note however that the Heroic Epic Fantasy genre as a whole should not be read as a Christian-genre, as the implications of the text would be dependent on the particular attitude and religious backgrounds of individual authors.

Bibliography

Anderson, Poul. *Three Hearts and Three Lions.* 1961. Berkley, 1978.
Attebery, Brian. "Fantasy as an Anti-Utopian Mode." *Reflections on the Fantastic: Selected Essays from the Fourth International Conference on the Fantastic in the Arts.* Ed. Michael R. Collings. Greenwood Press, 1986. pp. 3–8.
Bakhtin, Mikhail Mikhaĭlovich. *The Dialogic Imagination.* 1975. Ed. Michael Holquist. Trans. Caryl Emerson and Michael Holquist. University of Texas Press, 1981.
Benioff, David, and David B. Weiss, writers. "The Door." Dir. Jack Bender. *Game of Thrones.* HBO. 22 May 2016.
Broad, Charlie Dunbar. "The General Problem of Time and Change." *Scientific Thought.* 1923. Routledge, 1952. pp. 53–84.
Bujold, Lois McMaster. *The Curse of Chalion.* 2000. HarperCollins, 2011. Chalion 1.
Campbell, Joseph. *The Hero with a Thousand Faces.* 1949. New World Library, 2008.
Clemens, James. *Shadowfall.* 2005. Roc, 2006. Godslayer Trilogy 1.
Clute, John. "Fantastika in the World Storm." 2007. *Pardon this Intrusion: Fantastika in the World Storm.* Beccon Publications, 2011. pp. 19–31.
Croggon, Alison. *The Gift.* 2004. Walker Books, 2012. Pellinor 1.
Eddings, David and Leigh Eddings. *Magician's Gambit.* Del Rey, 1983. Belgariad 3.
———. *The Seeress of Kell.* Dey Rey, 1991. Malloreon 5.
Frazer, Sir James George. *The Golden Bough: The Roots of Religion and Folklore.* 1890. Project Gutenberg. 23 March 2003. Ebook.
Frye, Northrop. *Anatomy of Criticism.* 1957. Princeton University Press, 1973.
Hayles, N. Katherine. *Chaos Bound: Orderly Disorder in Contemporary Literature and Science.* 1990. Cornell University Press, 1994.
Herbert, Frank. *Dune.* 1965. Gollancz, 2010. Dune Saga 1.
Jordan, Robert. *A Crown of Swords.* 1996. Orbit, 2007. The Wheel of Time 7.
———. *The Wheel of Time.* Tor, 1990–2005. The Wheel of Time 1–11.

Jordan, Robert and Brandon Sanderson. *The Wheel of Time*. Tor, 2009–2012. The Wheel of Time 12–14.
Kantorowicz, Ernst H. *The King's Two Bodies: A Study in Medieval Political Theology*. 1957. 7th edition. Princeton University Press, 1997.
Lewis, Clive Staples. *The Lion, The Witch and the Wardrobe*. 1950. Harper-Trophy, 1978. The Chronicles of Narnia 2.
"Liminal." *OED Online*. Oxford University Press, December 2015. Web. Accessed 11 February 2016. www.oed.com/view/Entry/108471.
Martin, George R. R. *A Song of Ice and Fire*. Bantam Books, 1996–2011. A Song of Ice and Fire 1–5.
Mendlesohn, Farah. *Rhetorics of Fantasy*. Wesleyan University Press, 2008.
Miller, Dean A. *The Epic Hero*. 2000. John Hopkins University Press, 2002.
Nietzsche, Friedrich. *The Gay Science*. 1887. Trans. Walter Kaufmann. Vintage Books, 1997.
Rowling, Joanne K. *Harry Potter and the Deathly Hallows*. Raincoast Books, 2007. Harry Potter 7.
Sanderson, Brandon. *Arcanum Unbounded*. Gollancz, 2016.
———. *The Hero of Ages*. 2008. Dragonstell Entertainment, 2010. Mistborn Trilogy 3.
Tolkien, John Ronald Reuel. *The Lords of the Rings*. Allen & Unwin, 1954–1955. The Lord of the Rings 1–3.

8 Perfect Epic Empires
Appraising Cycles of Utopia and Anti-Utopia in Brandon Sanderson's *Hero of Ages* (2008)

Having briefly considered the cyclicality of Heroic Epic Fantasy in Chapters 5 and 7, the final chapters will expand on that discussion with an examination of how these cycles can be seen as chaotic. As Chapter 3 introduced, chaos theory offers a study of *patterned* behaviour that is *not predictable*. It is in this light that we will consider the repetitive cycles of Heroic Epic Fantasy in the final two chapters of this book. John Clute's last stage of Fantasy, that of "Return" ("Fantastika in the World Storm" 26) suggests a conclusion to the Heroic Epic Fantasy plotline that is cyclical, of returning to a lost Edenic state. Richard Mathews in *Fantasy: The Liberation of Imagination* (1997) likewise asserts that: "time is not seen as linear or progressive but as cyclical. The reader witnesses the ending of one age *and* the beginning of a new one" (81, original emphasis). However, messianic time is generally presented as *linear*, especially in the Judeo-Christian tradition, as a writer who presents a 'Kingdom of Heaven' following an apocalyptic battle may be reluctant to suggest that the world will fall again. And yet, more often in Heroic Epic Fantasy fiction, messianic time merges with a cyclical pattern of eternal recurrence that is found in other cultural traditions.

As Chapter 6 considered, Fantasyland begins in a state of high order and then deteriorates due to the impact of entropy. However, in a real-world system entropy is irreversible, and thus, also linear. In light of this, how does the Hero reverse entropy and 'return' to an Edenic state? While Chapter 7 began to offer a solution in the form of Maxwell's Demon, here, this chapter will expand on this argument and further explore a real-world solution by utilising chaos theory.

Chapter 4 concluded that a character must confront a bifurcation point several times in their journey (Figure 4.1). Ilya Prigogine and Isabella Stengers link a bifurcation point to the emergence of a self-organising system. In *Order out of Chaos* (1984), they describe how entropy results in a creation of new structures:

> We now know that far from equilibrium, new types of structures may originate spontaneously. In far-from-equilibrium conditions we may have transformation from disorder, from thermal chaos,

into order. New dynamic states of matter may originate, states that reflect the interaction of a given system with its surroundings. We have called these new structures *dissipative structures* to emphasize the constructive role of dissipative processes in their formation. (12, original emphasis)

Prigogine and Stengers identify these "far-from-equilibrium conditions" as the solution to how to combine linear time (irreversible processes) with cyclical time (reversible processes). Far-from-equilibrium conditions transform the system from a state of disorder and chaos to that of order. In doing so, a new system is formed as "new dynamic states of matter may originate." As I argue in this chapter, the same occurs in Heroic Epic Fantasy fiction as these far-from-equilibrium conditions cause a new system to originate entirely. These far-from-equilibrium conditions are a result of the Fantasyland having reached a point of extreme conditions (the increase in entropy that begins to thin or tear apart the world), and is further fuelled by the actions of the heroes as strange attractors (as discussed in Chapter 3), as heroes increase greater turmoil in the system in order to bring about change.

In response to these chaotic actions, the populace of Fantasyland demonstrates that they prefer a hegemonic order to that of chaos. Accordingly, Heroic Epic Fantasy cycles back and forth between states of utopia and anti-utopia as the populace responds to change. In *The Image of the Future* (1973), Frederik Polak argues that:

> Poised on the dividing line between past and future is man, the unique bearer and transformer of culture. [...] His mental capacity to categorize and reorder reality within the self (present reality) and in relation to perceptions of the not-self (the Other) enable him to be a citizen of two worlds: the present and the imagined. (1)

Similarly, as the Heroic Epic Fantasy hero navigates past narrative bifurcation points (Figure 2.1), the hero's actions result in a tipping of balance in the world's equilibrium (Figure 5.1). The hero is thus a "transformer of culture," bridging the current disintegrating Fantasyland with the image of a re-unified Fantasyland. This chapter expands on these discussions, arguing that, by fulfilling their function as a strange attractor, the Heroic Epic Fantasy hero is able to operate as a "transformer of culture."

I explore these ideas in further detail utilising Brandon Sanderson's *Hero of Ages* (2008), the last book of the *Mistborn* trilogy (2006–2008), as a case study. The *Mistborn* trilogy begins at a "far-from-equilibrium condition," where blankets of ash cover the air causing vegetation to perish. While Sanderson does not explicitly mention the term "far-from-equilibrium conditions," the trilogy overtly depicts conceptions of chaos and, moreover, demonstrates how the populace responds to these conditions by attempting to restore a utopia or anti-utopia. Using *Hero of Ages* as a case study, in this chapter, I examine cycles of stability and instability in *Hero of Ages* in order to discuss the effect that chaos and the attempt to attain equilibrium has on the structure of the Heroic Epic Fantasy plot and the final resolution of the main conflict of the narrative.

Cycles of Utopia and Anti-Utopia

Often in Heroic Epic Fantasy fiction the narration will depict an idea of an Edenic time that takes place prior to the events of the novel. A nostalgia of a lost past is, in fact, part of the Epic tradition, as M. M. Bakhtin indicates in *The Dialogic Imagination* (1975, translated 1981): "The world of the epic is the national heroic past: it is a world of 'beginnings' and 'peak times' in the national history, a world of fathers and of founders of families, a world of 'firsts' and 'bests'" (13). Likewise, in Heroic Epic Fantasy, heroes are described as stronger, more powerful, more heroic in these earlier times, in the 'Age of Legends' – a time period depicted within the Heroic Epic Fantasy text through the use of excerpts and references to mythologies, histories, religious texts, and prophecies. For instance, in Sanderson's *Mistborn* trilogy: "*Kelsier had heard stories. He had heard whispers of times when once, long ago, the sun had not been red. [...] Those days, however, were nearly forgotten. Even the legends were growing vague*" (*Mistborn: The Final Empire* 5, original emphasis). The characters have heard stories, almost 'legends,' of an ideal time before Fantasyland had deteriorated. The characters also note that the mistborns (magic users) were more powerful in earlier ages because the power gifted by a divinity was more concentrated in these first mistborns. In the sequel *Alloy of Law* (2011), which is set three hundred years later, this pattern continues as the characters note that the heroes of legend – those characters from the first trilogy – are more powerful than can be found at this time. It seems that the society of the current age always imagines the world of the past as a stronger, and thus a more blissful, one. But the Edenic past also necessitates the idea of a 'fall.' A near-apocalyptic event – usually a massive battle on the world or metaphysical scale – is a physical trigger of the fall, as is described in the inner histories of J. R. R. Tolkien's *The Lord of the Rings* (1954–1955), David and Leigh Eddings' *Belgariad* series (1982–1984), James Clemens' *Banned and the Banish* series (1998–2002), David Farland's *Runelords* series (1998–present), and in countless other novels. As the previous chapters considered, this fall is connected to entropy, which acts on Fantasyland before the events of the novel. The 'fall' is another expression of 'breaking,' the thinning of the boundary walls of Fantasyland, making it incomplete and un-whole.

As Heroic Epic Fantasy is cyclical, the conclusion of Heroic Epic Fantasy achieves a state that is not quite utopic in order to leave room for a 'fall' to occur again in a sequel series. As Brian Attebery concludes in "Fantasy as an Anti-Utopian Mode" (1986):

> In fantasy, the ideal world is one in which the individual can achieve heroic status. In utopia, the ideal is a world in which no one need be a hero. Fantasy depends on its dangers and its villains, its eternal struggle between light and shadow. Utopia attempts to arrange the light so as to eliminate the shadows. In a fantasy, the good is a goal never reached but always visible. (6)

Heroic Epic Fantasy is a *constant struggle* to achieve a utopia – a utopia that can never be reached. Consequently, the hero of Heroic Epic Fantasy fiction can only return the world to an Edenic or Utopic state for a brief, flickering moment. In fact, the idea of a perfect static existence is often found to be problematic in utopian theory, as Lyman Tower Sargent describes in "The Three Faces of Utopianism Revisited" (1994): "the words *perfect* and *perfection*, with their suggestion of completed, finish, static, and unchanging, were frequently used, and the issue of perfection, as has already been mentioned, still bedevils scholarship" (21, original emphasis). A utopia that achieves perfection is not possible, as perfection itself is not a desirable state as it suggests inflexibility. Many Science Fiction (SF) scholars have discussed the relationship between Utopic Fiction and SF, whether they are distinct literatures or if Utopic Fiction is a subset of SF fiction. In *Metamorphoses of Science Fiction* (1970), Darko Suvin concludes that:

> Strictly and precisely speaking, utopia is not a genre but the *sociopolitical subgenre of science fiction*. [...] SF is at the same time wider than and at least collaterally descended from utopia; it is, if not a daughter, yet a niece of utopia. (61, original emphasis)

Much of SF criticism relates Utopia to SF. Thus, by identifying Fantasy as an Anti-Utopia, this classification not only draws comparison to Utopic Fiction but to SF as well.

In *The Final Empire* (2006), the first book of Sanderson's *Mistborn* trilogy, a group of thieves and miscreants gather to overthrow the tyrannies of Lord Ruler, a man who claims immense, seemingly omnipotent, power and sets himself up as god. Consequently, the group must not only abolish the existing government which has remained stagnant for a thousand years, but they must also overturn the one remaining religion on the world and kill a god. In this way, Heroic Epic Fantasy fiction often depicts a unity of political and religious power. At the end of the first novel, Kelsier, the leader of this team and a hero of the slave class (called skaa), sacrifices himself, allowing himself to be killed so that the skaa will rise up in revolution in response and destroy the existing government. When Vin, the main protagonist of the novel, manages to kill Lord Ruler, Kelsier becomes deified in turn, and a "Church of the Survivor" springs up amongst the skaa, replacing the previous church.[1] Thus, the first book depicts the replacement of a god, a political and religious figure, who has maintained power for a thousand years ago. At the end of the novel, the surviving members of the protagonist group conquer the city and place an ally, a man from the noble class, on the throne. The rebellious group hope that placing nobility on the throne will give the replacement of Lord Ruler some measure of legitimacy.

In the next book, *The Well of Ascension* (2007), which takes place a year after the events of the previous novel, the characters find that King Elend Straff is unable to maintain order among the citizens. Throughout this second novel, Elend endeavours to give the populace democracy and instigate laws that give the skaa freedom. But entropy continues to increase in Fantasyland and the world faces a literal collapse. Although Elend attempts to regain the people's confidence by proclaiming himself a member of the Church of the Survivor, he is eventually voted out of his own throne by the council that he himself had set up. Elend is compelled to reclaim the throne through force using a koloss army (an army of inhuman 'superhumans') after his attempt to regain power by reinstating the unity of church and state fails. Thus, ultimately, at the end of the novel, Elend and Vin re-establish a non-democratic, tyrannical government over the capital city barely a year after overthrowing the previous one.

Through this new government the heroes create what Sargent describes as a "convinced utopian [trying] to build a eutopia":

> When a convinced utopian tries to build a eutopia, conflict will arise because, failing to achieve eutopia, he or she will use force to achieve it. Force will be necessary either because people question the desirability of the eutopia or because there is disharmony between the perfect blueprint and the imperfect people. Eutopians will not, and cannot, give up the vision [...]. Life in a perfect society is best even for imperfect people because they will accept it as better or law (force) will impose it. Antiutopians conclude that only the last alternate is possible. They believe that a deliberately constructed society of this sort can only be maintained by the continual use of force. ("The Three Faces of Utopianism Revisited" 24)

This idea, of a convinced utopian who has failed, is comparable to the idea of the ou-hero that was explored in Chapter 4. Throughout *The Well of Ascension* and *The Hero of Ages*, Vin and Elend spend much time in contemplating the tyranny of their government, as they wish to implement the perfect (eutopic) society for their people, but can only do so through force. Vin and Elend fear repeating Lord Ruler's mistakes, as they later learn that the Lord Ruler was an ou-hero himself; he was an ordinary man who took on omnipotent powers and set himself up as the god Lord Ruler in order to *save* humanity:

> *So, instead of plants that died from the distorted sun and ashy ground, we got plants that didn't provide quite enough nutrition. He did save the world. True, the near-destruction was his fault in the first place – but he did an admirable job, all things considered.* (Hero of Ages 164, original emphasis)

Both parties suggest that their tyrannical rule is what is best for their people. Though Lord Ruler is initially presented as an antagonist, and Elend and Vin are presented as protagonists, both parties incorrectly identify themselves as heroes: they mistakingly believe their actions will *save* the world. They are eutopic rulers, ou-heroes, who resort to using force to implement their idea of a utopian society, which instead results in an anti-utopian depiction of society.

However, unlike Lord Ruler, Elend and Vin hope that their dictatorship is a *temporary* measure and that eventually a democratic government can be put in place once the world is saved. The word 'dictator,' in fact, is a Roman political position where a chief magistrate would take emergency powers during a time of crisis for a short amount of time (*Encyclopædia Britannica*). Thus, the position is meant to be a short-term one and eventually the freedoms and rights of the people would be returned to them. In the same way, Elend and Vin do not believe that their society needs to be "maintained by the continual use of force" (Sargent 24). The world at this point in the novel is literally coming to an end, a "far-from-equilibrium" situation. Earthquakes in the planet suggest that the world has come too close to the sun and is, again quite literally, falling apart. The mists and the ash have increased to the point where very little sunlight can reach the vegetation and the human race faces starvation and extinction.[2] This is an extraordinary situation and consequently, the dictatorship established by the protagonists is hoped to be a temporary one that would heal the land and return it to its previously unbroken state. In contrast, Lord Ruler's tyrannical government is brought about because of stagnation. During his thousand years of rule, he suppresses all areas of progress and technology:

> *The Lord Ruler didn't just forbid certain technologies, he suppressed technological advancement completely. It seems odd now that during the entirety of his thousand-year reign, very little progress was made.* [...] *He constructed his perfect empire, then tried to make it stay that way.* (Hero of Ages 242–243, original emphasis)

Note the language used with regard to utopia (or anti-utopia), as Lord Ruler creates a "*perfect* empire, then tried to make it stay that way" (my emphasis).

The god or king whose authority is seen as antagonistic *because* of this stagnation is a common motif across many Heroic Epic Fantasy fictions. As entropy is increasing in Fantasyland, the authoritative figure that is unwilling to act or move is detrimental to restoring Fantasyland. For example, in Michael Moorcock's "While the Gods Laugh" (1961–1962), Elric attempts to gain knowledge of a book that could swing the balance into favouring either the forces of Law or the forces of Chaos. But instead of attempting to tip the balance into favouring the forces of Law, the Masters (or divinity) fear the other outcome, and accordingly hide and guard the book: "*We exist only to fight – not to win, but to preserve the eternal struggle*" (69, original emphasis). As the *Elric* series moves from Localised to Epic, Elric is depicted as the only one who is able to restore the balance of the world: "Lower dipped the Balance as Chaos gained strength, weaker became Law, and only Elric who bore the Black Sword could right the Balance by his actions" (Epigraph to "Doomed Lord's Passing" 384). Note the conscious use of the ideas of balance and chaos. But balance here does not simply mean defeating chaos, it means a complete destruction of the current age of humanity, so that: "history will not begin for many thousands of years, the type may take on a lowlier form, become more beastlike before it re-evolves" ("Dead God's Homecoming" 270). In order to reset the delicate balance, the hero must bring about the end of the world in order for it to evolve into something greater – an idea that will be explored in the latter part of this chapter.

In Ursula K. Le Guin's *The Farthest Shore* (1971), another foundational Fantasy text, although stagnation is not yet established, the hero Ged fears that the world will be corrupted by stasis:

> A false king ruling. Ruling forever. And over the same subject forever. No births; no new lives. No children. Only what is mortal bears life, Arren. Only in death is there rebirth. The Balance is not a stillness. It is a movement – an eternal becoming. (423)

Just as in other Heroic Epic Fantasy fictions, in Le Guin's *Earthsea* series (1968–2001), achieving and maintaining balance does not indicate stagnation; it means a *constant movement*, "an eternal becoming," or a constant creation into something new and different.

However, a constant cyclicality can be seen as a stasis too if it is unable to bring anything new into the cycle. For instance, in Robert Jordan's *The Wheel of Time* series (1990–2012), the antagonist warns the hero Rand al'Thor that he has been battling the Dark One in a war that occurs again and again:

> Do you have any glimmering that we have fought before, battles without number back to the beginning of Time? [...] That battle will

soon end. The Last Battle is coming. [...] And this time the cycle will not begin anew with your death. [...] This time the Wheel will be broken whatever you do, and the world remade to a new mold. (*The Great Hunt* 243)

As the Wheel of Time repeats itself, a reincarnation of Rand has been battling the Dark One since the beginning of time. This cycle of repetition is a pattern of stasis itself and can only be broken if a new pattern is established.

In the *Mistborn* trilogy, though the government under Lord Ruler is tyrannical, and it is this very lack of progress that leads to an anti-utopian state of tyranny, following the defeat of Lord Ruler it is apparent that the population *prefers* this state as it offers stability. Though many of them were slaves, people mourn the death of Lord Ruler as they find comfort in the routine. Additionally, as the food supplies had diminished greatly since his death, the people find that the world under King Elend's rule is a much harsher one than under Lord Ruler even though Elend is not to blame for these conditions. These reactions indicate that *the stability of their oppression is preferred to the chaos of their freedom*. For this reason, throughout *Hero of Ages*, various citizens rebel against King Elend's rule and set up their own city-states, temporarily restoring stability to the populace. After the collapse of Lord Ruler's thousand-year rule, a period where the civilisation was in complete stasis, the cycle repeats itself in smaller patterns, as various citizens and city-states rebel against the current government, as they try to return to the equilibrium they are familiar with (Figure 8.1).

Each of the independent city-state governments mimics Lord Ruler's tyrannical rule regardless of the class-system their new government is based on: Yomen is a member of Lord Ruler's original government, Penrod is a nobleman, and Quellion is a skaa, but all three governments restrict the skaa population back into slavery. The men leading these cities are directly paralleled to Lord Ruler: "Seems that the longer old Quellion is in charge, the more he looks like that rat the Survivor killed"

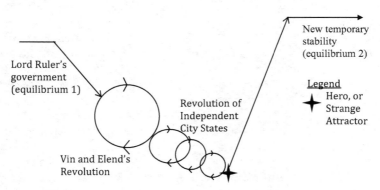

Figure 8.1 The Cycles of Sanderson's *Mistborn* Trilogy.

(217). All three governments, though they originate from different classes in society, all repress their populace back into a state comparable to before the revolution, when Lord Ruler governed the world. These new governmental bodies embody the conception Karl Marx has of the lower middle class in *The Communist Manifesto* (1888, Jones translation, 2002):

> The lower middle class, the small manufacturer, the shopkeeper, the artisan, the peasant, all these fight against the bourgeoisie, to save from extinction their existence as fractions of the middle class. They are therefore not revolutionary, but conservative. Nay more, they are reactionary, for they try to roll back the wheel of history. (231)

These governments "fight against the bourgeoisie," Elend's kingship, *not* because they are revolutionary, but in fact because they are counter-revolutionary; they "try to roll back the wheel of history."

True revolution can only come from a leader who ascends from all classes, a hero who acts a bridge between all members of the community. In political terms, the hero seems to embody Marx's idea of the communist as the assembly of heroes draws together the common interests of the community in the figures of a small group of agents:

> The Communists are distinguished from the other working-class parties by this only: 1. In the national struggles of the proletarians of the different countries, they point out and bring to the front the common interests of the entire proletariat, independently of all nationality. (234)

As suggested in Chapter 5, the group of heroes are all individuals representing their own species or race. Each member of the fellowship is isolated in some way from their own community, but they are unified in the larger group of protagonists. This group of heroes represent "the common interests of the entire proletariat, independently of all nationality." But Heroic Epic Fantasy heroes are not communist, not truly, because they are rarely from the working-class, but instead are often a member of nobility or the bourgeoisie.[3] Their relationship to the proletariat differs from the Marxist ideal.

Thus, in order to "ascend from all classes," religious terminology is used to bypass and amalgamate different strands of society. *Ascension* from all classes can only occur with messianic figures. These characters are noble-born but identify with the other classes, either due to upbringing (fostering with lower-class parents, for example) or adoption into the community via a pilgrimage experience (Paul Atreides in Herbert's *Dune*, 1965, is a foundational example). The heroes recognise that they are part of a larger group, an ecological network, as the characters start to recognise the connections between occurrences in the world and their own place and purposes within these networks:

> *I speak of us as "we." The group. Those of us who were trying to discover and defeat Ruin.* [...] *I like to look back and see the sum of what we were doing as a single, united assault, though we were all involved in different processes and plans. We were one.* (Hero of Ages 64, original emphasis)

The hero here accurately summarises the unity of the group in defeating the antagonist force, even if they were "all involved in different processes and plans." As emblems of their community, the unity of the heroic group suggests that the defeat of the antagonist force must be a result of collective human agency. Revolution must come from the entire populace (represented through the collective group of heroes) if it is to be successful, or risk deteriorating into greater and greater entropy.

This conception of the necessity of unity is similar to Sargent's summary of Plutarch's description of the founding of Sparta in *Utopianism* (2010): "in Lycurgus's Sparta every person was to completely dedicate themselves to the country. They were to lose themselves in the whole: 'he trained his fellow-citizens to have neither the wish nor the ability to live for themselves'" (17). Each hero or protagonist must dedicate themselves to the whole, sacrificing their life if required in order to restore Fantasyland. For example, as the latter half of this chapter will describe further, in order to prevent the metaphysical entity Ruin from regaining his body and thereby gaining power, the kandra society is required to commit suicide at the prophesised moment so that Ruin cannot take control of their bodies and act through them. Like the Spartans, they were supposed to "have neither the wish nor the ability to live for themselves" (Sargent 17). But instead of abiding by the wishes of the whole, many of the kandra population attempt to overthrow their governing body, as they do not desire any harm to come to their utopic existence. The population desires stability even if it results in suffering. Consider, for example, J. K. Rowling's *The Order of the Phoenix* (2003), where many of the people refuse to accept the return of the antagonist Voldemort, and instead assent to stricter and stricter rules as the governing body attempt to suppress any free thought that suggests Voldemort's return. To the populace, a *hegemonic order is better than chaos*. It is the heroes' role to rebel against this order and collectively work together in order to break out of the flat line of stability and progress into the future.

From Flow to Turbulence

As identified above, the reason Utopic Fiction is distinct from Fantasy fiction is because of a struggle and search for perfection. As Attebery argues:

> [S]uch themes are incompatible with utopian thought. The idea of restoring the world, in particular, might seem to lend itself to the presentation of a perfected society from which evil and injustice are expelled by the exertions of a hero. But healing a land is not the same as perfecting it. In a fantasy, the well-being of an individual or of a land (and in fantasy the two are ultimately inseparable) is expressed as a matter of being in harmony with nature. [And] nature nowhere demonstrates perfection [...]. ("Fantasy as an Anti-Utopian Mode" 8)

While it is possible to *heal* Fantasyland from its broken state, it is unlikely that the Fantasyland will persist in a perfect condition; once this state is reached, entropy will once more begin to act on Fantasyland. A stable Edenic state – one that is static – is not possible.

As the population attempts to return to a life that they are familiar with even if it leads to further repression and entropy, how do the heroes *heal* Fantasyland if it is caught in a cycle of repetition, which is itself stagnant? In this universe governed by entropy, how does order arise? How does equilibrium re-establish itself? N. Katherine Hayles answers these questions for a real-world system in *Chaos Bound* (1990):

> [C]haos is seen as order's precursor and partner, rather than as its opposite. The focus here is on the spontaneous emergency of self-organization from chaos; or, in the parlance of the field, on the dissipative structures that arise in systems far from equilibrium, where entropy production is high. The realization that entropy-rich systems facilitate rather than impede self-organization was an important turning point [...]. (9)

Illuminating Prigogine and Stengers' ideas in *Order out of Chaos*, Hayles describes how order arises out of chaos: "The essential change is *to see chaos as that which makes order possible*. Life arises not in spite but because of dissipative processes that are rich in entropy production. Chaos is the womb of life, not its tomb" (Hayles 100, original emphasis). Chaos allows life to occur, and thus makes order possible.

As emphasised in Chapters 6 and 7, the plot of Fantasyland is one that is triggered by flows and seepages. This flow increases exponentially until it becomes turbulent, pushing the system into a "far-from-equilibrium condition." Accordingly, when entropy has increased so dramatically in Fantasyland that the world is near collapse, the hero steps in as strange attractor, assisting the bifurcation point into selecting the 'correct' path. Recall from Chapter 3 how in a system of flow, as velocity of the flow increases, strange attractors pull these movements towards them, increasing turbulence and causing further dissipation of energy. This visual conception can also be applied as a metaphor to describe the

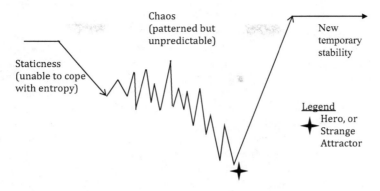

Figure 8.2 Increase in Turbulence Creating a New Equilibrium.

heroes of Heroic Epic Fantasy fiction. Prigogine and Stengers assert that: "At all levels [...] *nonequilibrium is the source of order. Nonequilibrium brings 'order out of chaos'*" (286–287, original emphasis). Chapter 3 considered that the heroes increase turbulence in a system, while simultaneously bringing stability. Here I expand on that argument and assert that, through the increase in turbulence, heroes as strange attractors push the entropy system *further into increasing* nonequilibrium, into a far-from-equilibrium situation. This imbalance, in turn, creates a new and different equilibrium, bringing order out of chaos as in Figure 8.2.

Note that in Figure 8.2, while a flat line of stability is established in a new equilibrium, the line has shifted slightly so that the stable line is at a different position than the original line of stability, making it a new and different system. Consequently, instead of returning the world to an Edenic state, I assert that the coming of the hero allows society to move forward in time, *past* the static existence in order to progress into the future. While Fantasyland may reach a utopia, this state is only temporary, as a static utopia would prevent progress. This idea of progressing past staticness is similar to different political interpretations of utopia. For instance, Suvin views utopia as degrees of perfection, as "more perfect" than our society but *not* an "absolutely perfect place" ("Degrees of Kinship" 36); Ernst Bloch perceives utopias as a dynamic quality, as utopia that are yet to be, the "Not-Yet-Conscious, Not-Yet-Become" (*The Principle of Hope* 129); Sargent brackets off the idea of perfection in utopia as something that opposes a totalitarian static state ("The Three Faces of Utopianism Revisited"). These perspectives of utopia view it *not* as a static existent, but instead a progressive one, where constant change will allow for a better future. Polak argues that: "Social change will be viewed as a push-pull process in which a society is at once pulled forward by its own magnetic images of an idealized future and pushed from behind by its realized past" (1). Society's idealistic or realistic image of the future in the present affects the outcome of the actual future. By bringing order out of chaos, the Heroic Epic Fantasy hero pushes Fantasyland into the future through the broken remains of its past, re-creating a new, unbroken Fantasyland; a new world entirely.

The idea of life arising out of chaos is not entirely a new one as it can be seen in various Mythologies. In *The Hero with a Thousand Faces* (1949), Joseph Campbell indicates that there are two stages of the world: "First, from the immediate emanations of the Uncreated Creating to the fluid yet timeless personages of the mythological age; second, from these Created Creating Ones to the sphere of human history" (271). The same holds true in Heroic Epic Fantasy; as in many creation stories, the world and the gods are created from chaos first, who then in turn create humanity. The multiple forgotten religions presented in *Hero of Ages* also depict similar creation stories:

> "Ruin and Preservation [...] They created our world, and our people."
> "Neither could create alone," [...]
> "For, to preserve something is not to create it – and neither can you create through destruction only." It was a common theme in mythology – Sazed had read it in dozens of the religions he'd studied. The world being created out of a clash between two forces, sometimes rendered as chaos and order, sometimes named destruction and protection. (*Hero of Ages* 621–622)

The origin stories found in Mythologies and recreated in Epic Fantasies are similar to the way that modern chaos theory is understood. In *Chaos* (1987), James Gleick suggests that in some systems of chaos: "order arises spontaneously in those systems – chaos and order together" (8), just as the origins of the universe is depicted in Epics.

Just like the presentation of entropy, ideas of chaos and order are often overtly depicted in Heroic Epic Fantasy as well. There are several types of chaos. While in *Chaos Bound* Hayles defines the first branch of chaos as "order out of chaos," Hayles distinguishes the second branch of chaos theory as: "order that exists *within* chaotic systems" (9, original emphasis). Gleick simplifies this second branch as: "order *masquerading* as randomness" (22, original emphasis). One simply has to take a step back and see the bigger picture so that the pattern of order could be identified in a seemingly random pattern. In Fantasy fiction, this second system often occurs in the way magic is depicted, as, since magic is often a result of metaphysical interaction, the influence of a conscious metaphysical entity results in a deliberately ordered system. For example, in *Hero of Ages*, when the 'natural' mists of the world start killing people or making them ill, it is later revealed that this phenomenon is too precise to be accidental:

> The calculation came out to be exact – precisely sixteen percent of the soldiers fell sick. [...]
> "It's like the chaos of normal random statistics has broken down".
> (191–192)

Note that the text explicitly evokes the idea of chaos itself, especially in how it relates to statistics as it would occur naturally in a bell curve. The pattern of order only begins to emerge when the army starts to keep a record of the number of people who fall sick and try to make sense of the seeming chaos.[4] Such an exact number (sixteen percent in *every* population group) cannot be attributed to coincidence or randomness, and instead indicates that an entity is influencing these events. Eventually, the characters realise that the number sixteen is a divine number because the number of allomantic metals ('special' metals that trigger magical abilities) are also sixteen in number. There is a precise mathematical order to the way the metals give magical abilities. Thus, this special percentage of sixteen is a clear sign of 'order,' of some divine or metaphysical force at work that is manipulating the universe into a recognisable pattern. This force, Preservation, had intervened for a purpose: although allomancy is an inherited quality, the magical ability can only be triggered once a person undergoes a traumatic event. The people who had fallen sick as a result to being exposed to the mist are those who have a repressed allomantic ability, exactly sixteen percent of the population; after recovery, they are able to use this magical ability.

While Hayles indicates that in the real world the two branches of chaos theory – order out of chaos and order within chaos – are usually incompatible with each other, in Heroic Epic Fantasy, these branches are fused through the actions of a divinity that attempts to create order in a chaotic system; they do so by introducing the heroes as strange attractors as a catalyst. As the previous two chapters considered, as abnormal metaphysical entities flow into Fantasyland, the entropy of Fantasyland increases exponentially, causing the flow of the abnormal entities to increase further. This exponential increase triggers a turbulent system. Recall that strange attractors: "served as efficient mixers. They created unpredictability. They raised entropy" (Gleick 258). Rather than simply restoring order, the heroes as strange attractors draw further turbulence to them.

Though they raise entropy, strange attractors "had the important property of stability" (Gleick 138), as Heroic Epic Fantasy heroes *also* create a level of organisation by triggering a far-from-equilibrium situation. Prigogine and Stengers indicate that once flow rate has increased until it forms turbulence, this turbulence, though it may appear to be disordered and irregular, is, on another level, seen to be ordered: "turbulent motion appears as irregular or chaotic on the macroscopic scale, it is, on the contrary, highly organized on the microscopic scale" (Prigogine and Stengers 141). The increase in turbulence leads to a far-from-equilibrium situation in which self-organisation emerges (9). Prigogine and Stengers identify that this self-organisation can *only* occur in far-from-equilibrium situations: "To use somewhat anthropomorphic language: in equilibrium matter is 'blind,' but in far-from-equilibrium conditions it begins to be able to perceive, to 'take into account,' in its way of functioning, differences in the external world" (14). Prigogine and Stengers argue that when disorder increases dramatically, the system will correct itself, almost as if the system itself is conscious of its own imbalance: "Viewed in this way, the transition from laminar flow to turbulence is a process of self-organization" (141–142). This is certainly true in Heroic Epic Fantasy, as the system introduces an element that will correct itself through the form of the heroes. These heroes act as strange attractors, further increasing the entropy of the system, so that the system will reach a far-from-equilibrium condition allowing a new self-organised system to emerge. As depicted in Figure 8.2, turbulence increases in the system until a new level of equilibrium has been reached.

It should be noted that far-from-equilibrium conditions are more frequent in long-running series or in sequel series. When one considers the plot of individual novels or the plot of the first half of a series, it is far more likely that the hero is able to re-establish the balance through a descent to the underworld which acts to tip the balance back into equilibrium (as represented in Figure 5.1) without having to reach a far-from-equilibrium condition that completes unmakes and then remakes the world. This 'simple' tipping back into balance is what occurs in Gail Z. Martin's *The Summoner* (2007) or Lois McMaster Bujold's *The Curse of Chalion* (2001), where the hero's confrontation with death leads to a rebalance of the system. As well, individual novels in a series may also start off lower down in the Epic scale and gradually increase in 'epicness' as the antagonist is defeated and a greater antagonist emerges. This is what occurs in Jordan's *The Wheel of Time*, for example, as the antagonist is defeated in the first novel; each defeat of an antagonist leads to a greater one arising, creating a system that is more tumultuous, until the system needs to be remade entirely if the hero has any hope of restoring balance. This idea is made overt in *The Wheel of Time*, as the characters continually comment that the 'Wheel of Time' itself is breaking. As these Heroic Epic Fantasy series continue, the idea of restoring balance through a simple tipping of the equilibrium starts to become replaced with a descent into greater and greater unbalance, eventually leading to an extreme "far-from-equilibrium" condition where the hero will completely break and then re-establish a new Fantasyland.

The Hero as Catalyst

By functioning as strange attractors, the heroes act as agents of change in a Fantasyland that is stuck in stagnation. As Farah Mendlesohn indicates in *Rhetorics of Fantasy* (2008): "the hero moves through the action and the world state, embedding an assumption of unchangingness on the part of the indigenes. This kind of fantasy is essentially imperialist: only the hero is capable of change; fantasyland is orientalised into the 'unchanging past'" (9).[5] Heroes – as opposed to ou-heroes – are confirmed in their status *as* heroes by being capable of bringing about change in a Fantasyland that is stuck in stagnation. This is the case with Lord Ruler's government persisting in a fixed state for a thousand years in a state of "eternal" tyranny; it is rooted in an "unchanging past." As described above, the population in the *Mistborn* trilogy often demonstrate their willingness to return to a government similar to the one under Lord Ruler, even if it results in a loss of freedoms, as long as it provides a comfort in stability. Thus, the hero asserts, "*That didn't stop the world from ending, but that's not necessarily a bad thing*" (*Hero of Ages* 64, original emphasis). An apocalypse is desirable because it suggests an implementation of a completely new system, a revolution that results in a new political system and often a new religion as well. But, as the previous chapter established, in order for this to occur, the hero must first remove an abnormal metaphysical entity, which may involve the death of a god or king.

Heroes as strange attractors are thus a source of instability and change and their arrival in the community might be a fearful one, as the arrival of the hero marks something strange and new in a static world. Part of the prophecies of the hero in the *Mistborn* trilogy states that the hero will be: "*one who would be an emperor of all mankind, yet would be rejected by his own people*" (608, original emphasis). Heroes may initially be rejected because they bring change to a population that does not desire it. In *Hero of Ages*, the arrival of Sazed and TenSoon into the kandra community denotes them as agents of change *because* of their isolation and individuality from this species. The kandra were originally humans, a race of Terris people, before they were transformed into a new species. While TenSoon is a member of the kandra community himself, Sazed is one of the last surviving members of the Terris people.

The kandra species are conscious, intelligent, shapeless creatures that are capable of mutating and mimicking other forms and species. But this ability, along with their consciousness, can only occur because of the physical penetration of a unique metal – a portion of a god's body – into their own body. As in the examples from the previous chapter, the metaphysical entity can only use another host body as an avatar through the physical penetration of it. Before the events of the series, the First Generation of kandra had made a promise to the ou-hero Lord Ruler that at a prophesised time – called The Resolution – their entire community will remove this metal from their body, thereby losing their consciousness, but in the process preventing Ruin, an antagonistic metaphysical entity, from using their bodies as vessels for his own will. The arrival of the heroes into their community signifies a time of change and that The Resolution is at hand.

Revolution here works in a plurality of ways. When TenSoon speaks to the kandra people and tells that the time of Resolution is near, the kandra decide to ignore his words and punish TenSoon instead: "TenSoon was to be their sacrifice. Their way of restoring order and orthodoxy" (83). Interestingly, though the kandra society is depicted as a "utopia" (67), there are still entire generations that are seen as rebellious, and thus TenSoon's death is meant to act as a type of scapegoat in order to restore stability. This idea of a scapegoat is reminiscent of the messianic hero, but, whereas the messianic hero is the end-point of an apocalyptic time whose sacrifice brings a new world into being, here, the peoples hope that TenSoon's sacrifice will maintain the status quo. When the First Generation (the governing body of the kandra people) come to realise that TenSoon's words should be followed and announce that the time of Resolution is at hand, the Second Generation take charge in a coup instead, attempting to overthrow the long-standing government so that *stability can be maintained*:

> "You fear change," Sazed said, meeting the kandra's eyes.
> "I fear instability," KanPaar said. "I will make certain the kandra people have a firm and immutable leadership." (662)

Rather than listen to the wisdom of their established leaders, the government is overthrown, so that the kandra way of life can continue to be the same, and thus their revolution brings stasis. It is only through the actions of the heroes that the kandra community eventually accept the sacrifice that they must make, removing the devices that had given them consciousness in order to allow the rest of Fantasyland to progress into the future. The prophecy in the *Mistborn* trilogy predicts: "The Hero will have the power to save the world. But he will also have the power to destroy it" (715). The coming of the hero destroys the familiar world and society. But the hero can only *save* the world by first destroying it in order for it to be rebuilt anew. This destruction also allows society to move forward in time, *past* the static Utopic existence, and progress into the future.

The hero Sazed is able to do so by taking on the power of two contradictory forces, creation and destruction, creating a unity or whole out of two broken parts. In the *Mistborn* trilogy, the metaphysical entities of Ruin and Preservation both belong together in order to bring balance: "Ruin and Preservation were dead, and their powers had been joined together. In fact, they belonged together. How had they been split?" (718). If Ruin is to stand for 'entropy' and Preservation for 'stability,' both cannot exist as individual entities, as they are opposite to each other. While Preservation is generally seen as the benevolent metaphysical entity and Ruin the malevolent one, Preservation recognises that the act of preservation – stasis – is detrimental to the act of creation. Humanity can only be created with the combination of Ruin and Preservation together, through order out of chaos. And so Preservation: "obtained a promise from Ruin to help make men" (*Hero of Ages* 622). But this promise had a caveat in it, "That Ruin could one day be allowed to destroy the world" (622). Preservation wanted to create humanity because he realised that it could not destroy Ruin, as its job is to preserve not destroy. With the help of Ruin, Preservation could create humans, one of whom will arise as hero and have the capability of destroying Ruin. And yet, while their removal is necessary in order for progress to be made, this new system must be a combination of both powers if it too is going to be able to take part in creation: "*He wouldn't simply bear the power of Preservation. He needed the power of Ruin as well.* [...] For these two powers had been used to create all things. If they fought, they destroyed. If they were used together, they created" (715, original emphasis). The hero thus takes on the power of two contradictory metaphysical entities creating a new equilibrium out of their unity, establishing their *wholeness*. The fractured Fantasyland is not simply healed but completely remade into a new whole. At this extreme far-from-equilibrium moment, one where the entire planet is facing collapse, Sazed destroys and then replaces these divine entities with himself, taking on their powers. In doing so, the hero is able to remake Fantasyland, creating a new paradise.

Other heroes through the *Mistborn* trilogy also sacrifice themselves in an attempt to save the world, but ultimately, they fail in their quest as they are unable to comprehend the wholeness of Ruin and Preservation, and thus they are redefined as ou-heroes. These ou-heroes are unable to comprehend the balance between the two – that Ruin and chaos are necessary for creation to occur – and consequently take the side of Preservation in order to defeat Ruin. The first human ou-hero to emerge is Lord Ruler, who takes on the metaphysical power of Preservation in order to save the world. Through his attempt to maintain order, Lord Ruler becomes a tyrant, and thus fails as hero, becoming an ou-hero. Later, Vin and Elend's attempt at establishing order after Lord Ruler's death proves to have the same consequences as that of Lord Ruler's regime. Like Lord Ruler, Vin misinterprets the prophecies. She takes on the power of Preservation in order to save the world, but in doing so, becomes an ou-hero herself at the end of the second novel. Throughout the third novel, the potential remains that Vin may still become a realised hero. The removal of Vin and Elend at the end of the trilogy then eliminates the risk of them becoming ou-heroes again.

Through the process of establishing a new equilibrium, heroes – both heroes and ou-heroes – are themselves 'used up' in an act of sacrifice, just as a catalyst in a chemical reaction. Often, even if the messianic act does not result in a permanent literal death, heroes may remove themselves from Fantasyland after a new equilibrium is established in order to avoid the risk of starting a new cycle of stagnation, as the hero has the capability of becoming the ou-hero if they remain. As Campbell identifies: "The hero of yesterday becomes the tyrant of tomorrow, unless he crucifies *himself* today" (303, original emphasis). After Sazed takes on the power of both Ruin and Preservation, replacing these abnormal or divine entities with himself, he then becomes "invisible" (Campbell 271), removing himself from the physical plane of humanity. The removal of the hero can be done in various ways, such as a permanent death, as in the examples of the ou-heroes above. Another possibility is that the hero is removed from normal society and their companions through the process of replacing a higher authority. The hero may become a god or a king, a type of social transcendence. This is what happens with Tylar in James Clemens' *Shadowfall* (2005), where, at the end of the novel, Tylar must rise as god-king, taking the place of the god that he had slayed.

Alternatively, the moment of transcendence may pass, and the hero is then depleted. In *Tehanu* (1990), the fourth book of Le Guin's *Earthsea* series, Ged describes how in his act of fulfilling his heroic role, his power was lost:

> "Like pouring out a little water," he said, "a cup of water on to the sand. In the dry land. I had to do that. But now I have nothing to drink. [...] All I had in the end was one cup of water, and I had to pour it out on the sand, in the bed of the dry river, on the rocks in the dark. So it's gone. It's over. Done." (546)

The language that Ged uses is that of an empty vessel that has run dry, a hero that has utilised all of his power until it has run out. He is thus able to return to a 'normal' life as a farmer, rather than resuming his position as Archmage. Cazaril in Lois McMaster Bujold's *The Curse of Chalion* (2001) describes a similar experience. Cazaril attempts to recapture the ephemeral moment where his bodily vessel was filled by god, but finds himself unable to do so: "'I have not the words for what I saw. Talking about it is like trying to weave a box of shadows in which to carry water.' *And our souls are parched*" (476, original emphasis). Although Cazaril is able to reconnect with society, this is only because his moment of transcendence is fleeting, and consequently, he finds himself profoundly changed – almost depleted. Like Ged, once he has fulfilled his messianic function of the hero, Cazaril is able to return to a 'normal' life.

The extent that heroes may remove themselves from society is dependent on the greatness of the resolution of the narrative. Is the hero able to rebalance the equilibrium through a 'simple' messianic death: a willingness to confront death or a temporary one? Or does the hero's death result in a complete breaking and then reshaping of the world? The former outcome may result in a hero who is able to return to the community, although they may be changed in some way.

Notably, either scenarios do not result in a permanent solution, as entropy will begin to act again on the re-established equilibrium. For instance, although the hero is able to reshape the entire world, fixing the shattered Fantasyland, Sanderson's plans for sequel series indicates that the land will fall again. Sanderson originally planned for the *Mistborn* trilogy to be part of a nine-book (three-trilogy) series:

> I wanted to move away from the idea of fantasy worlds as static places, where millennia would pass and technology would never change. The plan then was for a second epic trilogy set in an urban era, and a third trilogy set in a futuristic era. (*The Alloy of Law* 7)

Sanderson has not yet published these sequel trilogies, as *The Alloy of Law* and its sequels, while part of that world, is a "side deviation" (7). And yet, the conception of the sequel series themselves demonstrates the idea that the Fantasy fiction is cyclical; though the world is healed at the end of the first trilogy, sequels indicate that entropy has seeped in again, leading to another 'fall.' In the next and final chapter, I will discuss the concept of sequels in greater detail.

Notes

1. Sanderson makes overt connections between Kelsier's deification with that of Christ. Kelsier seemingly returns to the people to speak to them after his death, mimicking Christ's resurrection. In the next book, the Church of the Survivor takes on the object that killed Kelsier (a spear) as a symbol of their church, similar to the cross of Christianity.
2. N. K. Jemisin's *The Broken Earth* trilogy (2015–2017) similarly demonstrates a far-from-equilibrium situation, where the "Fifth Season" – a type of ice age period – occurs repeatedly over the course of thousands of years. George R. R. Martin's *A Song of Ice and Fire* (1996–present) likewise predicts the coming of an ice age with the repeated mantra "Winter is coming." Given the current cultural context, it is likely that these authors are making some commentary on global warming and climate change.
3. While more recently Heroic Epic Fantasy heroes are starting to originate from the lower classes, often, there still is some suggestion that these heroes might have noble bloodlines. For example, while Vin in *Mistborn* is part of the skaa class, her father is later revealed to be part of Lord Ruler's priest class.
4. An important facet of this type of chaos is the chaos of information. As established in previous chapters, it is the hero that usually is able to decipher and decode prophecy. Consequently, it is pertinent that in the *Mistborn* trilogy, the hero is revealed to be a scholar who has thoroughly investigated the prophecies and histories of the world and is only able to heal the world

through amalgamating pieces of information: "And, in a moment of transcendence, he understood it all. He saw the patterns, the clues, the secrets" (*Hero of Ages* 716).
5 As mentioned briefly in Chapter 5, there is an obvious problematic 'white saviour narrative' with the premise of an outsider who enters the community and saves it; however, this reading is complicated in post-1990s' Fantasy with the prominence of protagonist, antagonist, and central hero characters who may not fit the model.

Bibliography

Attebery, Brian. "Fantasy as an Anti-Utopian Mode." *Reflections on the Fantastic: Selected Essays from the Fourth International Conference on the Fantastic in the Arts*. Ed. Michael R. Collings. Greenwood Press, 1986. pp. 3–8.

Bakhtin, Mikhail Mikhaïlovich. *The Dialogic Imagination*. 1975. Ed. Michael Holquist. Trans. Caryl Emerson and Michael Holquist. University of Texas Press, 1981.

Bloch, Ernst. "Discovery of the Not-Yet-Conscious or of Forward Dawning." *The Principle of Hope*. 1959. Trans. Neville Plaice, Stephen Plaice, and Paul Knight. Vol. 1. Basic Blackwell, 1986. pp. 114–178.

Brett, Peter V. *Demon Cycle*. HarperCollins, 2009–2017. Demon Cycle 1–5.

Bujold, Lois McMaster. *The Curse of Chalion*. 2000. HarperCollins, 2011. Chalion 1.

Campbell, Joseph. *The Hero with a Thousand Faces*. 1949. New World Library, 2008.

Clemens, James. *The Banned and the Banished*. Del Rey, 1998–2002. The Banned and the Banished 1–5.

———. *Shadowfall*. 2005. Roc, 2006. Godslayer Trilogy 1.

Clute, John. "Fantastika in the World Storm." 2007. *Pardon this Intrusion: Fantastika in the World Storm*. Beccon Publications, 2011. pp. 19–31.

"dictātor." *Encyclopædia Britannica*. 20 July 1998. Web.

Eddings, David and Leigh. *Belgariad*. Del Rey, 1982–1984. Belgariad 1–5.

Farland, David. *The Lair of Bones*. 2003. Tom Doherty, 2005. The Runelords 4.

———. *Runelords*. Tor, 1998–2009. Runelords 1–8.

Gleick, James. *Chaos: The Amazing Science of the Unpredictable*. 1987. Vintage Books, 1998.

Hayles, N. Katherine. *Chaos Bound: Orderly Disorder in Contemporary Literature and Science*. 1990. Cornell University Press, 1994.

Herbert, Frank. *Dune*. 1965. Gollancz, 2010. Dune Saga 1.

Jemisin, Nora K. *The Broken Earth*. Orbit, 2015–2017. The Broken Earth 1–3.

Jordan, Robert. *The Great Hunt*. 1990. Tor, 1991. The Wheel of Time 2.

———. *The Wheel of Time*. Tor, 1990–2005. The Wheel of Time 1–11.

Jordan, Robert and Brandon Sanderson. *A Memory of Light*. 2012. Orbit, 2014. The Wheel of Time 14.

Le Guin, Ursula. "The Farthest Shore." 1973. *The Earthsea Quartet*. Penguin, 1992. pp. 301–478. Earthsea 3.

———. "Tehanu." 1990. *The Earthsea Quartet*. Penguin, 1992. pp. 479–691. Earthsea 4.

Martin, Gail Z. *The Summoner*. 2007. Solaris, 2012. Chronicles of the Necromancer 1.
Marx, Karl and Friedrich Engles. *The Communist Manifesto*. 1888. Ed. Gareth Stedman Jones. Penguin Classics, 2002.
Mathews, Richard. *Fantasy: The Liberation of Imagination*. 1997. Routledge, 2002.
Mendlesohn, Farah. *Rhetorics of Fantasy*. Wesleyan University Press, 2008.
Moorcock, Michael. "Dead God's Homecoming." 1963. *The Stealer of Souls: Chronicles of the Last Emperor of Melniboné Volume 1*. Ballantine Books, 2008. pp. 214–273. Stormbringer 1.
———. "Doomed Lord's Passing." 1964. *The Stealer of Souls: Chronicles of the Last Emperor of Melniboné Volume 1*. Ballantine Books, 2008. pp. 384–433. Stormbringer 4.
———. "While the Gods Laugh." 1961. *The Stealer of Souls and Other Stories*. Granada Publishing, 1968. pp. 40–72. Elric.
Polak, Fred. *The Image of the Future*. Trans. and Abr. Elise Boulding. Elsevier Scientific Publishing Company, 1973.
Prigogine, Ilya and Isabella Stengers. *Order out of Chaos: Man's New Dialogue with Nature*. 1984. Flamingo, 1985.
Rowling, Joanne K. *Harry Potter and the Order of the Phoenix*. Raincoast Books, 2003. Harry Potter 5.
Sanderson, Brandon. *The Alloy of Law*. Gollancz, 2011. Mistborn 4.
———. *The Hero of Ages*. 2008. Dragonstell Entertainment, 2010. Mistborn Trilogy 3.
———. *Mistborn: The Final Empire*. 2006. Tom Doherty, 2007. Mistborn Trilogy 1.
———. *The Well of Ascension*. 2007. Tom Doherty, 2008. Mistborn Trilogy 2.
Sargent, Lyman Tower. "The Three Faces of Utopianism Revisited." *Utopian Studies*, vol. 5, no. 1, 1994, pp. 1–37.
———. *Utopianism: A Very Short Introduction*. Oxford University Press, 2010.
Suvin, Darko. *Metamorphoses of Science Fiction*. 1979. Yale University Press, 1980.
———. "Science Fiction and Utopian Fiction: Degrees of Kinship." *Positions and Presuppositions in Science Fiction*. MacMillan, 1987. pp. 33–43.
Tolkien, John Ronald Reuel. *The Lords of the Rings*. Allen & Unwin, 1954–1955. The Lord of the Rings 1–3.

9 Chaotic Cycles

Evaluating Patterns Within
and Between Sequel Series
in David and Leigh Eddings'
The Seeress of Kell (1991)

The previous chapter considered how fractured Fantasyland is re-formed, making Fantasyland whole again. A new equilibrium is established, one that is different from the previous equilibrium (as in Figure 8.2). And yet, the practice of Heroic Epic Fantasy sequels and long-running series indicate that the resolution of the narrative is ephemeral. Fantasyland will become fractured again as the healed equilibrium is only temporary. In this chapter, I briefly consider the cycles of repetition between Heroic Epic Fantasy narratives and series as a constant movement between different equilibriums. Expanding on the discussions of the previous chapter, I argue that these cycles are chaotic. A common example of this chaotic pattern is the Butterfly Effect, which are "systems that almost repeated themselves but never quite succeeded" (James Gleick, *Chaos* 22). Similarly, there are nuances between cycles, so that the sequel series may deliver different meanings and conclusions from the one before it.

This idea is explicitly described in David and Leigh Eddings' *The Seeress of Kell* (1991), the last book in the *Belgariad* (1982–1984) and *Malloreon* series (1987–1991).[1] Though much of the series is published in the 1980s, I chose it here as a case study as it is an example of a series that is deliberately published alongside a sequel series, and, for practical reasons, it is also a series that is whole and completed. In contrast, many of the series begun in the 1990s and 2000s are as yet incomplete, or, has the potential to continue even if the series is seemingly closed.[2]

Eddings' narrative is motivated by two opposing destinies who have each selected a champion, a Child of Light and a Child of Dark, to face each other in an apocalyptic battle. *Belgariad* follows the journey of Garion, the Child of Light, as he confronts his destiny in facing the evil god Torak, the Child of Dark. Following the defeat of Torak, *Malloreon* poses a *second* confrontation between the Child of Light and Dark. Accordingly, the sequel series can be seen as a repetition of the first. And yet, despite the repetitive plot structure, the conflict in each series is resolved in dramatically distinct ways, proving that repeated events can lead to different outcomes. In this final chapter, I briefly discuss David and Leigh Eddings' *The Seeress of Kell* (with reference to the rest of the series) in order to argue that the movement between sequel series is a constant deterioration and re-establishment of new equilibriums.

Specifically, I argue that sequels represent chaotic systems; while the sequels are repetitive of the work that came before it, it is not an exact duplicate. There is enough variation between parts that the author can deliver an expected *and* unexpected ending simultaneously.

Movement between Equilibriums

In *The Fantastic: A Structural Approach to a Literary Genre* (1970, translated 1975), Tzvetan Todorov describes how narratives are "a movement between two different equilibriums":

> The image will be as follows: *All narrative is a movement between two equilibriums which are similar but not identical.* At the start of the narrative, there is always a stable situation; the characters form a configuration which can shift but which nonetheless keep a certain number of fundamental features intact. (163, original emphasis)

Todorov begins by explaining how all narratives begin with the idea of a stable equilibrium, similar to the period of stasis described in the previous chapter. In the next step: "something occurs which introduces a disequilibrium (or, one might say, a negative equilibrium); thus for one reason or another the child leaves his house" (163). Todorov here identifies how the narrative represents an imbalance in the initial stable equilibrium. In other words, as described in Chapter 6, the narrative is triggered by an increase in entropy which acts to unbalance Fantasyland.

When the narrative reaches a resolution, the "equilibrium is [...] re-established":

> after having overcome many obstacles, the child – who has grown up in the meantime – returns to the family house. The equilibrium is then re-established, but it is no longer that of the beginning: the child is no longer a child, but has become an adult among the others. (163)

As depicted in the previous chapter with Figures 8.1 and 8.2, while a new equilibrium is established, it is not at the same level as the initial equilibrium. Something has changed, as the character and world have also changed. Todorov concludes:

> The elementary narrative thus includes two types of episodes: those which describe a state of equilibrium or disequilibrium, and those which describe the transition from one to the other. [...] Every narrative includes this fundamental schema, though it is often difficult to recognize. (163–164)

Todorov thus asserts that *every* narrative is a transition between a state of equilibrium and disequilibrium. The latter half of this book has considered this movement, as the Heroic Epic Fantasy hero attempts to re-establish balance. This transition is not simply a movement back and forth between two equal or exact states of equilibrium, but as with Figure 9.1, the size, shape, direction, and momentum of these equilibriums can differ.

As this book has considered repeatedly, Heroic Epic Fantasy fiction is largely concerned with balances, but, as the previous chapter explored, when this equilibrium becomes exceptionally unbalanced, often the only way to re-establish a balance is by creating a *new* equilibrium: "The equilibrium is then re-established, but it is no longer that of the beginning" (Todorov 163). As indicated previously, when one considers a single Heroic Epic Fantasy novel, it may be that the narrative arc of the individual novel may be resolved through a simple transition from unbalance to balance, as in Figure 5.1. However, Heroic Epic Fantasy fiction is rarely contained to a single novel and is instead often depicted through trilogies or series spanning numerous books. As a result, instead of a narrative that is a "movement between two equilibriums," the narrative arc throughout the series may contain *several* equilibriums, all of which "are similar but not identical." Accordingly, Heroic Epic Fantasy narratives may be seen to cycle from sequel to sequel, a constant movement between different equilibriums; formed from the fragments of the first state, but still new and distinct from what has come before.

These cycles are chaotic, similar to the patterns of the Butterfly Effect (Figure 9.2): though the cycles follow a pattern, these patterns are not exact copies of one another, and thus, the final result is not predictable.

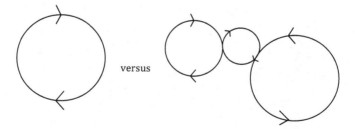

Figure 9.1 Differences in Cycles.

Figure 9.2 Chaotic Patterns.

The Butterfly Effect is a good model to investigate repetitions between sequel Heroic Epic Fantasy series. For instance, in Eddings' first series (*Belgariad*), the hero Garion, the chosen champion of Light, must confront the god Torak as the chosen champion of Dark. Although this event seems momentous – involving, as it does, a duel with, and consequent death, of a God – it is revealed in the sequel series (*Malloreon*) that this confrontation has occurred repeatedly from the beginning of time:

> The two have been meeting in these confrontations since before the beginning of this world. Each time, there's a Child of Light and a Child of Dark. When you and Torak met at Cthol Mishrak, you were the Child of Light and Torak was the Child of Dark. It wasn't the first time the two had met. Apparently it was not to be the last, either. (*Guardians of the West* 79–80)

The narration goes on to explain that two different fates have been meeting in confrontation for eons, with a chosen champion at each confrontation. As the events get closer to the 'final,' 'ultimate' fate, the speed of these confrontations speeds up accordingly, and come closer and closer together.

Although Eddings depicts these cycles overtly, this idea is also explicitly or implicitly present in other Heroic Epic Fantasy fictions. For example, the characters in N. K. Jemisin's *The Broken Earth* trilogy (2015–2018) observe a repetition in their history as well: "The same stories, cycling around and around. The same endings, again and again. The same mistakes eternally repeated" (*The Stone Sky* 345). Note the conscious awareness of "cycling," of having the "same endings," and – alongside of this – the hero's determination to break out of this cycle and bring about a new ending. Similarly, in *Game of Thrones* (2011–2019), the television adaptation of George R. R. Martin's unfinished *A Song of Ice and Fire* (1996–present), the characters explicit state their intent to "break the wheel." The awareness of cycles is presented more implicitly in Brandon Sanderson's *Mistborn* trilogy (2006–2008), as was described in the previous chapter. As the trilogy reached a crescendo towards a far-from-equilibrium situation – one that ultimately triggers a new equilibrium and breaks the cycle – the cycles of revolution leading up to this movement also speed up. Before, Lord Ruler's regime lasted for a thousand years, but towards the end of the trilogy, within a span of a year multiple revolutions spring up. These cycles, however, are suggested by my readings of Sanderson's text, rather than being present explicitly by the author, like Eddings does.

The movement between two equilibriums is more apparent in those Heroic Epic Fantasy series that have sequels, a series of sequels, or are a long-running series with individual stand-alone novels. Consider L. E. Modesitt Jr.'s *The Saga of Recluce* series (1990–present), for example, where the more than twenty book series demonstrate a constant cycling back and forth between the powers of Chaos and Order. Modesitt explicitly describes the equilibrium of these states using the language of "Balance." As in other Heroic Epic Fantasy narratives, when examined as a whole, the narrative in these series often cycle back and forth between two distinct equilibriums. Other long-running Heroic Epic Fantasy series follow a similar pattern of moving from balance to unbalance. Consider, for instance (in no particular order), Mercedes Lackey *Valdemar* series (36 books published from 1987), Stephen R. Donaldson's *The Chronicles of Thomas Covenant* (10 books published from 1977), Piers Anthony's *Xanth* series (41 books published from 1977), Robin Hobb's *The Realm of the Elderlings* (19 books published from 1995), Canadian Author's Steven Erikson's *Malazan Book of the Fallen* (12 books published from 1999, with additional novels written by Ian Cameron Esslemont), Raymond E. Feist's *Riftwar Cycle* (28 novels published from 1982), and Terry Brooks *Shannara* series (35 books published from 1977), to name just a few of the longer series not covered in this book. It should be noted that many of these texts (individual novels or the series as a whole) may in fact lean towards the Localised or Adventure end of the Fantasy spectrum, rather than the Heroic Epic, and yet the same principle of a movement between unbalance and balance still applies. While many of these novels may operate as stand-alone novels or contained trilogies, the length of the series demonstrates that, even when a 'happily ever after' is reached at the end of the novel or narrative trajectory, another unbalance occurs that triggers the plot of the narrative again.

The Lorenzian Waterwheel

The list of long-running Heroic Epic Fantasy series is endless. As a result, many critics and non-readers of Heroic Epic Fantasy may view the genre as repetitive or crude derivations of similar narrations. As Fantasyland is entropic, it *will* begin to deteriorate again immediately, leading to a new cycle, a new series. However, this new cycle is not a simple repetition of what has come before it. As established in the first chapter using the philosophy of Bertrand Russell, repetitive patterns do not indicate that: "the same cause, if repeated, will produce the same effect" (Russell, *Our Knowledge of the External World* 185). Far from simplifying the text into a reductive formula, these repetitions add complexity to the story. As N. Katherine Hayles indicates in *Chaos Bound* (1990), recursive structures and repetitions add layers of understanding to texts in a meta-fictional or intertextual manner: "Far from being ordered sets of words bounded by book covers, they [texts] are reservoirs of chaos. [...] Any word, [Derrida] argues, acquires a slightly different meaning each time it appears in a new context" (180–181). Repetitions allow nuanced meanings to emerge, building complexity with each re-iteration.

These recursive structures are emblematic of the evolution of Heroic Epic Fantasy from the Epic. In *Anatomy of Criticism* Northrop Frye (1957) asserts that:

> The regular pulsating meter that traditionally distinguishes verse from prose tends to become the organizing rhythm in *epos* or extended oratorical forms. Meter is an aspect of recurrence, and the two words for recurrence, rhythm and pattern, show that recurrence is a structural principle of all art, whether temporal or spatial in its primary impact. (251)

Repetition is thus part of the form of the Epic itself, "a structural principle of all art," adding as it does rhythm and pattern, but a pattern that resonates with meaning. Author Jane Yolen in *Touch Magic* (1981, expanded 2000) likewise suggests that: "The fantasy novel speaks many times to the listener. Once in the ear, and again and again and again in the echo chamber that is the heart" (58). Repetitive structures and motifs add a resonance, a nuance and depth to the pattern with each act of iteration, adding layers of perceptiveness and consideration.

The cycle of repetitions found from sequel to sequel in Heroic Epic Fantasy can be described by the Lorenzian Waterwheel model. As Gleick describes, the waterwheel is a chaotic system, the movement of which was discovered by Edward Lorenz. Picture a wheel with buckets around the rim. In this system, "water pours in from the top at a steady rate," gradually filling the buckets as the water flows at a continuous speed (Gleick 27). But as the water pours in, the buckets fill, and the speed at which the wheel turns can speed up or slow down, even though the water from the top continues to fall at the same rate:

> As buckets pass under the flowing water, how much they fill depends on the speed of spin. If the wheel is spinning rapidly, the buckets have little time to fill up. [...] Also, if the wheel is spinning rapidly, buckets can start up the other side before they have time to empty. As a result, heavy buckets on the side moving upward can cause the spin to slow down and then reverse. In fact, Lorenz discovered, over long periods, the spin can reverse itself many times, never settling down to a steady rate and never repeating itself in any predictable pattern. (27)

The rate at which the wheel spins can speed up, slow down, or even reverse itself. But the pattern at which the wheel turns is not a predictable pattern, even if the input of water flows at a steady rate. The progression of Heroic Epic Fantasy sequels is similar. From novel to novel, and from series to series, the narration may speed up, slow down, or even reverse itself. As the Lorenzian Waterwheel, Heroic Epic Fantasy series is a chaotic system. While there is a pattern of repetition between and within Heroic Epic Fantasy texts, as these repetitions are not quite exact, the cyclical narrative time can result in different outcomes.

For instance, Mercedes Lackey and James Mallory's *Obsidian* trilogy (2003–2006) ends with the establishment of one system of power over the other; this system is then reversed completely in the sequel trilogy, *Enduring Flame* (2007–2009). A third trilogy, the *Dragon Prophecy* (2012–present) which takes place a thousand years before the events of the first, is currently incomplete, but leaves the possibility open for the system to speed up, slow down, or reverse again. This pattern is similar to the back and forth movement presented by the three *Star Wars* trilogies. While balance is restored in the main trilogy (1977–1983), the prequel series (1995–2005) sets up an increase of entropy and leads to the unbalance of the Force. As the newest trilogy (2015–2019) has demonstrated, this balance is only temporary, or, indeed, a false restoration. As the series is still incomplete (at this time of writing), it is entirely possible that Balance may be restored, or, equally that the hero will fail, or, a third option, that once restored, it will unbalance again. This is the nature of chaotic cycles.

The application of chaos theory to the study of fiction is not a wholly new idea. In a series of articles, Donald Palumbo identifies that repetitions between SF epics can be seen at descending scales of plots and subplots, asserting that: "For the monomyth itself has numerous, striking affinities with many of the same chaos-theory concepts articulated and demonstrated in the Dune series" ("The Monomyth and Chaos Theory" 34). Examining Joseph Campbell's "cosmic cycle," Palumbo demonstrates that the repetitions between and within Herbert's *Dune* series and Asimov's *Foundation* series showcase "self-similarity":

> Its repetition with variations *across* the volumes, as it is the specific plot structure in volume after volume of the series, and *across* the characters, as character after character pursues his or her own scheme within a scheme, corresponds to the fractal's characteristic of duplication across the same scale. ("Plots within Plots" 59, original emphasis)

Palumbo examines what Hayles would describe as *"recursive symmetries between scale levels"* (Hayles, *Chaos Bound* 13, original emphasis): repetitive patterns across novel to novel demonstrating layers of similarities, but layers that build to create a deeply complex narrative. Likewise, Janet Brennan Croft in "Túrin and Aragorn: Evading and Embracing Fate" (2011) also argues that Tolkien's work demonstrates fractal patterns (a component of chaos theory): "you find the same structure, the same motifs, reinforced through repetition and variation, down to the very heart of the work" (155). These fractal patterns, rather than being simple structures, build a complexity to the narrative structure. Fractal images do not focus simply on the similarities but also on the differences: "a form of repetition with variation" (Croft 156). Though Heroic Epic Fantasy follows a cyclical pattern, a pattern of eternal recurrence by means of the repetitions between different narratives, the repetitions are never quite exact.

As identified above, many Heroic Epic Fantasy writers produce a long series of books within the same world or create multiple sequel trilogies or series; while repetitive narrative patterns can be identified from sequel to sequel, they are "a form of repetition with variation." The characters in Eddings' *Malloreon* are interesting, in that they recognise the repetition between patterns themselves:

> "There are some similarities, all right," [Belgarath] admitted. "The two of them are the same kind of people, and they both warned us about something [...]."
> "All right. For the sake of argument, let's say it wasn't coincidence. [...] Let's look at the notion that these repetitions crop up at significant points in the course of events." [replies Beldin]
> "Sort of like signposts?" Dunrik suggested. (*Seeress of Kell* 40–41)

The characters of Eddings' series are conscious of the fact that they are being manipulated by fate, and that these events have occurred repeatedly in the past. The characters also consciously note the idea that the sequel series is a repetition of the first series, but with some variations. Earlier, they reason that this cycle of repetitions is a form of stasis:

> We're on our way to another meeting between the Child of Light and the Child of Dark [...]. That meeting is going to be a repetition of an event that's been happening over and over again since the beginning of time. Since it's the same event, it stands to reason that the circumstances leading up to it should also be similar. [...] There are two Prophecies – two sides of the same thing. Something happening an unimaginably long time ago to separate them. [...] As long as those two forces are separate – and equal – the future can't happen. We all just keep going through the same series of events over and over again. (*King of the Murgos* 80–81)

Thus, the cycle has to continue until a major shift – a far-from-equilibrium situation – occurs, launching the system into a new state. Although the confrontation between the two prophecies through their champions would seem to indicate a final outcome through the nature of their confrontation (in the defeat of one champion, often through death), these meetings keep occurring until something *different* happens. The repetitions can only be stopped by shifting completely into a new trajectory: "and we knew that

166   *Chaotic Cycles*

this Event would be the last. The division of creation had endured for too long; and in *this* meeting between the two fates the division would end and all would be made one again" (*Seeress of Kell* 7, original emphasis). The last novel in the *Belgariad* and *Malloreon* series demonstrates the characters' awareness of the finality of their own journey.

Eddings' *Malloreon* series is not the only text where the characters are self-aware of the repetition between patterns. Due to the heroes and protagonists almost conscious awareness of being pawns in a narrative (as discussed in Chapter 3), Heroic Epic Fantasy often depicts conversations or moments of introspection where a character explicitly identifies these recursive structures themselves. For instance, *Shadows of Self* (2015), part of the spin-off sequel to Sanderson's *Mistborn* trilogy, culminates in a rebellion against the government. Similar to the first series, the rebellion is meant to overthrow a long-standing government. However, in this sequel, the events fuelling this rebellion are motivated by antagonistic forces rather than the heroes. The antagonists in *Shadows of Self* utilise the memory of the first rebellion in order to evoke a feeling of repetition within the population:

> *She has to be doing it on purpose*, Marasi thought, walking through the room. *Trying to echo that night when the Lord Ruler fell. A people on the brink of insurrection. Noble houses at each other's throats. And now...*
>
> Now a speech. The governor would have his moment before the crowd, and they would sense the resonance even if they couldn't put their finger on it. They'd been taught about that night since childhood. They would listen to him, and expect him to be like the Last Emperor, who had spoken long ago on the night of the Lord Ruler's death. (285, original emphasis)

Here, the antagonists themselves are exploiting the resonance between the first trilogy and the second series, highlighting repetitions within these patterns in order to guide the population into re-creating the pattern. Note the language, of "resonance" and "echo," as the character consciously reflects on the similarities between narrative patterns. But, as chaos theory suggests, "the repetitions were never quite exact. There was pattern, with disturbances. An orderly disorder" (Gleick 15). The character Marasi concludes that: "Governor Innate was *not* Elend Venture. Far from it" (*Shadows of Self* 285, original emphasis). The distinction between having the antagonist and protagonist forces trigger a revolution leads to different forks in the road (Figures 2.2, 4.1). While the patterns are the same, there are enough variations that different narrative trajectories are created. This is often true of stories that are depicted through sequels, whether they are Fantastika sequels or not. Like the model of the Lorenzian Waterwheel: "the spin can reverse itself many times, never settling down to a steady rate and never repeating itself in any predictable pattern" (Gleick 27). These variations lead to different bifurcation points in the trajectory of Fantasyland.

Leaving Room for a Sequel

These repetitions between sequels work to deliberately produce a feeling of déjà vu in the reader so that the experienced reader can recognise the allusions made to the previous text. In *Narrative Discourse* (1972, translated 1980), Gérard Genette asserts that:

> [T]he mere fact of recurrence is not what defines the most rigorous form of iteration, the form that is apparently most satisfying to the spirit – or most soothing to Proustian sensibility. The repetition also has to be regular, has to obey a law of frequency, and this law has to be discernible and formulable, and therefore predictable in its effects. (124)

The reader, through their experience with the first narrative, is led to certain expectations in the second narrative, which then may be enforced or subverted. In this way, the act of recurrence functions to build iterations for the reader who is already familiar with the narrative or the Heroic Epic form, creating a resonance through the act of reading.

As Roland Barthes suggests in *The Pleasure of the Text* (1975): "The stereotype is the word repeated without any magic, any enthusiasm" (42), and this may be the way that repetitions and formula fiction is generally imagined by those who do not find pleasure in Heroic Epic Fantasy fiction. However, Barthes identifies that repetition can be pleasurable for two contradictory reasons: "the word can be erotic on two opposing conditions, both excessive: if it is extravagantly repeated, or on the contrary, if it is unexpected, succulent in its newness" (42). While a perfect repetition of the narrative or narrative devices may alienate the reader, a chaotic repetition of motifs may lead the reader to experience a feeling of recognition and take pleasure in that "extravagantly repeated."

In creating a new novel, a Heroic Epic Fantasy author needs to create a balance between the repetition of these motifs that are part of the narrative structural frame and the 'play,' or manipulation, of them into something new. This is the way the genre develops. John G. Cawelti likewise stipulates in *Adventure, Mystery, and Romance: Formula Stories as Art and Popular Culture* (1976) that genre fiction contains conventional motifs with newly invented ones:

> A successful formulaic work is unique when, in addition to the pleasure inherent in the conventional structure, it brings a new element into the formula, or embodies the personal vision of the creator. If

such new elements also become widely popular, they may in turn become widely imitated stereotypes and the basis of a new version of the formula or even of a new formula altogether. (12)

Through the manipulation of these expected motifs, authors are able to evolve the genre, utilising previously known tropes and changing them slightly into something different. The structure, the skeletal frame, of these Epic-derived texts remains the same, buried, but the expression of the motifs that flesh out these devices are ever evolving. Brian Attebery likewise asserts in *Strategies of Fantasy* (1992) that Fantasy can be described in two distinct ways:

> Fantasy is a form of popular escapist literature that combines stock characters and devices [...] into a predictable plot [...].
> Fantasy is a sophisticated mode of storytelling characterized by stylistic playfulness, self-reflexiveness, and a subversive treatment of established orders of society and thought. (1)

Heroic Epic Fantasy is both of these things at once: a combination of a repetitive form that uses "stock characters and devices" and "a predictable plot," and the expression of these forms in new and nuanced ways in "a sophisticated mode of storytelling."

In this way, the relationship between the first set of series or trilogies and its sequel can be seen as: "*a movement between two equilibriums which are similar but not identical*" (Todorov 163, original emphasis). The conclusion of the *Malloreon* series, *The Seeress of Kell*, rewrites the events of the *Belgariad* series. While the readers assume that the death of Torak is a final, conclusive ends where the Child of Light triumphs over the Child of Dark, the sequel series undermines that. The same occurs for other Heroic Epic Fantasy sequels that are set in the same world. In these works, there is movement between two comparable equilibriums, both of which depict a movement between static equilibriums followed by nonequilibrium. But as they are exhibited in different ways, they lead to different bifurcation points. As Attebery further argues using *The Lord of the Rings* as a model:

> Each parallel movement effectively rewrites those that went before. Each prepares the way for those yet to come. The explicit prophecies and embedded narratives merely reinforce the intricate structuring of the narrative, pointing out to the reader the way the magic code governs the unfolding of events. (59–60)

Each repetition functions as an iteration, which builds on – or rewrites – the movement that has come before. While there are repetitions between series, these repetitions lead to new journeys.

With a narrative time that is a constant movement between two equilibriums, how does the author manage to deliver a conclusive ending? A novel in an earlier part of the series often ends on a final climatic moment, but with no real resolution of the overarching plot. At the end of a trilogy or a series, however, one might find that the author might leave room for another sequel. Indeed, an ambiguous ending might be more satisfactory than a conclusive one. Consequently, the Heroic Epic Fantasy tale frequently concludes with a few loose ends. In fact, even J. R. R. Tolkien in "On Fairy-Stories" (1947), on which he develops his philosophy on Fantasy, describes the ending of Fairy-Tales as follows: "The consolation of fairy-stories, the joy of the happy ending: or more correctly of the good catastrophe, the sudden joyous 'turn' (*for there is no true end to any fairy-tale*)" (68, my emphasis). In a footnote to the parenthesis, Tolkien continues:

> The verbal ending – usually held to be as typical of the end of fairy-stories as "once upon a time" is of the beginning – "and they lived happily ever after" is an artificial device. It does not deceive anybody. End-phrases of this kind are to be compared to the margins and frames of pictures, and are no more to be thought of as the real end of any particular fragment of the seamless Web of Story than the frame is of the visionary scene […]. A sharp cut in the endless tapestry is not unfittingly marked by a formula, even a grotesque or comic one. (80)

Tolkien suggests that the final resolution is only a temporary one, as he recognises that the conclusion of the narrative does not result in a frozen time. He describes the story as a web, the imagery of weaving of time here suggesting that the web is endless, just as when telling a history of the world, a historian may convey parts of the story but cannot repeat it in its entirety. The formulaic "happily ever after" end of a story is an "artificial device" that tells the reader that the story continues, but the narration has stopped – for the moment.

That sequel trilogies are often published so close together would suggest that some Heroic Epic Fantasy authors *plan* for a sequel trilogy or series. Eddings' *Belgariad* series, five books published from 1982 to 1984, is followed by the sequel series *Malloreon*, another five books published from 1987 to 1991. Sanderson published his *Mistborn* trilogy from 2006 to 2008, and in the stand-alone sequel series starting with *Alloy of Law* published in 2011, he clearly indicates his plan to publish further sequel trilogies. Even when there is some time between publications, this may be due to the author's or publisher's plan for more series. For instance, the final instalment of James Clemens' *Godslayer* trilogy (2005–present) has been postponed, as the author has revealed his plan to publish a sequel trilogy and re-release the first trilogy with the second.

And just recently, Patrick Rothfuss has announced that his incomplete *Kingkiller Chronicles* (2007–present) will act as the *prologue* for subsequent series.

Even if the author does not immediately plan for a sequel series, they often still leave room for the possibility of one to follow as Fantasyland is not fixed permanently. For instance, at the end of David Farland's *The Lair of Bones* (2003), the hero Averan declares: "'The damage is repaired,' Averan said. 'The new course will be better for us than the old'" (449), yet the hero Gaborn declares that his child will "finish what I cannot" (452) indicating that, though the Fantasyland appears to have been healed, there is more work to be done – and, indeed, the first *Runelords* series is followed by more novels. In Lois McMaster Bujold's *The Curse of Chalion* (2001), Cazaril indicates that he was allowed to live (after dying three times), because he may need to function as hero again (482). Although Cazaril is not called upon to be hero (yet), several more stand-alone novels in the same universe identify other characters as heroes who allow metaphysical entities to enter the world through their bodies in order to fix or restore Fantasyland.

These authors deliberately leave some questions unanswered, but questions that may seem unimportant at the time. Sanderson's *Mistborn* trilogy delivers a final scene that appears to be absolute; the death and rebirth of the world seem to indicate the end of the journey for the heroes, as their heroic function is fulfilled. However, Sazed leaves a letter, discussing the fourteen known metals that fuel magical powers: "*P.S. There are still two metals that nobody knows about*" (Hero of Ages 723, original emphasis indicating written text). Sazed's postscript indicates that there's still another mystery to solve, and thus the reader may anticipate another sequel to Sanderson's trilogy before the formal announcement is made. In the postscript to the latest published *Mistborn* novel, *The Bands of Mourning* (2016), Sanderson concludes: "There's always another secret" (439), further demonstrating the nature of Heroic Epic Fantasy fiction as one that does not have any closure.

The *Malloreon* series wraps up a number of unanswered questions that are presented in the *Belgariad* series, chiefly who is the child Errand/Eriond, and where does he come from. The introduction of Errand in the first series is depicted as mysterious and nebulous; his origins are clouded in mystery. *The Seeress of Kell* resolves this ambiguity, and places the character in an appropriate and satisfying position:

> "[...] Eriond was intended to be the seventh God. Torak was a mistake caused by the accident." [says the voice of the Prophecy of Light]
> "He's always been around then? Eriond, I mean?" [asks Garion]
> "Always is a long time, Garion. Eriond was present – in spirit – since the accident. When you were born, he began to move around in the world." [the voice replies] (*Seeress of Kell* 302)

The final chapters of *The Seeress of Kell* effectively tie Garion's Heroic path together with Eriond's Epic one. Yet, even with this resolution, the possibility of other stories set in the world can still occur. The series concludes with the following epigraph:

> And so, my children, the time has come to close
> the book. There will be other days and other stories,
> but this tale is finished. (374)

Though the Epic saga of that world is concluded, the lengthy epilogue at the end of the novel combined with the final inscription leaves room for further adventures to occur for that particular cast of characters. The story is never quite finished.

These open endings and unanswered questions leave room for the reader to hope. In *Demand the Impossible: Science Fiction and the Utopian Imagination* (1986), Tom Moylan describes how for the philosopher Ernst Bloch, utopia is when ideas result in a change of the status quo:

> Present time is provincial and empty. If humanity becomes too much taken with the present, we lose the possibility of imagining a radically other future. We lose the ability to hope. We lose what Bloch identifies as the *novum*: the unexpectedly new, that which pushes humanity out of the present toward the not yet realized future. (21, original emphasis)

It is notable that, in his foundational definition of Science Fiction, Darko Suvin extrapolates on Bloch's conception of the "novum," which is considered by many to be an intrinsic part of Fantastika fictions. Accordingly, the unanswered questions in the first series or trilogy allow the reader to hope for a future, that is, for the development of another series of books that will fulfil their desire for a 'return' to that Fantasy world. The end of the series only comes about when 'balance' is restored by re-unifying parts into a completed whole – and it is, of course, possible that these parts can be split again, so that an imbalance results in a new story. Instead of delivering an Edenic ending where characters live happily ever after and all problems are solved for all eternity, Heroic Epic Fantasy authors conclude their series with hope for the novum, "the unexpectedly new," which will push the reader towards the hoped-for next cycle.

Notes

1 Although Leigh Eddings is uncredited at the time of publication, it is largely acknowledged that the husband and wife team co-authored these works together.
2 As David Eddings has passed away, the possibility of the series continuing is unlikely.

Bibliography

Anthony, Piers. *Xanth*. Ballantine, 1977–2017. Xanth 1–41.
Attebery, Brian. *Strategies of Fantasy*. Indiana University Press, 1992.
Barthes, Roland. *The Pleasure of the Text*. 1975. Trans. Richard Miller. Jonathan Cape, 1976.
Benioff, David and D. B. Weiss, writers. *Game of Thrones*. HBO, 2011–2019.
Brooks, Terry. *Shannara*. Ballantine, 1977–2019. Shannara 1–35.
Bujold, Lois McMaster. *The Curse of Chalion*. 2000. HarperCollins, 2011. Chalion 1.
Campbell, Joseph. *The Hero with a Thousand Faces*. 1949. New World Library, 2008.
Cawelti, John G. "The Study of Literary Formulas." *Adventure, Mystery, and Romance: Formula Stories as Art and Popular Culture*. University of Chicago Press, 1976. pp. 5–36.
Clemens, James. *Godslayer Chronicles*. Roc, 2005–2006. Godslayer Chronicles 1–2.
Croft, Janet Brennan. "Túrin and Aragorn: Evading and Embracing Fate." *Mythlore*. vol. 29, no. 3/4, 2011, pp. 155–170.
Donaldson, Stephen R. *The Chronicles of Thomas Covenant*. Ballatine, 1977–2013. Thomas Covenant 1–10.
Eddings, David and Leigh. *Belgariad*. Del Rey, 1982–1984. Belgariad 1–5.
———. *Guardians of the West*. Del Rey, 1987. Malloreon 1.
———. *King of the Murgos*. Del Rey, 1988. Malloreon 2.
———. *Malloreon*. Del Rey, 1987–1981. Malloreon 1–5.
———. *The Seeress of Kell*. Dey Rey, 1991. Malloreon 5.
Erikson, Steven. *Malazan Book of the Fallen*. Bantam, 1999–2016. Malazan 1–12.
Farland, David. *The Lair of Bones*. Tor, 2003. Runelords 4.
Feist, Raymond E. *Riftwar Cycle*. Doubleday, 1982–2013. Riftwar 1–28.
Frye, Northrop. *Anatomy of Criticism*. 1957. Princeton University Press, 1973.
Genette, Gérard. *Narrative Discourse*. 1972. Trans. Jane E. Lewin. Basil Blackwell, 1980.
Gleick, James. *Chaos: The Amazing Science of the Unpredictable*. 1987. Vintage Books, 1998.
Hayles, N. Katherine. *Chaos Bound: Orderly Disorder in Contemporary Literature and Science*. 1990. Cornell University Press, 1994.
Hobb, Robin. *The Realm of the Elderlings*. Voyager, 1995–2017. Realm of the Elderlings 1–19.
Jemisin, Nora K. *The Stone Sky*. Orbit, 2017. The Broken Earth 3.
Lackey, Mercedes. *Valdemar*. Daw, 1987–2019. Valdemar 1–36.
Lackey, Mercedes and James Mallory. *The Dragon Prophecy Trilogy*. Tor, 2012–2017. Dragon Prophecy 1–2.
———. *The Enduring Flame Trilogy*. Tor, 2007–2009. Enduring Flame 1–3.
———. *The Obsidian Trilogy*. Tor, 2003–2006. Obsidian 1–3.
Martin, George R. R. *A Song of Ice and Fire*. Bantam Books, 1996–2011. A Song of Ice and Fire 1–5.
Modesitt, Leland Exton, Jr. *The Saga of Recluce*. Tor, 1991–2019. The Saga of Recluce 1–21.

Moylan, Tom. "The Literary Utopia." *Demand the Impossible: Science Fiction and the Utopian Imagination.* Methuen, 1986. pp. 29–52.
Palumbo, Donald. "The Monomyth and Chaos Theory: 'Perhaps We should Believe in Magic." *Journal of the Fantastic in the Arts*, vol. 12, no. 1, 2001, pp. 34–76. Print.
———. "'Plots Within Plots … Patterns Within Patterns': Chaos-Theory Concepts and Structures in Frank Herbert's *Dune* Novels." *Journal of the Fantastic in the Arts*, vol. 8, no. 1, 1997, pp. 55–77.
———. "Psychohistory and Chaos Theory: The 'Foundation Trilogy' and the Fractal Structure of Asimov's Robot/Empire/Foundation Metaseries." *Journal of the Fantastic in the Arts*, vol. 7, no. 1, 1988, pp. 23–50.
Rothfuss, Patrick. *The Kingkiller Chronicle.* DAW: 2007–2011. The Kingkiller Chronicle 1–2.
Russell, Bertrand. "On the Notion of Cause, with Application to the Free-Will Problem." *Our Knowledge of the External World.* 1914. Routledge, 2009. pp. 169–196.
Sanderson, Brandon. *The Bands of Mourning.* Gollancz, 2016. Mistborn 6.
———. *The Hero of Ages.* 2008. Dragonstell Entertainment, 2010. Mistborn Trilogy 3.
———. *Mistborn.* Tor, 2006–2016. Mistborn 1–6.
———. *Shadows of Self.* Gollancz, 2015. Mistborn 5.
Star Wars. Lucasfilm, 1977–2017. Star Wars 1–8.
Suvin, Darko. *Metamorphoses of Science Fiction.* 1979. Yale University Press, 1980.
Todorov, Tzvetan. *The Fantastic: A Structural Approach to a Literary Genre.* 1970. Trans. Richard Howard. Cornell University, 1975.
Tolkien, John Ronald Reuel. *The Lords of the Rings.* Allen & Unwin, 1954–1955. The Lord of the Rings 1–3.
———. "On Fairy-Stories." 1947. *Tree and Leaf.* 1964. HarperCollins, 2001.
Yolen, Jane. *Touch Magic: Fantasy, Faerie & Folklore in the Literature of Children.* 1981. Expanded edition. August House Publishers, 2000.

Afterword – Probing the Potentials of the Heroic Epic Pattern with a Brief Look at Anne McCaffrey's *All the Weyrs of Pern* (1991)

Throughout this book, I have identified recursive structures that form an integral part of Heroic Epic Fantasy. These repetitions give a sense of familiarity, of a Mythological story that one has already experienced before. Via the evolutionary and interconnected process of Heroic Epic Fantasy, especially the conscious part of the creative process that is aware of storytelling patterns in Mythology and Legends, the Heroic Epic Fantasy as a genre is metafictional. In "Fantasy and the Metatext" (2009), John Clute asserts that: "[W]e can understand megatext to refer to any story which is in some sense Twice-Told (which is to say any story that we are aware of)" (7). Clute suggests that the metatext – "metatextuality governs any expression in a text of its relationship to megatext" (8) – is a conversation; one that Heroic Epic Fantasy highlights rather than hides. Metafictional motifs and devices in Heroic Epic Fantasy stress the importance of storytelling and reveal its mechanics, but uncovering its mechanics is a means by which a reader may gain further pleasure in the text.

For example, Anne McCaffrey's *Dragonflight* (1968) deliberately evokes the idea of Mythology in the opening sentences of the two-page Introduction: "When is a legend legend? Why is a myth a myth? How old and disused must a fact be for it to be relegated to the category 'Fairy-Tale'?" (xi). Many critics and McCaffrey herself view the novel as a Science Fiction (SF) text despite the many motifs and themes borrowed from Fantasy. Indeed, I chose it as an example here because it is one text where the distinction of it as Fantasy or SF is fiercely contested. But, even if the text is defined as SF, this does not disbar it from also being examined as an Epic and it is pertinent that McCaffrey evokes the ideas of Mythologies and Legends in the introductory pages herself.

McCaffrey's *Pern* series (1967–2012)[1] presents a feudal society where dragons and dragonriders are called on to keep the world safe. Despite common Fantasy motifs, the texts themselves are often viewed as SF as the series takes place on a planet in our (the primary) universe and 'fantastical' elements are given scientific or pseudo-scientific explanations throughout the series. And yet Jane Yolen's *Dragon's Blood* (1982) features similar devices, of a planet colonised by people from earth, and instead is distinctly received as Fantasy rather than SF. Here, as in McCaffrey's *Pern*, a dragon-like lizard species already existed on the colonised planet – although while in *Pern* the colonisers used more obvious scientific methods (genetic manipulation) in order to increase the size of the lizards, the peoples of Austar IV in *Dragon's Blood* employed a method of selectively breeding to achieve similar results. Why then is one text received and marketed as an SF and the other as a Fantasy? It is perhaps important to remember Arthur C. Clarke's famous maxim: "Any sufficiently advanced technology is indistinguishable from magic" ("Clarke's Three Laws"). Fantasy fiction is not antithesis to SF. As I have demonstrated throughout this book, Heroic Epic Fantasy is logical and contains real-world scientific and philosophical ideas which are embedded directly into its narrative structure. When building a new world, an author must use their awareness and knowledge of the known theories of the universe. They may use this knowledge to subvert or play with these rules, or, as new theories are explored, the narrative structure itself may evolve according to this cultural feedback. As this book has demonstrated, models of how we currently understand the universe are embedded in the narrative structures of the production of Fantasy fiction. This is the logic and rationale behind the Heroic Epic.

While some of the texts that I have mentioned throughout this book may be viewed as SF or Horror/Gothic rather than Fantasy, as I emphasised in the introduction, identifying the narrative structure of Heroic and Epic is of greater importance than categorising the Fantastical nature of its world-building. For instance, are *Buffy the Vampire Slayer* (1997–2003) and *Blade* (1998) categorised as Horror or Gothic simply become of the presence of vampires regardless of the presence of destiny and messianism? Or are their categorisations dependent on being set in a primary world (a world recognisable to our own) rather than being set in a secondary created world, as in Gail Z. Martin's *The Summoner*? It is possible that a reader may argue for the classification of *The Summoner* as a Gothic or Horror text as well, categorising it by the motifs of ghostly and vampiric figures. But these distinctions are arbitrary and by concentrating on a debate that is centred on defining genres, academics in the field are lost in stagnation, unable to move forward in examining the texts themselves. By focusing on the structure of the Heroic Epic, we can bypass these questions of categorising motifs and identifying to what degree a text is 'possible in our world.' Instead of questioning whether the presence of fantastical elements is scientific, magical, or supernatural in nature, we can focus on how these elements are connected to the embedded narrative structures of the Heroic Epic and explore further what these devices say about the narration and ourselves.

For instance, we can ask ourselves questions such as 'does the "Force" in *Star Wars* (1977–2019) have a satisfying scientific explanation, or is it a religious phenomenon?' Or, 'does the spice in Frank Herbert's *Dune* (1965) unlock a scientifically justified precognition or a religious experience of prophesising?' Does the answer to these questions effect how we interrogate the structure of fate and free will? If it does, what does it say about our *own* preconceived notions and belief of science and religion? In what way do these notions impact our understanding – and criticism – of Fantasy and SF as a whole? By focusing on the common structure of fate and free will that is apparent in both texts *regardless* of genre, we can focus on the text instead and interrogate whether these structures are expressed in different ways, and, if so, how these different expressions further our understanding of the narratives. I use *Star Wars* and *Dune* as further examples here because there has been much debate over the nature of these texts as SF, or Fantasy, or indeed, a hybrid Science Fantasy. It seems to me that the juxtaposition of 'Science' and 'Fantasy' is where the pseudo-scientific elements of the world-building combine with the Heroic and Epic narrative structure of the text. For instance, the presence of messiah characters in *Star Wars* and *Dune* may lead to the characterisation of the texts as Fantasy. This is a *Heroic Epic structure*, and not simply a Fantasy motif.

Accordingly, I assert that, just as a Mystery plot can be integrated with other genres, by focusing on the Heroic Epic, we can discuss the narratives in terms of plot and character, regardless of other categorisations of the text. In this way, a text can have several identities (being a 'multi-genre,' just as a person may be multiracial) instead of being sorted and pigeon-holed into a distinct category. While a text may belong to several genre categories, the narrative structure of the Heroic Epic is a unifying thread that allows us to examine story cohesively.

For instance, at first glance, McCaffrey's *Pern* series does not appear to utilise the structure of the Heroic or the Epic. Yet, on closer examination, some elements of the Heroic and Epic structure do appear to be embedded deep within in the narrative, although they may be more finally nuanced than in the overt examples presented in this book. The character Jaxom demonstrates traditional markers of the hero character. First, he is orphaned immediately after his birth in the first book of the series, *Dragonflight* (1968), marking him as a distinct and unique individual. In his next appearance, he bonds to the dragon Ruth in *Dragonquest* (1971), a dragon who is exceptional in being white in colour. Ruth is initially considered disabled (or sterile) when compared to the other dragons, and yet seems to exceed the dragons in intelligence and self-awareness. These qualifiers mark both characters as distinct; the bond between them is likewise distinguished as special and superior to other dragonrider-bonds.

The final paragraph of *All the Weyrs of Pern* (1991), the novel that concludes the narrative arc of *Pern*, confirms the trajectory of both Jaxom and Ruth as destined hero characters:

> Only he, Jaxom, Lord of Ruatha Hold, and Ruth, the white dragon, could have done what had to be done to free Pern forever from Thread, serving their world as only dragon and rider could, united in mind and hear to their purpose. (433)

The final words of *All the Weyrs of Pern* emphasise Jaxom and Ruth's roles as destined heroes of the *Pern* series. While the individual novels may not express this Heroic structure, as there are many heroes throughout the *Pern* series who play an important role in defeating the menace of Thread, this final paragraph near the end of the *Pern* chronology expresses the idea that Jaxom and Ruth are the heroes of the series as a whole.

And what about the Epic spectrum? *All the Weyrs of Pern* culminates in complete world-salvation, a re-making of the solar system as the Red Star, a planetary object, is shifted out of orbit. This shift must occur as the Red Star causes Thread, an abnormal entity to the world, to release into the atmosphere and destroy Pern. It is notable that, through this destruction, the civilisation on Pern has regressed from one of advanced technology to a feudal society. Entropy clearly has an impact on the world's societies and technologies.

While the salvation of the world is *not* triggered by a divine entity setting a pawn lose in the world, due to the time-travelling mechanism operating in the book, an idea that actions are pre-ordained *does* occur. When travelling to the Red Star, Ruth remarks: "*This place is strangely familiar*" (331, original emphasis to indicate the dragon's telepathy). Jaxom later discusses with Aivas (a computer technology) that the event was destined to occur:

> "[…] It was – it had to be – it was as if I knew it had to be there! I discounted such a ridiculous notion at the time. And you, Aivas, would not have me believe that I have been there before?" [says Jaxom]
>
> "The time paradox has bewildered many. Your presentiment of involvement with the crater is unusual, but similar incidents are reported in the annals of psychic phenomena." [Aivas responds]
>
> […] "You have done it twice. The second time was six hundred Turns ago. It is the only explanation. Furthermore, *you* know that you've done it." [Aivas continues] (362–363, original emphasis)

Although the text uses the register of pseudo-scientific language rather than evoking ideas of divinity, the idea of destiny still remains. As such, a discussion of the Heroic Epic, and a larger examination of the impact of precognition on fate and free will, can also take place, regardless of the registers of 'science' versus 'fantastic.'

In this context, *All the Weyrs of Pern*, and indeed, all of the novels of the *Pern* series, may be seen as repeating the narrative structure of the first *Dragonflight* novel. And yet, despite this reduction, the stories continue to add complexity and depth with each repetition, until the later novel reveals a deeply buried Heroic and Epic structure. Although Fantasy and Fantastika authors may subvert or manipulate the structure, often appearing to disguise them, the Heroic Epic structure remains embedded within many narratives. Take for instance George R. R. Martin's Fragmented Narrative *A Song of Ice and Fire* (1996–present). The series as a whole has been lauded for its uniqueness in not presenting an instantly recognisable hero, and yet, notions of prophecy, messianic figures, and the breaking of a cycle are still explicit in the series. Notably, these motifs are subverted as, rather than breaking the cycle, the television adaptation (*Game of Thrones*, 2011–2019) concludes the series with a return to a status quo. Likewise, a messianic hero does not emerge from Joe Abercrombie's *First Law* trilogy (2006–2008). Arguably, this is because Abercrombie does not wish or attempt to save the people of his Fantasy world. Abercrombie's Fantasyland is doomed to destruction, without any hope of a saviour. *But* even though the messianic ending is never reached, Abercrombie and Martin still evoke the reader's *knowledge* of the Epic structure in order to manipulate the audience into believing that a satisfying happy ending may be possible. Even here, the Heroic Epic structure cannot be completely avoided.

These repetitions are a *resonance*: "1a. The reinforcement or prolongation of sound by reflection or by the synchronous vibration of a surrounding space or a neighbouring object. Also: a sound, or quality of sound, resulting from this" (*OED*). Throughout this book, I have emphasised both the shape and rhythm of the Heroic Epic form; the "regular pulsating meter" of the Epic (Northrop Frye, *Anatomy of Criticism* 251). The repetitions of the Heroic Epic pattern that I have identified all build on iterations, creating a resonance that evokes a memory, emotion, or overtones of a previously held understanding of the form. Rather than being simplified, repetitive, and formulaic, the repetitions within the Heroic Epic pattern create a resonance by building layers of depth and complexity: "7. *Art*. Richness of colour, *esp.* that produced by proximity to a contrasting colour or colours" (*OED*, original emphasis). This final definition of resonance suggests that not only is resonance created through "[t]he reinforcement or prolongation of sound by reflection," but also by *contrast*, by identifying the ways in which the pattern is different, made complex. It is in this juxtaposition that the beauty of the Heroic Epic pattern is created and exposed.

Note

1 Note that the last few books were co-written or written solely by McCaffrey's son, Todd McCaffrey, as McCaffrey passed away in 2011.

Bibliography

Abercrombie, Joe. *First Law*. Gollancz. 2006–2008. First Law 1–3.
Benioff, David and David B. Weiss, writers. *Game of Thrones*. HBO. 2011–2019.
Blade. Dir. Stephen Norrington. Perf. Wesley Snipes. Marvel Enterprises. 1998. Film.
Buffy the Vampire Slayer. Prod. Joss Whedon. Fox. 1997–2003. Television.
"Clarke's Three Laws." *World Heritage Encyclopedia*. Accessed 6 November 2017. http://self.gutenberg.org/article/WHEBN0000005653/Clarke
Clute, John. "Fantasy and the Metatext." *Science Fiction Foundation*, vol. 107, 2009, pp. 7–14.
Frye, Northrop. *Anatomy of Criticism*. 1957. Princeton University Press, 1973.
Herbert, Frank. *Dune*. 1965. Gollancz, 2010. Dune Saga 1.
Martin, Gail Z. *The Summoner*. 2007. Solaris, 2012. Chronicles of the Necromancer 1.
Martin, George R. R. *A Song of Ice and Fire*. Bantam Books, 1996–2011. A Song of Ice and Fire 1–5.
McCaffrey, Anne. *All the Weyrs of Pern*. 1991. Del Rey, 1992. Dragonriders of Pern 11.
———. *Dragonflight*. 1968. Del Rey, 1986. Dragonriders of Pern 1.
———. *Dragonquest*. 1971. Del Rey, 1978. Dragonriders of Pern 2.
"Resonance." *OED Online*. Oxford University Press, March 2016. Web. 10 March 2016.
Star Wars. Lucasfilm, 1977–2019. Star Wars 1–9.
Yolen, Jane. *Dragon's Blood*. 1982. Magic Carpet Books, 1996.

Index

A Game of Thrones see Martin, George R. R.
Abercrombie, Joe 72, 179
Ahmed, Saladin 29–30
Anderson, Poul 121
apocalypse 48, 136, 151–152, 158; *see also* fall
Aristotle, *Poetics* 93
Asimov, Isaac 3, 164
Attebery, Brian: "Fantasy as an Anti-Utopian Mode" 128, 139, 145–146 (*see also* utopia, anti-utopia); *The Fantasy Tradition in American Literature* 16; *Strategies of Fantasy* 2, 4–5, 44, 52, 56, 68, 168; *Stories About Stories* 4, 52, 57; "Structuralism" 14, 51, 68

Bailey, Cyril 21; *see also* Virgil
Bakhtin, M. M., *The Dialogic Imagination* 31–32, 43, 131, 138
balance 15, 67–68, 70–72, 76, 78, 84, 86–87, 89, 91–93, 95–97, 101, 103, 106, 108–109, 116, 118, 123, 125, 137, 142, 150, 152–153, 160, 162, 164, 167, 171; equilibrium 92, 101, 109, 136–138, 143, 146, 147, 150, 153–155, 158–162, 168–169 (*see also* far-from-equilibrium; Todorov, Tzvetan); fulcrum 71, 92; stability 47, 50–51, 64, 138, 143, 145–147, 149, 151–153, 159; tipping; tipping point 70, 92–93, 97, 101, 103, 137, 142, 150; *see also* restoration; unbalance
Barthes, Roland 56–57, 167
becoming *see* Broad, C. D.; transcendence
bifurcation 74–76, 81, 136–137, 146, 167–168; *see also* branching

binary 10, 13, 66–71, 79, 82, 86
Bloch, Ernst 147, 171; *see also* novum; utopia
blood 20, 23–24, 46, 92, 99, 110, 113, 119–120, 124, 176, 180; bloodlines 88, 97, 155; *see also* fluidity
Bobzien, Susanne 27–28, 49; *see also* Stoic philosophy
body *see* hero, body of
Borges, Jorge Luis 41; *see also* branches, forking
boundary 10, 23–24, 32, 50, 60, 64, 100–102, 104–106, 108–109, 113, 116, 118, 120–121, 125, 127–128, 133, 138; border 2, 10, 23, 33, 103–105, 107–108, 122–123; crossing 10, 23–24, 28, 32, 84, 93, 106–107, 116, 120, 125, 128, 130 (*see also* fluidity); *see also* metaphysical realm; restoration; threshold
Bourne, Craig 39, 42; *see also* branching-futurism; no-futurism
branches, branching-futurism 35, 39, 42–43, 46–47, 59–60, 74, 81, 84, 149; crossroad 40; forking, forks in the road 30, 35, 38, 41–43, 45–47, 69, 73–74, 76, 91, 166 (*see also* Borges, Jorge Luis); jonbar point 46; possible 15, 19, 24, 29, 25–36, 38–43, 45, 60, 67, 73–75, 79, 81, 84, 87, 96, 109, 129, 154, 164, 170–171 (*see also* hero, potential); *see also* bifurcation; Bourne, Craig; hero, journey of; time, theories of
Brett, Peter V., *Demon Cycle* 89–90, 94, 98
bridge 13, 88, 103, 118, 144; *see also* hero as channel; hero as mediator; hero as portal

Broad, C. D. 31, 129 *see also* becoming
Brooke-Rose, Christine 4
Bujold, Lois McMaster: *The Curse of Chalion* 20–26, 28–33, 42, 72–73, 95, 97, 113–114, 124, 126–127, 134; 150, 154, 170; *Paladin of Souls* 22, 30–33, 42, 125; *see also* James, Edward
Butcher, Jim 70
butterfly effect *see* chaos theory

Campbell, Joseph, *The Hero with a Thousand Faces* 6, 22, 24, 81, 130–131, 133, 148, 154, 164; *see also* metaphysical entity, invisible; mythology
Canavan, Trudi 87, 97–98
Card, Orson Scott 77–78
Carlyle, Thomas 7, 20–21, 31–32, 53, *see also* hero
Cawelti, John 56–57, 167–168
channel *see* hero as channel
chaos, chaos theory 5, 8, 22, 41, 47, 49–52, 55, 64, 68, 70, 71, 74, 97, 101–102, 119, 121–122, 133, 136–138, 142–143, 145–150, 153, 155, 158–160, 162–164, 166–167; butterfly effect 158, 160–161; fractal 164–165 (*see also* Palumbo, Donald); Lorenzian waterwheel 162–163, 166; ripples, butterfly effect 37–39, 51, 59; strange attractor 47–51, 64, 137, 143, 146–147, 149–151 (*see also* hero, shape of); *see also* far-from-equilibrium; Gleick, James; Hayles, N. Kathrine; Prigogine, Ilya; Stengers, Isabella; turbulence
Christ, Christian 4, 19, 123, 133–134, 155; Judeo-Christian 136; *see also* metaphysical realm; mythology
Clarke, Arthur C., "Clarke's Three Laws" 176; *see also* Science Fiction (SF)
Clemens, James: *The Banned and the Banished* series 54, 88, 138; *The Godslayer Chronicles* 72, 118, 169; *Shadowfall* 72, 110–112, 118–124, 126–127, 129, 131–134, 154
Clute, John: *Encyclopedia of Fantasy* 2; "Fantastika in the World Storm" 2, 20, 100, 104, 110, 116, 120, 133 (*see also* Fantastika; thinning; recognition; return; wrongness); "Fantasy and the Metatext" 175
Colish, Marcia L. 28–29, 75; *see also* Stoic philosophy
Croft, Janet Brennan 164–165; *see also* pattern
Croggon, Alison 102, 133
Currie, Mark 58, 62; *see also* metafiction
cycles *see* time, theories of

death 7, 10, 23, 30, 31, 38, 47, 53, 63–64, 71, 77, 78, 81, 83–87, 91–99, 106–108, 110, 112, 114, 120, 123, 125, 127–133, 135, 142, 143, 150–155, 161, 165, 166, 168, 170; *see also* messianic; re-birth; shadow; metaphysical realm
Derrida, Jacques 52, 82, 162
destiny 1, 6–11, 15, 19, 21–22, 26, 32, 35, 41–42, 45, 47–48, 53, 56, 61, 63, 73–75, 87, 89, 91–93, 158, 176, 178–179; chosen 9, 26, 43, 48, 53, 61, 124, 161; fated 25, 27–28, 38, 41; pre-determined 15, 19, 20, 25, 26, 39, 43, 47, 75; prophecy, prophet 3, 8–9, 14–15, 19–21, 23–26, 31–33, 35–36, 38, 40, 45, 47–48, 52–56, 58, 61, 65, 72, 74, 94–95, 105–108, 111, 116, 118, 132, 145, 151–153, 155, 164–165, 168, 170, 172, 177, 179 (*see also* hero as reader); *see also* fate; free will; hero as pawn; metaphysical entity
disorder 17, 49–50, 65, 82, 101–103, 112, 114, 122, 134, 136, 137, 150, 156, 166, 172; *see also* entropy
distortion 63–64, 76–77, 115, 141; *see also* mirror
deity, divine entity, divinity *see* metaphysical entity
Dubois, Page 57
Dunsany, Lord 21–22

Easton, Scott Burton 30; *see also* hero as vessel
Eddings, David and Leigh: Belgariad and Malloreon 61, 72, 111, 126, 132, 138, 158, 161, 169, 170; Demon Lord of Karanda 30; Enchanters' End Game 84;

Guardians of the West 161; King of the Murgos 61, 165; Magician's Gambit 84, 126; Pawn of Prophecy 111; The Seeress of Kell 132, 158, 165–166, 168, 170–171
Eliade, Mircea 109; *see also* mythology
entropy 15, 92, 100–103, 105–107, 109–110, 112, 115–116, 118–119, 121–122, 124–125, 128, 131, 133, 136–138, 140, 142, 145–150, 153, 155, 159, 162, 164, 178; *see also* disorder; far-from-equilibrium; irreversible processes; reversal
epistemological 47, 60–61, 63; *see also* McHale, Brian; ontological
equilibrium *see* balance; far-from-equilibrium; Todorov, Tzvetan
Erikson, Steven 9, 13, 162

fall 22, 68, 72, 80, 82, 94, 110, 119, 126–128, 136, 138–139, 155; fallen 126–127 (*see also* hero, body of, broken); *see also* apocalypse; wrongness, deterioration
Fairy-Tale 4–5, 11, 26, 34–36, 38, 40–46, 49, 64–66, 69, 133, 169, 173, 175; folktale 3, 6, 7, 18; *see also* Fantastika, Tolkien, J. R. R., "On Fairy-Stories"; Propp, Vladimir
Fantastic 1–4, 11–12, 56–57, 60, 68, 104–105, 121, 159, 175–176, 179; *see also* Fantastika
Fantastika 1–2, 9, 11, 50, 100, 120, 136, 166, 171, 179; *see also* Clute, John, "Fantastika in the World Storm"; Fairy-Tale; Gothic; Science Fiction
far-from-equilibrium 15, 136–137, 141, 146–147, 149–150, 153, 155, 161, 165; *see also* chaos; entropy; equilibrium; Prigogine, Ilya; Stengers, Isabella
Farland, David: *The Lair of Bones* 29, 70, 170; *Runelords* 67, 71, 73, 82, 88, 93, 96–97, 138, 170; *The Sum of All Men* 67, 71, 78, 82, 96; *Wizardborn* 69, 71–72, 77, 96; *The Wyrmling Horde* 67–68, 73–75, 80–81
fate *see* destiny; hero as pawn; metaphysical

Fisher-King 100, 118, 128–129; *see also* Osiris
fluid, fluidity 22–23, 28, 33, 35, 42, 47, 73, 97, 100, 104, 110–111, 116, 120, 148; bleed 110, 120 (*see also* blood); drain 49, 120, 127; flow 33, 35, 39, 42, 49–52, 59, 97, 104, 110–111, 113–116, 119–120, 124, 127, 129, 145–146, 149–150, 163; leakage 104, 127–128 (*see also* Mendlesohn, Farah; Roberts, Adam); pouring 23, 28, 154, 163 (*see also* hero as avatar; hero, as vessel); seepages 90, 110, 115, 120, 146, 155; spillage 23–25, 113; *see also* boundary, crossing, turbulence
Forster, E. M. 43; *see also* hero as stock character
fulcrum *see* balance
Fragmented Fantasy 9–10, 89, 92, 100, 179; *see also* Localised Fantasy
Fractured Fantasyland 108–109, 118, 120–121, 153, 158, breakage 5, 12, 15–16, 18, 20, 42–43, 53, 72, 79–82, 100, 102, 104–105, 108–113, 115, 119, 127, 129, 138, 145, 150, 155, 161, 179; disruption 62, 72, 102, 108, 112, 114, 106; division, divide 9, 41, 59, 72, 77, 109, 137, 166; fracture 60, 62, 72–73, 77, 100–104, 108–111, 113–116, 118, 120–121, 124–125, 127–128, 153, 158; fragments 77, 160; hole 23, 102, 106, 108, 112, 113; penetrate 32, 101–102, 105, 111–112, 115, 120, 123, 161; portion 77, 151; rips 106; rupture 102, 108, split, splitting 22, 58, 109–110, 119, 125, 153, 171; tearing 105–108, 137; unravel 129; un-whole 138; *see also* hero, broken body of; network; thinning; wrongness
Frazer, James, *The Golden Bough* 6, 123–124, 131; *see also* messianic; Osiris
free will 7, 15, 19–20, 24–30, 32–33, 35, 38, 40, 45, 47, 75, 111–112; choice 12, 15, 19–20, 23–31, 35–36, 38–43, 45, 53–54, 59–64, 68–70, 73–75, 76, 79, 81, 84, 86, 89–92, 96, 106–109, 112, 119, 127, 132, 158, 175; decision 25, 27, 45,

53, 69, 74, 76, 86, 90–91; *see also* destiny; fate; hero as pawn; Stoic philosophy; Russell Bertrand
Freud 24, 77; *see also* uncanny
Frye, Northrop, *Anatomy of Criticism* 21, 44, 93, 118, 128–131, 163, 179; *see also* metaphysical realm
future light cone 37–38, 40; *see also* Hawking, Stephen

Gaiman, Neil 41
Genette, Gérard 167
Gleick, James, *Chaos* 47, 49–50, 64, 74, 97, 100, 148–149, 158, 163, 166–167; *see also* chaos theory
god *see* metaphysical entity
Goodkind, Terry: *Stone of Tears* 51, 53–54, 74, 101, 105–110; *Sword of Truth* 73, 100; *Wizard's First Rule* 26, 101, 108
Gothic; Gothic Horror 2–4, 81, 100, 176; *see also* Fantastika
Grant, John 2
Greimas, A. J. 44; *see also* stock characters

Hawking, Stephen, *A Brief History of Time* 35–39, 45, 51, 59, 102; *see also* future light cone
Haydon, Elizabeth 36–37
Hayles, N. Katherine, *Chaos Bound* 5–6, 52, 68, 121–122, 146, 148–149, 162, 164; *see also* chaos theory; Maxwell's Demon; recursive structures
healing *see* restoration
hegemony 3, 137, 145
Herbert, Frank, *Dune* 3, 11, 88, 121, 144, 164, 177
hero: actualised hero 31–32, 39, 44, 53, 63, 67, 72–73, 84, 129–130 (*see also* ou-hero); as agent of change, as catalyst 15; as agent of divinity 20–24, 29–30; as avatar, possessed 20–23, 30, 68, 74, 78, 82, 90, 94, 111, 115, 124, 130, 151 (*see also* fluidity, pouring); body of 23, 31–32, 74, 78, 82, 88, 94–95, 110–111, 113, 115–116, 118–120, 123–129, 131, 134–135, 144–145, 151–152, 170 (*see also* hero, shape of); bodily, body of 110–111, 120, 154; broken body, body of 9, 15, 42–43, 62, 72–73, 75, 80–81, 97, 102, 109–112, 116, 118–120, 123–124, 126–131, 134, 143, 146, 148–149, 152, 155–156, 161, 172 (*see also* fall; Fractured Fantasyland); as catalyst 149, 151, 154; as channel, as catalyst 24, 28, 87, 95, 111, 114–115, 123 (*see also* bridge; hero as portal; hero as vessel); function of (*see* messianic); cup, shape of 28–30, 32–33, 75, 127, 134, 154 (*see also* hero as vessel); cylinder, shape of 28–29 (*see also* hero, body of; strange attractor); as horizontal hero, as catalyst 85, 86–91, 97 (*see also* Mathews, Richard; mythology); as inside/outside figure, as catalyst 87; journey of 1, 6–7, 11–12, 24–26, 30, 39–40, 42, 44, 47–48, 53, 58, 63, 70, 72, 74, 76, 79–81, 83–86, 88–89, 92–94, 102, 104–105, 116, 120–121, 128, 130, 136, 158, 166, 168, 170 (*see also* mythology; transcendence); as knight, as catalyst 22, 45, 126; as liminal figure, as catalyst 118, 122–124, 135 (*see also* threshold); as mediator, as catalyst 23, 35, 47, 51, 57–58, 64, 93, 106, 118, 123, 125, 127–128 (*see also* bridge); path, journey of 7, 24–26, 30, 35, 36, 38–43, 45–47, 57, 60–64, 70, 74–76, 78, 79, 87–89, 91, 93, 98, 106, 109, 128, 146, 171 (*see also* branching-futurism); as pawn, puppet, as catalyst 20–22, 25–26, 28, 30, 45, 111, 119, 124, 166, 178 (*see also* fate; free will); as poet, as catalyst 21, 31–32; as portal, as catalyst 12, 32, 104, 118–120, 122–125, 127 (*see also* bridge; hero as channel; threshold); as potential hero, as catalyst 9, 15, 31–32, 36, 38–45, 62, 64, 67, 70, 73–77, 79, 81, 89–90, 95, 107, 129, 131–132, 153, 158, 175 (*see also*, branches, possible; ou-hero); as prophet, as catalyst (*see* destiny); as reader, as catalyst 47, 51–58 (*see also* destiny, prophecy); shape of 1, 15, 19, 20, 28–34, 44, 48–50, 70, 72, 75, 79, 120, 127, 160, 179, 155 (*see also* Carlyle, Thomas); trajectory, journey of 57, 74, 128, 130, 162, 165–167, 178; transformer

of culture, as catalyst 137; as transgressor as catalyst 23, 25, 114, 128, 133; as twin-natured being, as catalyst (*see* Kantorowicz, Ernst H.); as vertical hero, as catalyst 85–86, 91–97 (*see also* Mathews, Richard; mythology); as vessel, as catalyst 20, 23, 29, 30, 33, 39, 75, 111, 126, 127, 134, 152, 154 (*see also* Easton, Scott Burton; fluidity, pouring; hero as channel; hero, shape of
Hobb, Robin 94, 162
Homer, *Odyssey* 93, 106; *see also* mythology
Howard, Robert 8–9

instability 64, 138, 151–152 *see also* unbalance
irreversible processes *see* entropy; time, theories of

Jacques, Brian 12
James, Edward 4, 13, 20; *see also* Bujold, Lois McMaster
Jameson, Frederic 82
Jemisin, N.K., *Broken Earth* Trilogy 111–112, 155, 161
Jones, Diana Wynne 16
Jordan, Robert: *A Crown of Swords* 55, 118; *The Dragon Reborn* 48; *The Eye of the World* 115; *The Gathering Storm* 55, 58; *The Great Hunt* 47–52, 54, 58–64, 142–143; *The Wheel of Time* 9, 33, 47, 54–55, 58, 71–73, 77, 87–88, 94, 97, 115, 118, 142, 150

Kantorowicz, Ernst H. 123
Kincaid, Paul 12; *see also* Mendlesohn, Farah

L'Engle, Madeline 29
Lackey, Mercedes: *The Fairy Godmother* 26, 35–36, 38–43, 45, 49; *The Fire Rose* 11; *Five Hundred Kingdoms* series 11, 33, 35; with James Mallory, *Obsidian* Trilogy 79, 164; *Valdemar* 162
Langford, David 76; *see also* mirror
Leigh, E.: Belgariad and Malloreon 61, 72, 111, 126, 132, 138, 158, 161, 169, 170; Demon Lord of Karanda 30; Enchanters' End Game 84; Guardians of the West 161; King of the Murgos 61, 165; Magician's Gambit 84, 126; Pawn of Prophecy 111; The Seeress of Kell 132, 158, 165–166, 168, 170–171
Le Guin, Ursula K.: "The Child and the Shadow", non-fiction 69, 79–80; *The Farthest Shore*, *Earthsea* series 142; "The Child and the Shadow", non-fiction 69, 79–80; *Tehanu*, *Earthsea* series 154; *A Wizard of Earthsea*, *Earthsea* series 78, 80
Lewis, C. S., The Lion, The Witch and the Wardrobe 11, 19, 104, 126
liminality *see* hero as liminal figure
Localised Fantasy 8–11, 72, 89, 100, 112, 114, 118, 129–130, 142, 162; *see also* Fragmented Fantasy
Lorenzian waterwheel *see* chaos theory
Lucas, George *see* Star Wars
Lynch, Scott 9–10, 89

Mahabharata 23; *see also* mythology
Mallory, James *see* Lackey, Mercedes
Manlove, C. N., *Modern Fantasy* 3, 19, 24, 26
Martin, Gail Z.: *The Blood King* 92, 97; *Chronicles of the Necromancer* 84, 93, 96, 97, 114; *Dark Haven* 97, 114–115; *Dark Lady's Chosen* 25–26; *The Summoner* 84–88, 90–97, 150, 176
Martin, George R. R., *A Song of Ice and Fire* 9, 14, 89, 92, 125, 155, 161, 179
Marx, Karl 144
Mathews, Richard, *Fantasy: The Liberation of Imagination* 4, 27, 70, 85–86, 136; *see also* horizontal hero; vertical hero
Maxwell, James Clark, "Maxwell's demon" 118, 121–122, 124, 136; *see also* Hayles, N. Kathrine
McCaffrey, Anne, *Pern* 175–179
McCullough, Joseph A. 8
McHale, Brian 60–62; *see also* epistemological; ontological
Mendlesohn, Farah: *Cambridge Companion to Fantasy Literature* 13; *Rhetorics of Fantasy* 12, 19,

26–27, 44, 53–54, 104, 120–121, 151; *A Short History of Fantasy* 4; see also fluidity, leakage; Kincaid, Paul; Roberts, Adam
messianic 1, 6, 7, 15, 81, 84–86, 89, 91–95, 97, 108, 118, 123–125, 127, 129–131, 136, 144, 152, 154–155, 176, 179; sacrifice 7, 63–64, 80, 84–86, 88–92, 94–95, 97, 109, 111, 120, 124–125, 129, 131, 139, 145, 152–154; see also death; Frazer, James; hero
metafiction 47, 51–52, 56–58, 65–66, 96, 162, 175; see also, Currie, Mark; Waugh, Patricia
metaphysical entity 7, 10, 20, 23–24, 36, 64, 71, 86, 93–94, 101–102, 104–107, 109–116, 118–120, 123–125, 127–129, 131–132, 138, 145, 148–149, 151–153, 170; divine entity, divinity 6–8, 10, 20–23, 25, 29–31, 33, 42, 71, 93, 95, 102, 110–112, 119–120, 122, 124–125, 127–132, 134, 138, 142, 149, 153, 154, 178–179; entity abnormal to Fantasyland 71, 102, 104–105, 110–112, 114–116, 118–122, 124, 129, 131–132, 149, 151, 154, 178; fate, fates 7–8, 10–11, 14, 19–21, 24–26, 28–36, 38, 40, 42–43, 45, 47–49, 52, 63, 70, 74, 111, 161, 164, 165–166, 172, 177, 179; god 5, 8, 10, 20–26, 28–32, 34, 38, 42, 64, 72, 82, 85, 92–93, 102, 110–113, 116–121, 123–125, 127–128, 130–134, 139–142, 148, 151, 154, 156–158, 161, 169, 170, 172; invisible, divine entity, divinity 22, 119, 132, 154; see also Campbell, Joseph; destiny
metaphysical realm: dreamscape 24, 37, 57, 64–64, 113–114 (see also, Tolkien, J. R. R., "On Fairy-Stories"); fairyland 37; heaven 8, 23, 85–86, 110, 123, 128–129, 136 (see also Christianity; Frye, Northrop); hell 8, 85, 86, 128 (see also Christianity; Frye, Northrop); underworld 78, 92–94, 103, 105–109, 122, 129, 150 (see also death); see also boundary
Miéville, China 114
Miller, Dean A., *The Epic Hero* 7, 22–23, 76, 85–86, 91–92, 123, 128, 130; see also mythology

mirror; mirroring 23, 59–61, 63, 70, 74, 76–77, 83; see also distortion; Langford, David
Modesitt, L. E., Jr., *Magic of Recluce* 29, 70–71, 161–162
Moorcock, Michael: *Elric* 9, 13, 102, 142; *Wizardry and Wild Romance* 4
Moylan, Tom 171
myth, mythology 4–8, 12, 16, 18, 20–24, 47, 52, 65, 68, 70, 76, 83, 85, 91–92, 109, 116, 118, 122–123, 128–131, 133–134, 138, 148, 172, 175, see also Campbell, Joseph; Christianity; Eliade, Mircea; hero, horizontal; hero, vertical; hero, journey of; Homer, *Odyssey*; *Mahabharata*; Miller, Dean A.; *Ramayana*; Virgil, *Aeneid*

network 72, 105, 144–145; holistic; whole 9, 12, 15, 69–70, 72, 78, 86, 100, 104–105, 110, 115–116, 120, 132, 144, 153; interconnected 49 (see also Stoic philosophy); threads 47–48, 94–95, 177–178 (see also patterns); weave, weaving 48–50, 59, 95, 154, 169; see also Fractured Fantasyland
Nietzsche, Friedrich 82, 133
Nikolajeva, Maria 5
no-futurism 35, 39, 42–43; see also Bourne, Craig; branching-futurism; time, theories of
Novik, Naomi 114–115
novum 3, 171; see also Bloch, Ernst; Suvin, Darko

Okorafor, Nnedi 93–94, 98
ontological 47, 60–63; see also epistemological; McHale, Brian
Osiris 118, 131, 134; see also Fisher King; Frazer, James
ou-hero 15, 45, 64, 67–69, 72–81, 87, 89, 90–91, 95–96, 98, 106–107, 109, 115, 132–133, 140, 141, 151, 153–154; see also hero, as actualised; hero, as potential

Palumbo, Donald 164; see also chaos theory, fractal
pattern 1, 7, 13–14, 18, 37–38, 41, 43, 47–50, 52, 55, 57, 59, 61–63, 67, 70, 73, 75, 96, 116, 133, 136, 138, 143, 147–149, 156, 158, 160, 162–167, 173, 175, 179; see

also chaos; Croft, Janet Brennan; network, threads
Plato 59; *see also* shadow
Polak, Frederik 137, 147–148; *see also* utopia
Pratchett, Terry 41
Prigogine, Ilya, *Order out of Chaos* 50, 136–137, 146–147, 149–150; *see also* chaos; entropy; far-from-equilibrium
Propp, Vladimir 6–7; *see also* Fairy-Tale
Pullman, Philip, *His Dark Materials* 11, 26, 93, 112

Ramayana 20, 23; *see also* mythology
rebirth 21, 32, 47, 65, 93, 97, 118, 130–131, 142, 170; *see also* death; restoration
recognition 15, 25, 52–53, 58, 77–78, 93, 100, 127, 153, 159, 167, 169; *see also* Clute, John
recursive structure 15, 47–48, 52, 58–59, 61–64, 68, 70, 72, 76, 162–164, 166, 175; *see also* Hayles, N. Katherine; repetition
repetition, repetitive 7, 14–15, 36, 41, 47–49, 52–53, 55, 58, 61–63, 67–68, 73, 81, 106, 115, 133, 136, 143, 146, 158–159, 161–168, 175, 179; *see also* patterns; recursive structures; time, theories of
resonant 15, 57–58, 62, 76, 107, 163
restoration 72, 86, 92, 95, 97, 112, 121, 125, 128, 138, 142, 145, 152, 164, 170; healing 1, 6, 72–73, 100, 112, 118, 123–125, 127–129, 130–131, 133–134, 141, 146, 153, 155, 158, 170; rebuild 116, 124, 133, 152; remade 93, 125, 129, 143, 150, 153; *see also* balance; boundary; rebirth; unbalance
return *see* Clute, John; restoration
reversal 15, 68, 75, 90, 93, 97, 102, 116, 118–119, 121–122, 131, 133, 136, 164–164, 166; reversible processes (*see* time, theories of); *see also* entropy
Roberts, Adam 104; *see also* fluidity, leakage; Mendlesohn, Farah
Rothfuss, Patrick 170
Rowling, J. K., *Harry Potter* series 8, 10, 51, 53, 65, 77, 97–98, 145
Russell Bertrand 27, 162; *see also* free will

Sanderson, Brandon: *Alloy of Law*, *Mistborn* series 138, 155, 169; *Bands of Mourning*, *Mistborn* series 170; *Elantris* 112–113; *Hero of Ages*, *Mistborn* series 125, 137–138, 140–145, 148–149, 151–156, 170; *Mistborn* Trilogy, *Mistborn* series 10, 53, 56, 72, 88, 95, 98, 111–112, 132, 137, 143, 155, 161, 169; *Mistborn: The Final Empire*, *Mistborn* series 138–140; *Shadows of Self*, *Mistborn* series 166; *The Well of Ascension*, *Mistborn* series 56, 140; *see also* Jordan, Robert, *The Wheel of Time*
Sargent, Lyman Tower: "The Three Faces of Utopianism Revisited" 139–141, 147; *Utopianism* 145; *see also* utopia
Science Fiction (SF) 2–4, 11, 29, 60, 77, 100, 130, 139, 164, 171, 175–177; *see also* Clarke, Arthur C., "Clarke's Three Laws"; Fantastika; Suvin, Darko
shadow 22, 59–61, 65, 67, 69–70, 72–73, 76–80, 83, 130, 139, 154, 166, 173; shade 77, 78, 96 (*see also* death); *see also* Plato; Vogler, Christopher
stability *see* balance
Star Wars 11, 79, 91, 96, 164, 17
Stengers, Isabella, *Order out of Chaos* 50, 136–137, 146–147, 149–150; *see also* chaos; entropy; far-from-equilibrium
stock character 35, 43–45, 168; character-type 15, 43, 45, 67; *see also* Forster, E. M; Greimas, A. J.
strange attractor *see* chaos theory
Stoic philosophy 19, 27–29, 33, 49, 65, 75, 82; *see also*, Bobzien, Susanne; Colish, Marcia L.; free will; network
Suvin, Darko: "Considering the Sense of 'Fantasy'" 4, 68; "Degrees of Kinship" 147 (*see also* utopia); *Metamorphoses of Science Fiction* 3, 139; 171 (*see also* novum; Science Fiction(SF))
Swinfen, Ann 5

time, theories of: cyclical 6, 15, 22, 47, 93, 96–97, 131, 133, 136–138, 142–143, 146, 154–155, 160–165, 171, 179; eternal recurrence 96, 136, 165 (*see also* rebirth); irreversible 121, 136–137; linear 136–137; reversible 137; tensed 35, 39, 60 (*see also* branching-futurism; no-futurism); tenseless 35; *see also* repetition; utopia

thinning 50, 64, 100–103, 105, 110, 138; diminishment 100, 102, 112, 143; *see also* Clute, John; entropy; Fractured Fantasyland

threshold 118, 122–123, 125, 130–131; *see also* boundary, crossing; hero, as liminal figure; hero, as portal

tipping point *see* balance

Todorov, Tzvetan 60, 104, 159–160, 168; *see also* equilibrium

Tolkien, J. R. R.: *The Lord of the Rings* 4, 7–9, 19, 26–27, 32, 79, 88, 104, 126, 138; "On Fairy-Stories" 64, 169 (*see also* Fairy-Tale; metaphysical realm, dreamscape)

transcendence, transcends 1, 6, 7, 22, 31–32, 68, 85–86, 95, 121, 128–133, 154, 156; ascendance 6, 7, 56, 66, 128–129, 140, 144, 157; becoming 31–32, 45, 75, 78–79, 81, 91, 106, 129–130, 142, 152, 154 (*see also* Broad, C. D.; hero, actualised; hero, potential; ou-hero); *see also* hero, journey of

turbulence 47, 49–50, 52, 145–147, 149–150; *see also* chaos; fluidity

unbalance 70–71, 92–93, 97, 101, 106, 109–110, 150, 159–160, 162, 164; *see also* balance; instability; wrongness

uncanny 60, 75–77, 82; *see also* Freud

utopia, Utopianism 72, 136–142, 145, 147, 152, 171; anti-utopia 128, 136–143, 146 (*see also* Attebery, Brian, "Fantasy as an Anti-Utopian Mode"); Edenic 72, 82, 136, 138–139, 146–147, 171; eutopia 140–141; perfection 69, 136, 139–142, 145–147, 167; stagnation 139, 141–142, 146, 151, 154, 176; stasis 9, 44, 97, 142, 143, 146–147, 151–153, 155, 159, 165, 168; *see also* Bloch, Ernst; Polak, Frederik; Sargent, Lyman Tower; Science Fiction (SF); Suvin, Darko; time, theories of

Virgil, *Aeneid* 21, 93, 106; *see also* Bailey, Cyril; mythology

Vogler, Christopher 80; *see also* shadow

Waugh, Patricia 51; *see also* metafiction

Wolfe, Gary K. 1–2

wrongness: decay 78, 102, 112, 118–119, 121; deterioration 15, 118, 136, 138, 145, 158, 162; soiled 23, 113, 119, 126; *see also* Clute, John; Fractured Fantasyland; thinning; unbalance

Yolen, Jane 5, 163, 176
Young, Helen 12